M000206802

ADULT ADD FACT BOOK

The Truth About
Adult Attention Deficit Disorder
Upated November 2011

Ron Sterling MD

**Unsheepable
Publications**

Disclaimers

This book is a modified excerpt from a forthcoming book to be published in early 2012. Although this book's content is presented in a detailed and highly-documented form, it is provided for *informational purposes only.*

The content of this book is *not* intended in any way to be a substitute for face-to-face, in-person, professional, medical, psychiatric, psychological or behavioral health care services. Always seek the advice of your physician or other qualified health care provider with any questions you may have regarding medical, psychiatric, psychological or behavioral health conditions.

This book's content should not be relied on for medical, psychiatric, psychological or behavioral health diagnosis or treatment. *Never disregard medical advice or delay in seeking it because of something you have read in this book.*

In addition, the contents and cover of this book may vary from other books with the same title that have not been assigned an ISBN which have been or may be offered for sale as hardcopy or electronic copies. Ron Sterling retains the right to offer such non-ISBN books with the same title and significantly similar content at will, without notification to past or potential buyers of such non-ISBN books. However, Ron Sterling will price all such similar books at or near the same price as this book. If one book that contains similar material is discounted by a retailer, such discounted price is not the responsibility of Ron Sterling or Unsheepable Publications, whatsoever, and they will not be held liable for any inconvenience or damages that may be claimed in regard to such discounting of similar non-ISBN books by third parties.

Any references in this book to websites, publications, or information resources of any kind are made for information purposes only. Neither Ron Sterling nor Unsheepable Publications receive any financial benefit in any way, whatsover, from such references.

Citations and references to Internet websites (URLs) in this book were accurate at the time of writing (November 15, 2011). Neither Unsheepable Publications nor Ron Sterling are responsible for URLs that may have expired or changed since that date.

Unsheepable
Publications
Bold thoughts for
sheepish times. ^{TM}

ISBN-10: 0615525261
ISBN-13: 978-0615525266

This book is based on *Understanding ADD*,
a chapter to be found in Dr. Sterling's forthcoming book —

The Culture Genes
Why America's Greatest Strength
is Also its Greatest Weakness ^{TM}

(To be published in early 2012)

The Culture Genes
turned into a major project. It
will not be final until late 2014.

Photography Credits

Book Design and Graphics by Ron Sterling

Certain "non-conforming" styles are being utilized in this book, including many headings, very few hyphenated words, shorter paragraphs, and additional space between lines and paragraphs. These styles are adopted as being ADD-friendly.

This is the fourth edition of Dr. Sterling's *Adult ADD Factbook*.

The fifth edition will be published soon. It will be available on Amazon.com in paperback and Kindle and will contain the following upgrades: (1) the term "Threat Monitor Center" will be used instead of "Emotional Brain"; (2) updated information on medications; (3) critical analysis and commentary regarding the 2012-2013 New York Times series of articles on ADD; (4) a wish list of ADD-related studies that need to be done or replicated; and (5) expanded discussions about (a) emigrations to the Western Hemisphere; (b) the downside of the non-ADD brain; and (c) long-term memory processes.

This edition has been widely read, well received and positively reviewed. It has "turned the lights on" for thousands of readers by giving them a ground-breaking better understanding of both the upside and the downside of the ADD brain.

To my wife, Sarah,
and my daughter, Kelly

Introduction

This book is a modification of a chapter from my forthcoming book *The Culture Genes — Why America's Greatest Strength is Also it Greatest Weakness*™. That book should be completed and available in the spring of 2012. I wanted to get this information published as soon as I could since there is so much misunderstanding about Attention Deficit Hyperactivity Disorder (ADD).

This book attempts to arrive at a balance between scientific truth (which requires some technical and scientific language) and user-friendliness. It is my hope that I have used language and concepts that are easy to understand and remember, without dumbing down too much the scientific findings about the upside and the downside of the ADD brain.

Yes, there is a clear upside to the ADD brain.

I highly recommend that you take your time and do your best to *fully understand* the major reasons for the high prevalence of the non-diagnosis and missed-diagnosis of Adult ADD. This Factbook should help you understand how the current narrow definition and the stigma related to the diagnosis of ADD clearly subvert a true estimate of the prevalence of ADD and of many other dopamine-deficiency conditions in the entire Western Hemisphere.

ADD is the current poster child for a large number of dopamine-deficiency conditions that are significantly responsible for "nicotinism," alcoholism, obesity, many eating disorders, insomnia, fibromyalgia, and the over-use of marijuana, cocaine, illicit methamphetamine, and opioids, not to mention rampant gambling, over-spending, and impulse-control problems of all kinds.

If you wish to fully understand ADD and how widespread dopamine-deficiency conditions are in the Western Hemisphere, you need to fully understand this book or the chapter that it will become in *The Culture Genes*.

This Factbook is comprehensively sourced and end-noted. To go to a pubmed.com citation found in an endnote, just go to pubmed.com, put your cursor in the search box, enter the seven or eight digit number found in the endnote citation, and click on "search." The pubmed search engine will bring up the citation's abstract and any links to available full-text articles.

The research cited in this book is not mine. The conclusions drawn about the cited reports are generally also not mine. They are the conclusions of the researchers, themselves. This is just not me blowing hot air or rendering my experienced, professional opinion — it is the truth as we know it at this time (November 2011). I wrote this Factbook purposefully to have significant value and usefulness to both ADDers and non-ADDers.

Please note: For the sake of brevity, when I refer to "dopamine deficiency" in this book, that term includes the meaning "and also likely norepinephrine deficiency."

For convenience, a few medical, anatomical, and diagnostic terms used in this book have been abbreviated. The most important ones are: (1) **ADD** = Attention Deficit Hyperactivity Disorder, (2) **PTSD** = Posttraumatic Stress Disorder, (3) **EB** = Emotional Brain, (4) **HPA Circuit** = Hypothalamic-Pituitary-Adrenal gland neuroendocrine pathway, and (5) **PFC** = Prefrontal Cortex. With respect to my use of the term "**non-ADD brain**," I am referring only to those brains that are dopamine-optimized, not all the other possible brains that exist among humans, and not the brain that may have above-optimal CNS dopamine.

I should also note that I have relied, as much as possible, on human-based, in vivo (live) research. Occasionally, I have used animal-based research to support a significant relevant finding. I have kept such references to a minimum since, in my opinion, animal models related to working memory, PFC operations (generally), cerebellum, and emotional brain structures (insula, cingulate gyrus, thalamus, and amygdala, among others) are not completely reliable when it comes to transferring such results and conclusions to humans. Non-humans do not have the same highly-developed top-down modulation of data and behaviors. However, the results of such non-human, animal-based research can occasionally be significant indicators of human-brain processes.

And, finally, a few thoughts about the word "truth." You might think I am using that term in the title of this book for marketing purposes, since "truth" can be a very influential word. However, this is not the case. I use the word truth to stand for facts. Scientific truth is very important to me. And, scientific truth with respect to ADD, dopamine and norepinephrine deficiencies and ADD medications has been compromised in many ways by the usual suspects — politics, irrationality, money, and power.

Truth can often be discovered more efficiently by proposing a hypothesis based on current but, possibly, immature sets of data. I propose a number of hypotheses in this book which, without the funding and resources of a major research institution, I will not be able to fully investigate. Proposing hypotheses is a very important part of the scientific (fact-discovery) process.

In this book, I propose several hypotheses. I have not done this casually. I do not propose them to just produce drama, excitement, intellectual stimulation, fantasy, or profit. I propose them for the specific purpose of facilitating further scientific investigation and mindfulness, and on the basis of existing scientifically-significant supportive data.

As they say "if the shoe fits, wear it."

In that regard, in the last section of this book, I discuss a few variables related to why there have been so many explanations of the "typical" ADD person or ADD characteristics which have *not* "stuck." The previous explanations of the processes that lead to the typical characteristics of ADD have not been widely accepted for many reasons. One of my theories is that "traditional" ADD explanations have not been widely accepted precisely because they don't resonate with those who fit the criteria for ADD. In other words, "the shoe did not fit."

Facts and truth are very important to me. In the first three editions of this book, I clearly oversimplified EB and adrenal gland function. In this edition, I greatly expand that discussion based on feedback from readers who felt that I had left out too much detail. This will likely not be the last edition of this book. Thankfully, scientific truth is always perfecting itself, testing and confirming or disputing important hypotheses. My plan is to update this book as significant scientific discoveries are made, for as long as I can.

Thank you for purchasing this book.

— *Best wishes, Ron Sterling, M.D.*

ADULT ADD FACT BOOK

The Truth About
Adult Attention Deficit Disorder
Upated November 2011

Ron Sterling MD

**Unsheepable
Publications**

Contents

* * * * * * * * * *

Acting Up!

Adult
Attention Deficit Disorder

> "The highest form of ignorance is
> when you reject something you don't
> know anything about." — Wayne Dyer

You could say that Attention Deficit Hyperactivity Disorder ("ADD") is one of the most misunderstood and underdiagnosed brain types in America. You could. And, you would likely be correct.

I say "you would *likely* be correct" because, of course, all things are arguable, and the forces that are allied against such a conclusion are formidable. Those forces consist of "official" governmental policy, a weak-kneed scientific community, the suppression of dissent in America, the fears of health care professionals who experience "official" bullying at all levels, the widespread belief that Americans have no particular weaknesses, and a capitalist-gone-wild culture that significantly exploits and benefits from the downside of ADD and all the other similar dopamine-deficiency conditions. (More about that later.)

I am hoping that you have noted that I used the term "brain type" in this book's first sentence. There is a reason for that, honest! To fully understand the reason for that, you must do your best to understand this book.

1 The Under-diagnosis and Missed-diagnosis of ADD

If you are one of those people who have been undiagnosed or misdiagnosed for many years and have struggled with one or more of the significant downsides of ADD, you know what it is like to finally find relief in a correct diagnosis and treatment.

Whether you were being mistreated for ADD-related insomnia, anxiety, moodiness, depression, anger, impulsiveness, hypersensitivity, eating disorder, narcissism, procrastination, passive-aggressiveness, disorganization, dissociation, compulsions, social phobia, self-injury, agitation, gambling, legal or illegal substance abuse or "sociopathic" behavior, you know that once the correct ADD diagnosis was made, your life changed.

1.1 "Diagnosis Shock" and Mourning

You also know how angry, temporarily confused, resentful, and sad you got when you thought about all the years you struggled. In too many such cases, you had been on the verge of suicide or almost killed yourself, you had become exhausted, chronically fatigued, clinically depressed, or you ended up with fibromyalgia.

Getting the correct diagnosis can be a shock and can lead to a period of considerable bereavement. Such newly-diagnosed and properly treated adult ADDers often go through a mourning process related to past educational and training struggles, lost opportunities and relationships, substance abuse, financial difficulties and criminality, and other significant troubles that took place while they were undiagnosed or misdiagnosed and not properly treated.

It is very apparent to anyone who specializes in the diagnosis and treatment of adult ADD that there are hundreds of thousands of people who clearly fit the criteria for the diagnosis of ADD who have been and continue to be misdiagnosed.

ADD mindsets and behaviors too frequently get interpreted by others, including professionals, as evidence of narcissistic or borderline personality disorders, anxiety disorder, panic disorder, major depressive disorder, eating disorder, addiction disorder, dysthymic disorder, seasonal affective disorder, and obsessive compulsive disorder, among many others.

1.2 The Literature on the Missed Diagnosis of ADD

The authors of an early 2009 brief report entitled *Attention deficit hyperactivity disorder erroneously diagnosed and treated as bipolar disorder* noted "There is a dearth of literature on patients erroneously diagnosed and treated for bipolar disorder."[1] I consider that a significant understatement.

I highly recommend reading the following articles.

Unrecognized attention-deficit/hyperactivity disorder in adults presenting with other psychiatric disorders (2008) [2] ("Barkley 2008 Study") —

"In a sample of individuals in the US diagnosed with any psychiatric disorder within the preceding 12 months, between 6.5% and 25.4% also met criteria for adult ADHD. The four most prevalent psychiatric disorders linked to elevated rates of comorbid ADHD include drug dependence, agoraphobia, dysthymia, and bipolar disorder.

Given these high rates of comorbidity, clinicians should *routinely screen* for ADHD in every diagnostic evaluation." (emphasis mine)

The Prevalence and Correlates of Adult ADHD in the United States: Results From the National Comorbidity Survey Replication (2006) [3] -

"One striking implication of the high overall comorbidity is that many people with adult ADHD are in treatment for other mental or substance use disorders but *not* for ADHD. The 10% of respondents diagnosed with ADHD who had received treatment for adult ADHD is much lower than the rates for anxiety, mood, or substance use disorders. *Direct-to-consumer outreach and physician education are needed* to address this problem. (emphasis mine)

The comorbidity findings raise the question whether early successful treatment of childhood ADHD would influence secondary adult disorders. The fact that a diagnosis of adult ADHD requires at least some symptoms to begin before age 7, means that the *vast majority of comorbid conditions are temporally secondary to adult ADHD.* (emphasis mine)

A related question is whether adult treatment of ADHD would have any effects on severity or persistence of comorbid disorders. A question could also be raised whether ADHD explains part of the adverse effects found in studies of comorbid DSM disorders. A number of studies, for example, have documented high societal costs of anxiety, mood, and substance disorder, but these all ignored the role of comorbid ADHD. Reanalysis might find that *comorbid ADHD accounts for part, possibly a substantial part, of the effects previously attributed to these other disorders.*" (emphasis mine)

Childhood ADHD and the Emergence of Personality Disorders in Adolescence: A Prospective Follow-up Study (2008)[4]

"In summary, these data suggest that as compared to controls, individuals diagnosed with ADHD during childhood are at greater risk for a diagnosis of a personality disorder in late adolescence. Specifically, we found elevated rates of Narcissistic, Paranoid, Borderline, and Antisocial personality disorders. Further, Antisocial and Paranoid personality disorder appears to emerge primarily when ADHD is persistent. *Clinicians treating young adults should be mindful of possible co-occurring ADHD and personality disorders.*" (emphasis mine)

Attention Deficit Hyperactivity Disorder among Pathological and At-Risk Gamblers Seeking Treatment: A Hidden Disorder (2011):[5]

"The association ADHD-problem gambling therefore appears to be not only frequent, but also linked to factors that are known to worsen the prognosis."

1.3 Why Aren't We Screening More Aggressively for ADD?

Given the relatively comprehensive co-existing-disorder studies done since 2006, you have to wonder why health care professionals are still not adequately screening for ADD before they come to conclusions about diagnoses such as narcissistic, antisocial or borderline personality disorders, anxiety disorder, panic disorder, social phobia, major depressive disorder, eating disorder, addiction disorder, dysthymic disorder, obsessive compulsive disorder, seasonal affective disorder, reading impairments, sleep disorders, fibromyalgia, and, the list could go on.

Well, wonder no more.

I quote from Dr. Joel Young's 2009 article, *Why Now? Factors That Delay ADHD Diagnosis in Adults,*[6] which, unfortunately, is unavailable at Medscape.com unless you become a member:

"Another key reason why ADHD was not identified in childhood among many of today's adults with ADHD was that some very prominent popular publications warned of the pernicious effects of psychiatric medication; for example, Mayes and colleagues identified an influential Washington Post article in 1970 that estimated that 5%-10% of Omaha school children were dosed with behavior-controlling medications, with or without parental permission. In actuality, the medicated students were children with special needs and they were not forced into treatment.

Nevertheless, people at that time often believed that what they had read must be true, and thus, parents were daunted. But they were not the only ones who believed the *scary drug stories*. The media hype also generated enormous concern in Washington over possible drug misuse and abuse. National conferences and congressional hearings were organized. In 1971, Congress ordered the Drug Enforcement Administration to categorize amphetamines and methylphenidate as Schedule II drugs. This action limited access to stimulants and placed them out of reach of children without resources or motivated parents. As a result, today's adult came of age in a climate that was indifferent and sometimes *actively hostile to the legitimacy of ADHD*." (emphasis mine)

I highly recommend reading a short, but very accurate and detailed history of the development of our awareness about the collection of symptoms that became the criteria for the diagnosis of ADD and the medications that were found to be very helpful — *Suffer the Restless Children: The Evolution of ADHD and Pediatric Stimulant Use, 1900-1980.*[7][8]

Of course, we can't blame the US Congress and the US Drug Enforcement Administration for the whole underdiagnosis and misdiagnosis problem. Such 1971 legislation was heavily influenced by these significant American belief systems: (1) willpower and discipline can overcome almost any personal obstacle or condition; (2) genes don't control our destiny — we do, (3) self-awareness is psychobabble; (4) "mental illness" is primarily environmental or psychological, not physiological or genetic; and, (5) using medication is a weakness. [9] [10] [11] [12] Even President Obama would have us all believe that "No one has written your destiny for you. Your destiny is in your hands." [13]

1.4   IQ is not Protective

Another very important reason that ADD has been particularly underdiagnosed in people with high Intelligence Quotients (IQ) has been the widespread misunderstanding that ADD does not coexist with high intelligence, or that a high IQ protects someone from the working-memory downside of ADD. [14] [15] [16]

ADD *does* coexist with high IQ and high IQ *does not* fix the working memory deficits of ADD.

1.5   Conflicts of Interest Decrease Credibility of ADD Research

Since you may not know this, Drs. Barkley, Kessler, Spencer, Wilens, et al., who were involved in publishing the 2006 and 2008 studies noted in Section 1.1 above have also co-published many articles while being loosely (or otherwise) associated with Harvard child psychiatrist Joseph Biederman, M.D. (the "Biederman Group"). It has been claimed that Biederman's writings and work have had a significant influence on the increased use of antipsychotic and ADD drugs for children.

Details of more recent fallout from such "medication activism" can be found in Attorney General Martha Coakley's lawsuit against drug manufacturer Ortho-McNeil-Janssen for illegally marketing Risperdal,[17] at the Voice of Detroit,[18] and at Nature.com News Blog (dated July 4, 2011) which describes the recent "remedial actions" taken by the Massachusetts General Hospital regarding Biederman, Spencer and Wilens.[19]

Notably, Dr. Biederman was the subject of targeted Congressional inquiries by Senator Charles Grassley (R-Iowa) beginning in 2008. The problem was that much of Biederman's work was underwritten by drug companies for whom he was a private consultant. *You could say he got caught with his hand in the cookie jar.*

The Congressional inquiry revealed that Biederman earned at least $1.6 million in consulting fees from pharmaceutical companies from 2000 to 2007, but failed to report all but $200,000 to Harvard officials. This constituted a major non-disclosure of a huge conflict of interest. [20] Thus, some of the conclusions found in their studies (including one cited above) done within the atmosphere of such conflicts of interest, could legitimately be questioned.

So, I did my homework and *did not* just rely on Biederman-related sources regarding the underdiagnosis and misdiagnosis of ADD as some other disorder. In addition, my many years of experience evaluating and treating ADD clearly indicates a *very high percentage* of misdiagnosis, mistreatment, and non-diagnosis of ADD.

Fortunately, for several years, Senator Grassley conducted extensive oversight and sought complete disclosure of financial ties between the pharmaceutical industry and physicians, medical schools, medical journals, continuing medical education, and the patient advocacy community.

Senator Grassley asked 33 medical groups for information about any financial backing they got from the medical device, insurance and pharmaceutical industries, including several advocacy groups such as Children and Adults with Attention Deficit/Hyperactivity Disorder (CHADD), Depression and Bipolar Support Alliance, Mental Health America, NARSAD, Screening for Mental Health Inc. and the National Center for Mental Checkups at Columbia University (TeenScreen).

Senator Grassley's previous inquiry into the National Alliance on Mental Illness (NAMI) found that the majority of their funding was from the pharmaceutical industry. [21]

Grassley investigated and exposed extensive financial conflicts with respect to Dr. Charles Nemeroff, Dr. Joseph Biederman, Dr. Melissa DelBello, Dr. Timothy Wilens, Dr. Thomas Spencer, Dr. Alan Schatzberg, Dr. Martin Keller, Dr. A. John Rush, Dr. Karen Wagner, Dr. Jeffrey Bostic and the former head of the National Institute of Mental Health, Dr. Frederick Goodwin.

Additionally, Grassley investigated the American Psychiatric Association and the funding they received from the pharmaceutical industry. [22]

Although Dr. Barkley has not co-authored any publications with any Biederman Group members since 2006, his earnings related to pharmaceutical company activities is substantial.[23] It is my understanding that, unlike the Biederman Group, he has not been accused of hiding his earnings from such activities.

2   Dr. Sterling's Conflicts of Interest Disclosure Statement

I have been posting my own Conflicts of Interest Disclosure Statement [24] on my websites since 2001. I have no conflicts, whatsoever. A relevant section from my Disclosure Statement reads:

> "Dr. Sterling does not have any arrangements with, and will not consider any arrangements with manufacturers of pharmaceutical or biomedical products, or any of their affiliates, distributors, or representatives. This has been true since 2001.

> Dr. Sterling does not accept nor utilize sample medications, nor does he talk with pharmaceutical representatives or sales people. In fact, he does not even return phone calls

from such representatives. This has been true since 2001.

Dr. Sterling attends conferences and engages in required continuing medical education (CME) courses. Many of such CME courses are subsidized by or funded in part by pharmaceutical and biomedical corporations. Dr. Sterling does not obtain any financial benefit from attending such conferences or CME courses and does not accept funding for any expenses related to any such conferences or CME courses.

Dr. Sterling participates in short-term investment strategies and 'day-trading.' He may occasionally purchase equity stocks in health care, pharmaceutical, and biotechnology companies as short-term investments. He has no long-term investments in any pharmaceutical, medical or biomedical entities."

3   Parts of the ADD Elephant

The authors of the book *Driven to Distraction*[25] and *Delivered from Distraction*,[26] Drs. Hallowell and Ratey, discuss how easy it is to get side-tracked by one or two of the many symptoms and signs of ADD which can result in an incorrect diagnosis. Although they do not use the term "misdiagnosis," this is the term I will use.

Chapter 6 in *Driven to Distraction* is entitled "Parts of the Elephant." At the beginning of that chapter, the authors list 13 "subtypes" of ADD. The list includes ADD with (1) hyperactivity, (2) anxiety, (3) depression, (4) learning disorders, (5) agitation or mania, (6) substance abuse, (7) creativity, (8) high-risk behavior, (9) dissociative states, (10) borderline personality features, (11) conduct, oppositional, or sociopathic personality features, (12) obsessive compulsive disorder, and (13) pseudo-ADD.

Unfortunately, it is rather disappointing to see that neither of the above-noted books contain a single entry in their indexes for the terms "diagnosis shock," "misdiagnosis," "stigma," "discrimination," "bereavement," "mourning," or "recovery." I bring this up for a few reasons which I will write about further in this book.

On the upside, Drs. Hallowell and Ratey *do* talk about some of the many factors that contribute to the dilemma of misdiagnosis and underdiagnosis, but, in my opinion, they do not say it loud enough. Also, on the upside, Drs. Hallowell and Ratey *do* reject the term" co-morbid" in favor of the term "co-existing" to describe disorders that may "co-exist" with adult ADD.

4   Co-existing? Co-morbid? Or, Just Plain Wrong?

Why do I highlight these words? Because there are hundreds of thousands of adults with ADD who are either undiagnosed or misdiagnosed. If, for instance, 33% of the population that would typically be referred to an anxiety disorder clinic fit the criteria for the diagnosis of ADD and have not been diagnosed properly (the "Canadian Ameringen 2007 Study"),[27] you can bet that such a finding is just the tip of the iceberg. You would think that the Canadian Ameringen 2007 Study would have inspired dozens of follow-up studies but, apparently, *it has not.*

My professional opinion is that the term "co-existing"(co-morbid) can *only* be correctly used if the condition with which ADD is allegedly co-existing continues to be a valid condition or diagnosis *after* the ADD is properly treated.

Most of the studies have looked for ADD in the midst of major depressive disorder, bipolar disorder, substance use disorders, anxiety disorders, conduct and oppositional defiant disorders, panic disorder, obsessive compulsive disorder and borderline personality disorder.[28] [29] [30].

In my professional and scientific opinion, I would classify many of the uses of the term "co-morbidity" with respect to "co-existing with ADD" as an *inaccurate* characterization which can all too easily be interpreted as a "cover" for mistakes made with respect to correctly making the primary diagnosis of ADD.

Most of these so-called "co-existing" disorders are diagnosed based on the pre-treatment presence of significant ADD symptoms which may either disappear completely or be substantially reduced when the ADD is treated properly.

5   Wait Until the Dust Settles

Certainly, after properly diagnosing and treating adult ADD, a professional should stay tuned for what might still need to be fixed, because it is very possible to have complicating co-existing disorders such as posttraumatic stress disorder, major depressive disorder, or some other significant set of problematic symptoms.

It is not uncommon for those who have experienced the consequences of untreated ADD to "burn out" and have resultant significant major depression, panic attacks, and fibromyalgia, among other things.

It is not uncommon for many people with untreated adult ADD to have experienced significant trauma in family relationships as they were growing up, since ADD is powerfully genetic[31] and a parent or other relative with significant untreated ADD can be pretty difficult to live with or be raised by — low frustration tolerance, quick tempers, impulse control problems, substance abuse, unpredictable, disorganized, and non-empathic, among other things.[32]

6   The Short Story of ADD

Attention Deficit Disorder (ADD) is technically called Attention Deficit Hyperactivity Disorder (ADHD). [33] I use the term ADD because the more technical term tends to mislead people into thinking that hyperactivity must be present to make the diagnosis. Not true.

Adult ADD only started receiving proper attention in the last 15 years. This means that the diagnosis and treatment of ADD in adults has lagged behind the diagnosis and treatment in children. [34] It is not a "fad" diagnosis. ADD has historically been under-diagnosed and under-treated, so all of us are catching up on the awareness and proper treatment of ADD, in general, but even more specifically with respect to adult ADD. [35] [36]

Historically, ADD in children has received the most attention because of the challenges that hyperactive, impulsive children caused for school systems. ADD has at least two types of expression — a hyperactive type and what I call a "day-dreamer" type. Officially, there are three types of ADD. More than just a little controversy exists about the 1994 set of criteria still being used for diagnosing ADD. You can find the "official" diagnostic criteria on the Internet at http://www.behavenet.com/capsules/disorders/adhd.htm[37] or in the DSM IV book[38], if you wish to understand the outdated criteria established in 1994 and not revised in 2000 or if you wish to fact check or compare my discussions with that of the 1994 criteria.

For a very comprehensive discussion of the 1994/2000 criteria, I recommend Chapter 3 - "Diagnostic Criteria for ADHD in Adults," in the 2008 book *ADHD in Adults — What the Science Says*, by Russell Barkley, Kevin Murphy, and Mariellen Fischer (Guilford Press) ("Barkley's 2008 Book"). Two studies, the UMASS and Milwaukee Studies, are the major contributors to the content of Barkley's 2008 Book. The methodologies and results of those studies are only available in the book. You can request the datasets that the reports were based on by writing to Russell Barkley. Barkley's 2008 Book is frequently quoted in the scientific literature. However, as noted in the introduction to Barkley's 2008 Book, "For these and other reasons we have opted to publish these projects in book form," and, thus, you will need to purchase the book or find it in a library.

It used to be thought that children with ADD grew out of it, but it became evident that what they were often growing out of was just the hyperactive component. [39] [40] [41] Many children with ADD became adults with untreated ADD. [42] [43] Many were never diagnosed during their school years because they weren't causing problems (often the day-dreamer type) and because awareness of the many characteristics and subtleties of the disorder have not been and *still* are not widely known.

People with ADD often experience significant challenges and failures in higher education even if they have high IQs. They often have lifestyles of rapidly changing jobs, problematic work practices, difficult relationships, and "under-achievement." Due to the emotional fallout of frequent troubles, challenges, and inconsistencies, adults with ADD often get depressed and experience chronic low self-esteem. In addition, adults with ADD often experience significant negative daydreaming (worrying), which sets them up for chronic mild depression and substantial moodiness. They also can get easily overwhelmed, which often translates into a feeling of chronic anxiety (dread) or short-tempers.

In their book *Driven to Distraction*, Edward M. Hallowell, M.D. and John J. Ratey, M.D. use the term "attention inconsistency disorder" to more accurately describe the attentional problems related to ADD. ADD is not a "deficit" in attention as much as it is distractibility which leads to inconsistent attention or "flitting" attention. I would just call it "Distractibility Disorder." What happens in the ADD brain can be called "serial single-tasking," which I write about further below in this book. The true "deficit" in Attention Deficit Disorder consists of less-than-normal levels of certain neurotransmitters in certain parts of the brain.

Here are a few signs of ADD in adults: (1) Easily distracted, resulting in inconsistent attention and memory problems — losing or forgetting things, being absent-minded, not finishing things, misjudging time, trouble getting started ("procrastination"); (2) Hyperactivity, restlessness, fidgeting; and, (3) Impulsivity, impatience and moodiness — saying things without thinking first, interrupting others, easily frustrated and angered, unpredictable moods, risky driving behavior. ADD seems to be distributed equally between women and men.

We do not yet have all the scientific tools we need to directly study the living human brain at the microscopic level, so we do not yet know all the causes of ADD symptoms. However, research clearly points toward deficits in amounts and functions of the neurotransmitters dopamine and norepinephrine in the prefrontal cortex ("PFC") and the Emotional Brain ("EB") areas of the human brain. [44]

A well-functioning PFC is crucial to judgment, organization, attention span, working memory, planning, impulse control, problem solving, critical thinking, forward thinking, and empathy. [45] The PFC is a region of the brain with several parts and circuits that run through it to other areas of the brain. [46]

A "well-functioning" EB is crucial to processing sensory data of all types related to threat assessment and survival/defender responses, including fear, pain, temperature, visual novelty, mismatch, uncertainty, and noxious smells and tastes, among other things. *Well-functioning* in this paragraph is in quotes because the definition of "well" is up for grabs when it comes to most of the functions of the EB. In this book, I will point out the upside and the downside of both the dopamine-optimized and the low-dopamine EB.

Not all ADD is the same. In addition to the neurotransmitter problems, the actual brain site(s), receptor sites and types, enzymes, and neurotransmitter synthesis in the PFC and EB where the deficiency or malfunction exists can vary from person to person. There are at least ten major dopamine function genes and six major norepinephrine genes.

You can imagine how one person who fits the criteria for ADD might have one set of high-risk ADD genes and another person might have a whole different set of such genes. They both fit the criteria for ADD, but the specific physiological roots for each of their difficulties could be quite different. This is likely the reason that some medications work with some people, but not with others. The so-called "hyperactive," "inattentive," and "combined type" subtypes that are part of the "official" 1994 DSM IV ADD diagnosis are so outdated, it is almost painful to read them. Those 1994 subtypes are very arbitrary and are completely unrelated to any particular treatment strategies that would be indicated for one alleged DSM subtype over another.[47]

Failure of a test dose of one type of ADD medication is *not* diagnostic. About 70% of the time, methylphenidate (Methylin, Concerta, MetaDate, Ritalin LA) is a slam-dunk solution.[48] About 30% of the time it is not, and you should move on to trials of other ADD medications. If you are in the 30% group, it can take a little longer to find the right medication or possibly the right combination of two different medications. If you are an adult who fits the criteria for the diagnosis, 98% of the time you will find a medication or combination of two medications that will make a significant difference in your life. (This is a much higher success rate than in children, since diagnosing ADD in children is less reliable and more often incorrect — more about that later.)

To help people understand the deficit in ADD, I use the "bridges-out" concept. This is a somewhat simplified explanation — the brain is a very complicated organ with very complex feedback and modulation loops. The brain is made up of billions of little pieces of road (nerve cells). The pieces of road can only transport data to each other with the use of bridges (chemicals called neurotransmitters). The major chemical neurotransmitters are *temporary, chemical bridges* between two or more nerve cells. "Temporary" means so temporary that when processing phasic data loads, nerve cells can shoot bridges out and suck them back into the nerve cell around 300 times per second. "Chemical" means the bridges are simple molecules — not "structural" and not longer-lasting proteins. The term "bridge" indicates their function — they bridge the gap (synaptic space) between nerve cells. [49] In the human brain, no long highways (circuits) can operate without good bridge function. So, if a lot of bridges are out (low neurotransmitter levels or functions), there are fewer highways (circuits) available for transporting data. When there are only a few bridge-optimized highways for information to travel on, much information doesn't get processed properly. For a more detailed description of this "bridges-out" concept, please read the section *Serial Single-Tasking and the ADD Brain*.

All medications that help with ADD symptoms do similar things — they increase certain neurotransmitters in the PFC and the EB. They create and make more bridges available to nerve cells so that there are more usable roads for information processing. If people with already optimal levels of dopamine and norepineprhine neurotransmitters take these medications, they generally get mostly side-effects. There are no advantages to increasing such neurotransmitter levels to above optimal. Unfortunately, there is no clear evidence yet that these medications can "fix" neurons, so their function is to temporarily "optimize" a deficient component (bridges/neurotransmitters).[50] However, two 2010 studies demonstrated actual pulvinar (large part of the thalamus) enlargement in ADD youth treated with "stimulants."[51] [52]

Not all people with ADD have difficulties and problems. There are people who, because of their particular circumstances, intelligence level, or support systems, do relatively well. They may be very creative and energetic and accomplish a lot. However, in those people who are experiencing significant downsides of ADD, I recommend a thorough evaluation and a treatment plan.

7   How to Diagnose ADD

Although there are self-report questionnaires, symptom checklists, and even some computer-generated attentional tests, they are only useful for general screening to see if you fit many of the criteria for the diagnosis. Most of those diagnostic tools just don't go deep enough and are not fine-tuned enough to pick up on whether a person is able to adequately self-define and self-report to answer the questions correctly. That is, a back-and-forth conversation with a live specialist allows for further clarification and exploration which are processes that are extremely important to making a correct diagnosis and to understanding what other variables in a person's life are significantly affecting them. I could find only one study that clearly indicated how *inaccurate* adult ADDers are at self-evaluation.[53] In my experience, if you have poor working memory (the ADD brain) along with high distractibility, you cannot be deemed to be adequately credible at self-reporting without the added processes of interviewer clarification and exploration.

No questionnaire or computer program is going to pick up the subtleties of a statement or self-report that may be off the mark or need clarification. Let's see "you used the word 'selfish' to describe your behavior, could it be that you just don't follow-through well?" "Empathy requires follow-through to know that it exists. It is generally not going to be recognized by others if it is only a quick thought that you had that disappears when your next thought shows up. How are you at follow-through?" Or, "you say you don't have trouble reading, but you mention that you don't like to read. Can we talk about that some more?"

The longer and more comprehensive Adult ADD screening questionnaires that are available have been created by Dr. Daniel Amen.[54][55] The Adult ADHD Self-Report Scale (ASRS-v1.1) Symptom Checklist has been widely used for screening for adult ADD.[56]

You might ask "If the 1994 official criteria for the diagnosis of ADD are outdated, then what criteria are used to arrive at a diagnosis?" You should ask that question. The short answer is "We use the 1994 outdated criteria with a few modifications that have been clearly established to be relevant." One of the old criteria specifies an age of onset prior to or around seven years old. That criteria is clearly unscientific and is no longer used.

Age of onset can be problematic to determine, because some symptoms may have shown up early, and some later, depending upon the challenges that were presented to any particular individual at any particular time.

Generally, data that supports an age of symptom or impairment onset in childhood and up through college or early adulthood is more diagnostic than an age of onset much later in life.

Other important criteria and considerations related to the diagnosis of ADD in adults can be found in Russell Barkley's 2008 book *ADHD in Adults: What the Science Says* and in an excellent 2008 article by Thomas Brown — *ADD/ADHD and Impaired Executive Function in Clinical Practice*.[57]

It takes me about 100 to 150 minutes to ask enough questions, and do enough clarification and exploration to obtain enough information to rule-in or rule-out the diagnosis of ADD and to make valid decisions about what else might be going on.

If you fit the criteria for ADD, then it is a matter of deciding on what treatment strategies you wish to pursue. Once that is decided, it is a matter of deciding what that particular treatment strategy might involve in terms of work and follow-up.

"Treatment" has a wide range of meanings from minimum medication management to working through issues related to years of untreated ADD — misdiagnoses, the fallout of untreated ADD on relationships, traumas related to parents who may have also had untreated ADD, and traumas related to past behaviors attributable to impulse control problems, impatience, low-frustration tolerance (irritability, anger), criminality, job failures, debt problems, etc.

8   What do We Know for Sure about Neurotransmitters and ADD Symptoms?

We know for sure from recent studies using radioisotopes to tag dopamine receptors and transporters in the human brain that dopamine deficiency in the PFC and EB is clearly related to the symptoms of ADD.[58 59 60 61 62 63]

8.1   Many Neurotransmitters are Very Specialized and Localized

Other important neurotransmitters (bridges) found in the human brain that are generally very specialized and usually found concentrated in *specific* regions of the brain include norepinephrine (clearly implicated in producing the symptom mix found in ADD), serotonin (not clearly implicated in ADD yet), acetylcholine, GABA, and glutamate. *Neurotransmission Basics at CNS Forum* is a good place to start understanding more about the brain's neurotransmitters and their specialized pathways. [64]

For a good scientific review of the interactions and contributions of dopamine and norepinephrine to PFC functions up to 2009, I recommend *The Emerging Neurobiology of Attention Deficit Hyperactivity Disorder: The Key Role of the Prefrontal Association Cortex.*[65]

8.2   ADD is Mostly Caused by Deficient Dopamine and Norepinephrine

Although radioligands have been developed for tagging norepinephrine transporters, serotonin transporters, and estimating GABA and glutamate, they were developed much more recently than the dopamine-related radioligands. As of November 2011, they had not yielded the kind of data that is currently available for the dopamine system. Thus, we don't have the same conclusive data for norepinephrine deficiencies and malfunctions in ADD as we do for dopamine. For instance, norepinephrine levels in the normal and the ADD brain have *not* been definitively imaged or mapped due to the continuing analysis of whether the current radioligands used for such imaging are specific enough. (November 2011) [66 67 68 69]

However, there is more than enough reliable research that shows trouble in norepinephrine systems related to ADD.[70 71] See especially the 2000 article *Comparison of the role of dopamine, serotonin, and noradrenaline genes in ADHD, ODD, and conduct disorder: a multivariate regression analysis of 20 genes.*[72]

Other than the final pieces of evidence which will be available after norepinephrine receptors are reliably tagged and researched, the other challenges of understanding brain norepinephrine functions are its complex interactions with dopamine[73] and the fact that norepinephrine is synthesized from dopamine by dopamine beta-hydroxylase. Since norepinephrine is synthesized from dopamine, increasing dopamine levels alone, with the use of medications that are known to do that, could also increase norepinephrine levels.[74]

Please note: **For the purpose of brevity, whenever I use the term "dopamine-deficiency or malfunction" in this book, you can assume that I also mean "and likely norepinephrine deficiency and malfunction."**

The chemical neurotransmitters serotonin, acetylcholine, GABA, and glutamate have been marginally implicated in producing the symptoms of ADD.[75 76] However, there is nothing that says you can't have troubles with more than one neurotransmitter system and, often, with people who have *not* been properly treated for their ADD, it is possible to end up clinically depressed (stress-induced hippocampus damage that can be fixed with selective serotonin reuptake inhibitor antidepressants [77]) due to the years of above-average stress created by the challenges of coping with undiagnosed and untreated ADD.

9 Are Medications the Only Solution for Fixing ADD Symptoms?

Given the clear neurobiological basis of ADD symptoms — neurotransmitter deficiencies and malfunctions — there is *no* consistently reliable non-medication method for raising those levels to optimal, well, unless you want to say that being an "adrenaline junkie" can do it. Behaviorally, you can temporarily raise working memory (dopamine and norepinephrine levels) by fidgeting (biting nails, twisting hair, stroking ear, doodling, tapping foot, chewing gum, etc.),[78] and by fear or pain inducing behavior like participating in certain kinds of gambling, extreme sports, thrill-driving, criminal or first-responder activities (police, fire, security, war, emergency services, etc.). There's even a book, "Fidget to Focus," that will help you learn how to fidget effectively.[79]

9.1 Non-Medication Things That Fix Dopamine Deficiencies

You can also temporarily raise low dopamine and norepinephrine levels with alcohol, [80 81 82 83 84 85] nicotine (cigarettes, chewing tobacco, nicotine gum), [86 87 88 89 90] marijuana, [91 92] cocaine (eat, snort, smoke, inject), crack cocaine (free-based cocaine), [93 94] non-pharmaceutical methamphetamine (crank, ice, cris, chrome, etc. etc. - oral, smoked, injected), [95 96 97] eating food (binge eating leading to obesity), [98 99 100 101 102 103] exposure to sunlight,[104 105 106] and threat, fear, or pain-related thoughts or activities, among many other things.

The opioids have not been studied as much with respect to their effects on dopamine and norepinephrine neurotransmitter functions, but there is significant evidence that heroin, morphine, and fentanyl increase extracellular dopamine, [107 108 109] and clear evidence that ADDers are very vulnerable to opioid abuse.[110] [111] The side effects of all these misguided attempts to fix dopamine deficiencies range from severe injuries to serious legal and financial problems, and brain and other organ damage.[112]

The above behaviors can raise dopamine levels temporarily and people with dopamine deficiencies are very "vulnerable" to such "dopamine-fixes." Not only can they better tolerate such increases in dopamine levels because they start with less dopamine than a non-ADD person, but they feel much better doing it because it "treats" their dopamine deficiency.

Such dopamine-fixes for the ADDer provide a *temporary* feeling of calmness, wellness, and increased cognitive function — emphasis on the "temporary."

9.2   ADDers *Can* Do It!

The significance of the positive results from improved dopamine levels due to such dopamine-fixes that do not produce too much neurotransmitter (side effects) is that such dopamine-deficient people *can think about it* and *can do it* - smoke cigarettes, do drugs, jump out of planes, put out fires, adventure, etc.   There is *no* aversive initial physiological "speed bump" to slow them down. (Much more about this in Sections 15.10, 16, 17, and 18.)

9.3   Non-ADDers *Cannot* Do It!

People who do not have significant dopamine deficiencies generally experience mild to severe discomfort (queasiness, jitteriness, etc.) to increasing their dopamine levels to above optimal by such dopamine-stimulating thoughts and behaviors and, thus, they almost always experience the *opposite* of calming or wellness from such "dopamine-fixes."[113] [114]

Almost always, dopamine-optimized individuals will *not* enjoy the first few cigarettes of their lives and also will *not* automatically feel good thinking about or participating in many of the proven dopamine-stimulating activities.   If they are so motivated for such activities that they are willing to be "sick" for the period of time it takes for them to develop enough tolerance to start enjoying the behaviors, they might get "hooked" (true desensitization). At that point, they are not actually "enjoying" the behaviors, themselves, but they are avoiding withdrawal symptoms after "resetting" their dopamine receptors due to too much exposure to above-optimal levels of dopamine — believe me, it feels "good" to avoid withdrawal symptoms.

In other words, an *already* dopamine-optimized brain (the non-ADD brain) provides a strong disincentive (speed bump) to thinking about or doing such dopamine-stimulating behaviors in the first place. (Much more about this in Sections 15.10, 16, 17, and 18.)

9.4   Caffeine Doesn't Fix Dopamine Deficiency

However, you can't effectively raise dopamine or norepinephrine levels with caffeine. It primarily raises the levels of a completely different chemical neurotransmitter — acetylcholine[115][116][117][118] — which is the major neurotransmitter utilized by the human neocortex and which is present throughout the entire nervous system, including at junctions for all peripheral muscle control. Often, what ADDers are treating with their above-average caffeine intake is their daytime drowsiness or fuzziness due to the well-documented poor sleep quality associated with the untreated ADD brain.[119] (More about that in Sections 12.2 and 15.1.2.)

Additionally, khat use in the Eastern Hemisphere, which is not unlike caffeine use and coca leaf use in the Western Hemisphere, has been shown to have long-term adverse effects on working memory and cognitive flexibility.[120] Unlike caffeine, however, khat is clearly similar to amphetamines in its actions with respect to increasing dopamine in the PFC. [121]

9.5 ADD Medication for Adults

In adults, I highly recommend pursuing a properly-supervised medication-treatment strategy. Before you start accusing me of some kind of conflict of interest with respect to pharmaceutical companies and their possible "profiteering" from an increased frequency of medication treatment for ADD, you should read my disclosure statement,[122] as quoted earlier in this book.

If you think about it a bit, the best way I could profit from an increased frequency of the diagnosis of ADD would be to recommend therapy for treatment, which could go on and on and on with little or no results. The most cost-effective and most effective treatment for the symptoms of ADD is the correct medication. The folks who hugely profit from the existence and under-treatment of ADD in our society are the entertainment industry and most retailers.

9.6 ADD Medication for Children

With respect to children under the ages of 12 or so, I do not particularly support the use of medication strategies for treatment, or, if utilized, utilized only in the most difficult behavioral circumstances or at minimum doses.

Although I am not an expert on the use of ADD medications in children, it is my professional opinion that there are too many variables being treated in the young-child situation to be sure that treatment is proper or completely relevant.[123 124 125] The variables include (1) children, until they get enough language skills and experience in life ("maturity"), are very poor self-reporters, (2) too many "authority" figures in a child's life have too many agendas of their own that may not be appropriate or entirely relevant to making a correct diagnosis and correct medication decisions, [126 127 128 129 130] and (3) children's brains are still going through neurobiological maturing processes and probably should not be "messed with" too much. [131 132]

Unfortunately, the kind of environmental and structural changes that can help kids both in and out of school who fit the criteria for ADD is not very available in the United States. Between our distraction-obsessed society, economic instability, family dysfunction and overwork, and insufficient school resources, the choices for medication strategies over structural changes become attractive only because there are *very few* other available support or treatment options. [133] [134]

Nevertheless, when a child reaches an age where neural development is more or less stabilized (mid-teens to late teens) and self-reporting skills are more developed, medication strategies should be offered to young people with ADD so that they can have a chance to bloom without the obstacles that ADD can present to their successes.

10   Medication Issues

Generally, if you fit the criteria for ADD and do not want to explore or work on other psychological, social, or environmental issues, it is possible to find the right medication(s), the right dosage(s) and the right timing of the dosage(s) within about three to eight 25-minute follow-up sessions.

10.1   Methylphenidate (Ritalin) is a 70% Solution[135] [136]

If Ritalin (methylphenidate) is a slam dunk, fewer follow-up appointments are generally required for fine-tuning medication. If it is not, it may take more follow-up appointments to arrive at the right medication result. In a very few instances, there are enough complicating factors that trials of all the available medications, even in combination with a mood stabilizer, do not bring about a good result. In my experience, that is around 2% of the adult population that fits the criteria for ADD. (The 98% figure is *not* true for children who fit the criteria for ADD, since the diagnosis in children is much less reliable due to the factors noted above.)

10.2 Seek Correct Medication Aggressively

Finding and fine-tuning the correct medication for any particular person should be done fairly aggressively. Any medications that have significant side-effects such as muscle tension, increased heart rate, overstimulation (a "buzz"), stomach upset (queasiness, nausea), increased anxiety, increased irritability, or adverse effects on sleep should be seen as *incorrect* and the trial of the next available medication should begin.

The point of taking medication is to *not* have side effects or any significant downside. Those are signals that it is either the wrong medication or the wrong dose of the right medication. *Please note, again:* Just because one ADD medication does not work for you, does not mean there is none that will work for you.

10.3 Mission of Medication — No Side Effects

The point of medication is to raise norepinephrine and dopamine levels to as close to optimal as possible without raising them to above optimal. Since we cannot accurately measure an individual's neurotransmitter levels to determine how much medication would be the correct medication, we have to proceed by trial and error and self-report assessments of the upside and downside of a particular medication and its dosages. There is no advantage to above-optimal levels of neurotransmitters. They are as problematic as below optimal levels of neurotransmitters. [137] [138] [139] [140]

Once you have established the correct medication, dosage and timing of dosages, that will be the exact regimen that will work for most of your life. Generally, ADD medications are "take-it-or-leave-it" medications. That is, except for Strattera (atomoxetine), they do not need to "build up" in your body nor do they need to be reduced by gradual weaning. No tolerance or addiction will take place if you are on the correct medication and the correct dosages of the correct medication. When you are utilizing your medication(s) you will have a more dopamine-optimized brain than off the medications. Off the medications means returning to your ADD brain. That can be shocking for some people after they have discovered what life is like with a more optimal brain (close to optimal norepinephrine and dopamine functioning).

There are many myths about ADD medications, which I will begin to address further below in this book.

I recommend finding the right medication and dosages *before* trying to come to conclusions about your possible "personality disorder," "anxiety disorder," "anger problems," "irritability," "moodiness," "selfishness," "passive-aggressiveness" or other so-called character or psychological flaws until you see what you are when the "dust settles." The ADD brain so significantly affects thoughts, feelings and behavior, that it would be premature and difficult to make an accurate personality or other behavioral diagnosis *before* the ADD portion of the equation is properly treated. [141] [142]

10.4 Antidepressants, Antianxiety and Sleep Agents

This question always comes up — "Aren't there some other medications that are effective for the treatment of ADD, such as anti-anxiety, antidepressant, sleeping, or mood stabilizing medications?" Yes, and, a big *no*. Yes, other medications can have "positive" effects on some symptoms of ADD such as anxiety, moodiness, or insomnia, but they are equivalent to using tape to fix a rusty-pipe leak. You need to fix the pipe to fix the leak, not the other way around.

10.5 Generally, SSRIs Worsen ADD

For instance, practically all partial or dedicated selective serotonin reuptake inhibitors (Prozac-like antidepressants called SSRIs) make ADD symptoms worse. This is because, no matter who you are, mildly depressed or more seriously clinically depressed, all SSRIs generally cause some cognitive "fuzziness" and peripheral numbness. Using an SSRI, alone, for ADD symptoms of moodiness will generally make adult

ADDers even more fuzzy, slower, more distracted, and, often, outright sick (nausea, drowsiness, headaches, increased anxiety).[143] This negative effect is likely caused by the SSRI inhibition of dopaminergic neurotransmission (the opposite of what the ADD brain needs).[144][145] The only studies of the direct use of *only* SSRIs for treating ADD have been with children, so, subtle, but bothersome side effects were likely not properly reported by children who clearly cannot self-report as well as adults. [146][147]

This is not to say that SSRI antidepressants may not be useful in their own right for the treatment of severe "burnout" (major depressive disorder) that can often result from years of untreated ADD in adults. However, unless the depression is so severe that it is obviously the priority treatment target, it is better to treat the ADD first, then the depression. Believe it or not, many adults who have been untreated for their ADD for many years, may be clinically depressed and *not know it*. That is, they have been so distractible that they have not noticed the ongoing severity of their depression. Once you treat their ADD properly, they may begin to notice things they did not notice before.

In my opinion, this is why a professional, in all but the most severe cases, should treat the ADD first before the clinical depression, even if it is clearly present. Often, unfortunately, it appears to me that those clinically depressed adults who may be experiencing the distractibility, impatience, impulsiveness, irritability and anxiety of ADD, if given an SSRI prior to treating their ADD, may be more prone to impulsive suicidal or violent behaviors in the midst of the additional "fog" that often accompanies SSRI treatment. [148]

The opposite is true with someone who may fit the criteria for bipolar disorder. The bipolar disorder must be treated before the ADD part of the equation is targeted, since ADD medications can often stimulate a phase of mania, which can be substantially harmful to the bipolar patient.

10.6 Bupropion (Wellbutrin) for ADD?

There is also a very common misunderstanding that Wellbutrin (bupropion) is an antidepressant which has shown effectiveness for the treatment of ADD. How bupropion got classified as an antidepressant is quite interesting, since, unlike all the other tried-and-tested antidepressant medications, it has a minimal effect on serotonin, and fairly potent effects on dopamine and norepinephrine.[149]

In my opinion, bupropion should not be classified as an antidepressant anymore than methylphenidate should be classified as an antidepressant. Bupropion is clearly very stimulating — clearly too stimulating for the treatment of ADD when it targets an already optimized part or function of an ADDers' PFC and EB, that is, when it is the *wrong* medication for that person.

11 Different Medications Work for Different People

If you hear anyone, professional or otherwise, claim that Ritalin (methylphenidate) can be used to test whether you fit the diagnosis of ADD or not, tell them they are wrong, wrong, wrong. This myth exists even among my colleagues.

The truth is different medications work for different people.

11.1 Location, Location, Location

Unfortunately, very little good research has taken place with respect to head-to-head comparisons of the treatment efficacy of different medications in a given population of ADDers.[150] Practically no research has been done to figure out what areas of the PFC and EB are being targeted by different ADHD medications. [151] [152] The current subtypes of ADD are based on criteria established in 1994, long before the scientific community had radioisotope ligands and fMRI tools with which to accurately study dopamine and norepinephrine in the central nervous system ("CNS").

Unfortunately, there is no conclusive answer to the question "Why do different drugs work differently for different people with ADD?" The current most logical answer is based on our knowledge that although all ADD *clearly* involves lower than optimal levels or malfunctioning of dopamine and *very likely* lower than optimal levels of norepineprhine in regions of the PFC and the EB, that there is also the *additional variable* of where the particular malfunction is located within pathways that coordinate, amplify, or modulate such areas.

There is very strong evidence that treatment-relevant ADD subtypes should be based on anatomical and functional differences within the PFC and the EB than on the logical, but arbitrary, behavioral definitions found in the DSM IV. Such subpart receptor abnormalities or neurotransmitter malfunctions are likely each targeted by a specific medication, rather than generally targeted by every ADD medication. Those PFC and EB subparts have been studied intensively over the last 10 years,[153 154 155 156 157] but there is much more to be discovered.

Such anatomical and functional differences in ADD-implicated neurotransmitters have been substantially confirmed by SPECT scans,[158] and other neuroimaging studies,[159 160 161 162 163 164] but a conclusive answer as what specific areas of, or pathways to and from, the PFC and EB that typical ADD medications might specifically target has not been firmly established (as of November 2011).

Other important studies that don't get talked about much in the scientific community because MRIs are all the rage, are Electroencephalograph ("EEG") studies of the brains of those who fit the criteria for ADD.

A series of studies done by A.R. Clarke, et al, in Australia and Becker in Germany showed significant EEG clusters — either three or four, but *more than one.*[165 166 167] The latest EEG study published in 2011 by Clarke, et al,[168] found that such earlier EEG research was robust and not substantially affected by the inclusion of children with comorbid disorders. One study abstract says it all: "These results support a re-conceptualisation of ADHD based on the CNS abnormality underlying the disorder rather than on the behavioural profile of the child."

ADD medications are clearly *not* interchangeable, and the scientific community needs to do some serious research to more firmly document this fact. To do otherwise is to doom ADDers to the continuing legacy of "one size fits all" mistreatment.

11.2 Head-to-Head Medication Comparisons are Substantially Invalid

In the huge 2009 *Final Report Update 3 Drug Class Review — Pharmacologic Treatments for Attention Deficit Hyperactivity Disorder* published by the Oregon Health and Science University (2009 Oregon ADHD Drug Class Review),[169] the authors miss the point entirely. Out of 3,776 research articles identified from searches, 369 were selected to be included in their massive review. Sixty-nine of those studies were of the "head-to-head" trial type.

Head-to-head trials are only valid or useful if all ADD is neuroanatomically or neurophysiologically the same, and this is clearly *not* the case.

The 2009 Oregon ADHD Drug Class Review concludes "Overall, the rate of response to stimulants appeared to be in the range of 60% to 80%. . . Response rates for non-stimulants varied. Significant variation in the method of assessment and definition of response was most likely the reason for the wide variation." I guess any excuse will do.

Honestly, without the 2009 Oregon ADHD Drug Class Review even raising the question of whether the assumption that "head-to-head" trials of ADD medications have any validity whatsoever, makes it a fatally-flawed report and continues the legacy of "bad" ADD medication science.

11.3 Medications that Make a Huge Difference

In my experience, if you fit the criteria for ADD, Ritalin (methylphenidate) is a "slam-dunk" solution about 70% of the time. About 30% of the time *it is not*. If you are in the 30% group, it can take more time to find the right medication. I have not been able to find any valid research that reports the percentages of different medications being used by people for their diagnosis of ADD. In my experience, there is a large percentage of mis-medication taking place with ADD medications.

For instance, I have not been able to find any scientific literature on the clear downside of Adderall (mixed salts of amphetamine). In my opinion, this medication could be a poster child for "bad science." What is the clear downside of Adderall, you ask? It is a medication that contains two distinctly different chemicals with very different effects and side effects. As noted earlier in this chapter, different medications work for different people. Since Adderall is a combination of two very different amphetamines (dextroamphetamine, a short-acting medication, and amphetamine, a long-acting medication), *one might be correct for you, and the other might not.*

In other words, doctors should be asking patients whether or not they are experiencing a period of time with Adderall where it seems optimal and then "turns bad" or was "bad" at the beginning of the duration of the dose, but got better later during the duration of the dose. If there is a "biphasic" effect of Adderall, it should be discontinued and the next trial of medication should be with a single-chemical drug, such as dextroamphetamine. By about three hours into the duration of Adderall, the dextroamphetamine part of the pill is gone and the effects of Adderall during the last couple of hours of its duration are primarily due to the long-acting amphetamine in Adderall.

In my opinion, there are way too many ADDers being treated incorrectly with Adderall who think that the side effects of the Adderall are just part of the treatment protocol. The frequent side effects of the long-acting amphetamine in Adderall are over-stimulation — feeling weird, fuzzy, and experiencing muscle tension, headache, "a crash," or sleep impairment. *Please note:* Starting on an extended release form of Adderall is even worse science, since it would be nearly impossible to detect which chemical in the Adderall might be incorrect, since they will be working together or against each other during the exact same period of time. In that regard, if one of the components of Adderall is targeting an already dopamine-optimized part or function in your PFC and EB, it will produce too many neurotransmitters in those already-optimal areas, which will significantly contribute to the production of tolerance and withdrawal.

Medications which can make significant differences in an ADD person's life include Ritalin (methylphenidate), Focalin (dexmethylphenidate), Adderall (mixed salts of dextroamphetamine and amphetamine — two categories and four chemicals in one tablet), Dexedrine (dextroamphetamine), Desoxyn (methamphetamine), Vyvanse (lisdexamfetamine), Strattera (atomoxetine), Provigil (modafinil), Wellbutrin (bupropion), Catapres (clonidine), Tenex (guanfacine) and, sometimes, a mood stabilizer such as Lamictal (lamotrigine).[170]

All ADD medications have similar final effects of raising extra-cellular levels or increasing cellular synthesis of dopamine and norepinephrine but their mechanisms for obtaining those results are different. [171 172 173 174 175 176 177 178 179 180 181 182]

There is no completely reliable method for predicting which medication will be helpful for a particular person unless that person has a close biological family member who has already been accurately diagnosed with ADD and has found the correct medication.

There is some evidence that SPECT scans[183 184] can help predict correct medication strategies, but the expense of such a scan is far greater than aggressively pursuing appropriate trials of the useful medications and deciding which medication is the most helpful.

12   ADD Medication Myths and Facts

12.1   The Number One Myth: ADD Medications are "Stimulants"

The number one myth about ADD medications is that they are "stimulants" or that they are "addictive."

They are only stimulants or addictive if they are used improperly for reasons other than increasing dopamine and norepinephrine levels *up to optimal.*

People who do not fit the criteria for ADD and have optimal baseline levels of dopamine and norepinephrine can get a "buzz" (a stimulation experience) from many ADD medications because that is what happens when you increase such neurotransmitters to *above optimal.*

This is true for *all* CNS neurotransmitters that can be increased to dramatic above-optimal levels by both legal and illegal drugs.

Neurons that are exposed to prolonged or intense, shorter periods of above-optimal neurotransmitter levels will reset themselves and don't return to their original default mode easily.[185][186][187]

With respect to the question of whether the *correct use* of restricted drugs such as amphetamines and methylphenidate by ADDers lead to subsequent addiction, the answer is almost unequivocally "no."

The questions "does the use of restricted medications by ADDers lead to subsequent substance use disorders?", "does the use of restricted medications by ADDers lead to a reduction in subsequent substance use disorders?", and "are untreated ADDers more likely to develop substance use disorders?" are all addressed further below in this book.

12.1.1 "Restricted" Equals "Dangerous"? Really?

You will note throughout this book that I use the term "restricted" to stand for medications that have been called "stimulants" in the past. "Stimulant" is a very old term and is scientifically indefensible as a category of medications, since many medications not labeled "stimulant" are clearly stimulants. The many so-called "non-stimulants" are just as powerful with respect to increasing neurotransmitters such as acetylcholine, norepinephrine, dopamine, gaba, glutamate and serotonin to above-normal levels. Such "non-stimulants" not only produce stimulation, but also tolerance, dependence, and withdrawal syndromes.

There is no advantage to increasing PFC or EB neurotransmitters (dopamine and norepinephrine) to above optimal.[188] [189] [190] [191] It confuses nerve cells, which produces a characteristic "buzz" but, that's about it. So, although it may help someone stay up late and cram for a test or meet a deadline, the myth that above-optimal levels of such neurotransmitters assists in learning is hogwash. If you are finding yourself frequently waiting until the last minute to get things done, you should get an evaluation about your likely ADD-induced "procrastination habit," which is frequently the result of the indecisiveness and poor planning of the ADD brain until better dopamine levels get created by the fear-factor of the impending deadline or test date.[192]

12.1.2 No Such Thing as Neuroenhancement for Already Optimal Brains

There is no consistent or reliable evidence that above-optimal levels of such neurotransmitters significantly enhance learning processes or performance.[193] [194] The clearest evidence is that above-optimal levels only allow for a longer study period, which, if done improperly, without much sleep, works against long-term memory, since sleep is important for learning and long-term memory.[195] [196] [197] [198] Of course, if you don't care about how much of your "learning" gets into your long-term memory, then go for it. Again, that sounds so ADD — short-term versus long-term thinking.

The truly scientific mind would *not* logically conclude that this particular class of ADD medications should be called "stimulants" anymore than Prozac (fluoxetine) should be called a stimulant since it is a stimulant for many people, and sometimes cannot be tolerated due to its stimulating effects.[199] And, so are many other "non-stimulants" also very "stimulating." Wellbutrin (bupropion) is also consistently a very stimulating medication, but it is not restricted, nor is it classified as a "stimulant."[200 201] In addition, caffeine and nicotine are "legal stimulants" which unarguably cause huge amounts of morbidity and mortality compared to all the ADD restricted drugs combined (not to mention, all the illicit "stimulant" drugs combined). [202 203 204 205 206]

12.1.3 Withdrawal by Another Name is "Discontinuation Syndrome"

It is well known that it is very difficult to "withdraw" from many of the psychotropic medications[207 208] which are not restricted, but widely "misprescribed," such as Zoloft (sertraline), [209] Effexor (venlafaxine),[210 211] Pristiq (desvenlafaxine) [212] Paxil (paroxetine),[213] Lexapro (escitalopram),[214] Celexa (citalopram),[215] Seroquel (quetiapine),[216] Neurontin (gabapentin),[217] and the list could go on (all the benzodiazepines, for instance [218]). Some people find it impossible to withdraw from these medications, and even more so when they are misprescribed (in cases of too casual symptom treatment and/or misdiagnosis).

Apparently, the term "discontinuation syndrome" is preferred in the medical community as noted in *SSRIs and SNRIs: A review of the discontinuation syndrome in children and adolescents* (2011)[219] which states:

> "The term discontinuation rather than withdrawal syndrome is favored to avoid any misconception about drug dependence or addiction, especially by highly anxious

children and families. Antidepressant medications are not believed to be habit forming or addictive as they are not associated with drug-seeking behaviors and have no clinically significant potential to cause dependence."

In the case of *Addictive Potential of Quetiapine* (2008),[220] the authors showed no hesitancy to use the term "addictive" when describing the "drug-seeking" behavior of the subject of their report. However, when one reviews the many reports about so-called "discontinuation" syndromes, it becomes almost laughable as to the extraordinary lengths that are taken to characterize clear withdrawal symptoms due to stopping such medications as "discontinuation" syndromes.

Withdrawal by some other name is still withdrawal.

12.1.4 Drug-Seeking by Another Name is "Seeking Reinstitution of Stopped Medications for Symptoms of Withdrawal"

For that matter, drug seeking by some other name is still seeking "reinstitution of stopped medications" when stopping a particular prescribed medication produces such significant withdrawal symptoms[221] [222] that it is similar to the withdrawal from nicotine, alcohol, or heroin. [223]

As noted above, I question the language choices in these "scientific" articles, because, clearly, one word should suffice — "withdrawal." It is more than significant to note that somewhere between 1996 and 1998 the scientific community moved away from the term "serotonin withdrawal syndrome" to the apparently more acceptable term "serotonin discontinuation syndrome." I guess, as noted above, they did not want to unduly scare anyone.

The term "drug seeking" is also clearly open to valid arguments about its definition. Is it "drug seeking" to set up an appointment with your doctor to get back on an antidepressant you have stopped which is causing you withdrawal symptoms, completely unrelated to your original symptoms of depression? I guess that would be "acceptable drug seeking" as opposed to using your spouse's antidepressants until your appointment date with your doctor, which, I suppose, would be "true drug seeking" since you are "stealing" it from someone. [224]

12.1.5 What Criteria Establishes the Classification of "Dangerous Medication"?

The Controlled Substances Act is absurdly out of date — "The law implementing the CSA is 40 years old. It employs antiquated definitions that have little scientific relevance in the modern scientific literature. 'Dependence' is a broad label for a series of neurobiological adaptations which occur during chronic exposure to any one of a number of drugs — such as antidepressants, high blood pressure medications and opioids."[225]

Any experienced psychiatrist can tell you hundreds of "horror" stories about the inappropriate use of many "unrestricted" psychotropic medications from antidepressants to mood stabilizers to anti-psychotics that have unarguably caused more death, health hazards, and withdrawal tragedies, and have been inappropriately prescribed and utilized *far beyond* what has taken place with the "restricted" ADD medications.

Here's some data for you to ponder about the "dangerousness" of methylphenidate.

A 2009 extensive review of the literature by Susan E. Hardy, MD, PhD, entitled *Methylphenidate for Treatment of Depressive Symptoms, Apathy, and Fatigue in Medically Ill Older Adults and Terminally Ill Adults*[226] revealed (1) depressive symptoms, apathy, and fatigue are common symptoms among medically ill older adults and patients with advanced disease, and are associated with increased morbidity and mortality; (2) evidence for effectiveness was weak due to the lack of large studies, but it was present; and (3) *evidence for safety was stronger*. (emphasis mine) There are no studies reporting any significant downside to the correct use of methylphenidate in patients as old as 106.

However, there has been consistent evidence from 1993 to the present that SSRIs such as Prozac (fluoxetine) can have some serious side effects in older adults ranging from increased incidence of falls with resultant fractures to over-stimulation.[227][228][229][230][231]

It is unfortunate that the scientific community continues to tolerate the kind of negative branding of certain medications with the "stimulant" tag, because the effect of such branding scares a significant number of people and discourages the appropriate use of such medications, not to mention how the "stimulant" tag and, thus, the "restricted medication" classification create significant obstacles to access and continuity of medication treatment for ADD. [232][233]

The stigma attached to these profoundly helpful "stimulant" medications is still very high and patients often experience it when presenting their prescriptions to pharmacists and when talking about such medications with others.[234]

12.1.6 "Comfort-Zone Bias" in the Diagnostic Process

The stigma attached to these profoundly helpful "restricted" medications for ADD clearly influence health care professionals to look for other, more acceptable diagnoses — ones that don't require medications that may be classified as "restricted" for their treatment. How much this medication "discomfort-zone" bias contributes to misdiagnoses and inappropriate or incorrect treatment strategies for a particular set of clear ADD symptoms, is not known. That's right. Apparently, no one has studied that possible outcome — "unscientific diagnostic bias based on the chilling effect of a restricted drug classification." (If you find research on the "chilling effect of restricted drug classification on the correct diagnosis of ADD," let me know.)

I was able to find only one study published in 2003 — *Physician perceptions of the use of medications for attention deficit hyperactivity disorder.* [235] Apparently, it has not been replicated in any form, although the authors recommended near-future follow-up studies focused on medications for *adults* who fit the criteria for ADD. This study selected 1,000 physicians who were found on lists of prescribers of ADD medications for children and adolescents who belonged to a large managed-care organization. Out of 1,000 surveys sent out, only 365 were returned, with a high percentage of the responders being psychiatrists of various types.

Bottom line? "The majority (58%) would prefer to prescribe a non-controlled medication" even though a large majority overwhelmingly perceived the controlled medications to be highly effective. If the high percentage of psychiatrists in this study would "prefer" to prescribe a non-restricted medication, you can bet there is a very high percentage of non-psychiatrists who prefer the same.

12.2   The Number Two Myth: ADD Medications Cause Sleep Problems

This myth is so embedded in the mainstream community and among my colleagues that it is almost laughable, if it weren't so serious.

Even in a 2009 Medscape Continuing Medical Education article published allegedly for the purposes of continuing education, the author stated "Because many adults with ADHD are treated with stimulants, adding sedating sleep remedies to the medication mix may be problematic." [236] Nothing could be further from the truth — the truth being that restricted medications which may be causing sleep problems should be viewed as incorrect medications and the search for the correct medication should continue.

The Texas Department of State Health Services began a process in 1998 which most recently resulted in a report entitled *The Texas Children's Medication Algorithm Project: Revision of the Algorithm for Pharmacotherapy of Attention-Deficit/Hyperactivity Disorder* (2006 Algorithm Project).[237] I regard the 2006 Algorithm Project report as the best attempt, to date, to be as scientific as possible about how to proceed with medication trials for the treatment of ADD symptoms and impairments. However, *even it has major flaws.* For instance, the report claims that "Atomoxetine (Strattera) can be given in the late afternoon or evening, whereas stimulants generally cannot." Wrong, wrong, wrong. Honestly, I don't get why it is so unclear to these researchers. The correct medication, whether it is a so-called "stimulant" or not produces better sleep and *should* be taken later in the evening, closer to bedtime, because it will improve sleep.

Additionally, if you review just about any of the "patient handouts" that are published by Medscape, pharmacies, and pharmaceutical companies, they almost always warn against taking the restricted ADD medications later in the day due to adverse effects on sleep.

One more time, with italics: Such patient information sheets should say *"If this medication causes sleep difficulties, consult your doctor. You may be on the wrong medication for your diagnosis."*

12.2.1 Correct Medication Leads to Profound Sleep Improvement

Yes, the wrong ADD medication or too much of the right medication can adversely affect sleep for those with ADD. The right ADD medication will not create sleep problems. In fact, the right medication will likely create better sleep. In fact, if an ADD medication prescribed to a person with ADD is affecting sleep adversely, it *is* the wrong medication. Have I said that enough yet?

As noted in *ADHD Sleep Problems: Causes and Tips to Rest Better Tonight!*, Dr. William Dodson, M.D. states "If the patient spends hours a night with thoughts bouncing and his body tossing, this is probably a manifestation of ADHD. The best treatment is a dose of stimulant-class medication 45 minutes before bedtime." [238] Dr. Larry Silver, M.D., notes that "Some children and teens with ADHD have difficulty going to sleep at night because they cannot turn their head off. They are fidgety and active in bed. They hear every sound in the house and cannot ignore the sounds." According to Silver, medications like Ritalin, Dexedrine, or Adderall at night may help — "'Yes, everyone thinks these medications cause sleep problems. However, when ADHD prevents you from going to sleep, being on these medications counteracts those symptoms." [239 240 241 242]

You might wonder how this could be, given the hype about the alleged stimulating effects of most ADD medications. Well, here is the true story.

When you have taken the correct ADD medication for you, that medication changes your brain to a more optimal brain with respect to neurotransmitters in your PFC. When the medication wears off, and they all wear off pretty fast except for Strattera (atomoxetine), you are back to your ADD brain.

12.2.2 Eighty Percent of Untreated ADDers have Significant Sleep Impairments

Somewhere in the vicinity of 80% of adults with ADD have sleep onset insomnia — difficulty getting to sleep — often at both bedtime and later in the night when they wake up. [243]

A large number of untreated ADDers develop certain "sleep habits." They may use a strategy of staying up late until they are so exhausted they can pretty much guarantee that they will fall asleep without being tortured by their thoughts for more than an hour when they do go to bed. Or, they often use "white noise" (television, music, fan, or white-noise machine in background) to distract them from the internal noise (thinking). [244]

Other strategies for sleep often involve the "misuse" of over-the-counter and prescription sleep medications to treat this common symptom of ADD when treating the ADD itself is what is required.

The primary reason for this sleep difficulty is that when your ADD brain is operating it *does not* have the ability to screen out irrelevant data (distractibility) and focus on sleep and the processes of getting to sleep like a non-ADD brain can.

In spite of all the valid and replicated ADD sleep studies, the "stimulant" tag noted above continues to mislead even professionals to think that you cannot take these medications later in the day without messing up sleep. The opposite is actually true.

12.2.3 The Key is Being on the Correct Medication

However, *the key is being on the right medication.* If you are not on the right medication for you, it can have an adverse effect on sleep. If you are on the right medication, you should be able to take it just about anytime of day (even in the middle of the night at low doses) and it will improve sleep.

12.3 The Number Three Myth: A Trial of Ritalin (methylphenidate) Will Be Diagnostic for ADD

The most reliable way to evaluate and discover whether you fit the criteria for ADD is a properly done clinical evaluation. In my experience, if you fit the criteria for adult ADD, it is a 98% chance that you will find a medication or a combination of two medications that will change your life. What that medication will be is somewhat unpredictable, as noted above. The figure of 98% only applies to adults, as noted earlier in this book.

A trial of even six out of the possible seven or so medications that will change an ADD brain into something that is a more dopamine- and/or norepinephrine-optimized brain would still *not* be "diagnostic" and would not rule out the diagnosis. Until you have explored all the appropriate medications for ADD, you will not be able to use medication failures as evidence that you do not actually have a significant dopamine and/or norepinephrine deficit.

Generally, the 2% of people who cannot be helped who fit the criteria for ADD are people who have confounding factors that prevent them from utilizing ADD medications, such as epilepsy, morbid high blood pressure or serious heart conditions. In addition, people with Posttraumatic Stress Disorder or Bipolar Disorder may not be able to utilize ADD medications because it could make their co-existing disorder worse. No guarantee on that, but those are the people who are often in the 2% can't-be-medicated-without-serious-problems group.

In the section above entitled *Why Different Medications Work for Different People*, I note that about 70% of adults who fit the criteria for ADD are significantly helped by Ritalin (methylphenidate) without any side effects.[245][246][247] The remaining 30% or so of those who fit the criteria for the diagnosis of ADD are significantly helped by some other medication or combination of medications. There is no precise way to predict what medication will work for what person.

Just think about it for a second or two. If you wanted to test the effectiveness of a particular ADD medication and do "head-to-head" comparisons of different ADD medications, how would you do that?

Since there are subtypes of ADD likely based on neurophysiological differences among ADDers that respond differently to different medications, researchers can't really do head-to-head comparisons until they discover a way to identify the ADD subtypes in advance of trying to make head-to-head medication comparisons.

So, if you were to test the effectiveness of Ritalin (methylphenidate) treatment you could expect a 30% failure rate. If you were to test the effectiveness of Adderall (mixed amphetamines) treatment or any other non-Ritalin medication, you could expect a very large failure rate somewhere in the 60-80% range. And, that is about what has happened when the effectiveness of these medications has been tested in the general population of ADDers.[248]

In addition, many of the studies of the effectiveness of a particular medication for ADD have, in my opinion, "forgiven" too many side effects in the assessment of the alleged effectiveness.

12.3.1 ADD Medications are NOT Interchangeable

I will say this one more time, in a different way, to make sure it is clear — *ADD medications are not freely interchangeable, and, often, are not interchangeable at all.*

12.4 Myth Number Four: ADD Medications are Addicting

Before discussing drug tolerance and withdrawal, I should add a little explanation about bridges (neurotransmitters) and roads (neurons). Those bridges (neurotransmitters) can only create their temporary bridge-connections by being *accepted* somewhere on the surface of the road (neuron) to which they are connecting.

12.4.1 What is "Tolerance"?

If the bridge (neurotransmitter) receptors are blocked or locked down for some reason, the bridge (neurotransmitter) has no way to connect and it ends up generally stranded and then being quickly biologically "trashed" and thrown away — broken down quickly into a non-active metabolic by-product. You can read more about bridges (neurotransmitters) and roads (neurons) below in Section 14 — *Serial Single-Tasking and the ADD Brain.*

As noted above, the goal of ADD medications is to increase norepinephrine and dopamine levels in the PFC and EB *up to optimal* but *not to above optimal.*

Using prescription medications or recreational drugs (cocaine, methamphetamine) to raise such levels to above optimal has no information processing advantages, but, generally, such levels produce what have been traditionally called "stimulating" side effects. This is why people who don't fit the criteria for the diagnosis of ADD *can* get "high" or "buzzed" or "energized" by taking ADD medications — they start with baseline optimal neurotransmitters and they increase them to way above optimal, thus, the "buzz." But, guess what? Nerve cells are very protective.

So, to get such a "buzz" from any of the ADD medications or cocaine or methamphetamine on an ongoing basis it requires more medication or recreational drug to produce the same earlier "buzz" as the drug use continues.

It is called "tolerance," which can be viewed as "nerve cells trying to protect themselves" (homeostasis) by shutting down receptors (gates) and using other mechanisms to protect themselves from the damaging effects of *too much* artificially "induced" neurotransmitter. [249] [250]

12.4.2 What is "Withdrawal"?

Thus, to get the same "buzz" from nerve cells that have closed most of their gates to protect themselves, it takes more and more drug to *crash through the gates.* When such drug use ceases or is reduced and the amount of available neurotransmitter returns to its pre-drug-use baseline, there is no chance of that baseline level being enough for adequate functioning. New, higher gate-thresholds are out of reach without "artificial" help.[251] Those closed gates don't reopen very fast ("nerve cell caution"). Withdrawal occurs (a period of time when nerve cell functions are non-optimal as they gradually reopen receptor gates and return to pre-drug-use higher availability).

Thus, all those neurological and physiological bad things called withdrawal symptoms take place while the affected nerve cells are moving back to normal — headaches, hallucinations, cognitive slowing, fuzziness, seizures, nausea and vomiting, etc.

In addition, there is clear evidence that too much "gate-crashing" can produce significant brain damage that does not heal quickly, if at all.[252] [253]

12.4.3 Side Effects are Not to Be Tolerated and are Always Indicators of the Wrong Medication or too Much of the Right Medication

Three key concepts are very important: (1) Correct ADD medication targets the correct area of the PFC and EB, and it varies from ADDer to ADDer; (2) Side effects are not to be tolerated — if you fit the criteria for the diagnosis of adult ADD, there is a correct medication (or combination of medications) that will have minimal or no side effects (downside); (3) Dosage of the correct medication should not be increased to a level where it produces side effects and, if it does, it should be reduced.

The correct use of such medications allows "take-it-or-leave-it usage."

On medication, you will have a more "optimal" brain.

Off medication, you will have a more ADD brain.

No tolerance develops.

In my opinion, there is a huge misunderstanding among health care professionals about ADD medication side-effects — that all ADD medications cause side-effects and they are to be accepted and tolerated. In other words, such side-effects are part of treatment. If anyone says this to you, they are wrong, wrong, wrong.

A 2010 study called *Real-World Data on Attention Deficit Hyperactivity Disorder Medication Side Effects* [254] revealed the following:

> "Most common side effects mentioned included loss of appetite, sleep problems, and mood disturbances. Only 21 percent of side effects were considered very bothersome or extremely bothersome. Regardless of how bothersome the side effects were, *only 20% of patients mentioned the side effects* to their prescribing physicians." (emphasis mine)

This was a small study with only 325 patients, which goes to show you how side-effects have not even been deemed important enough to thoroughly study — in other words, they are *widely believed to be unavoidable.* The study clearly demonstrated that 80% of patients who experienced bothersome side effects *never even reported them to their physicians*, which clearly indicates that those patients had the misunderstanding that such "bothersome side effects" were part of the treatment protocol.

I will say it again, "wrong, wrong, wrong." Significant side effects, except for a very few instances of allergies to "non-active" components of such medications, are reliable indicators of above-optimal neurotransmitter levels and continuation of such a scenario will lead to processes of tolerance and withdrawal (addiction).

"Side effects" are practically always manifestations of too much neurotransmitter. There is no advantage to too much neurotransmitter (too many bridges). The condition produces "buzz." Staying on a medication that produces significant side effects is likely to produce tolerance to that medication and require increased dosing. *Please don't do that.*

First, you must be sure you have the correct diagnosis. Second, you must find the right medication for you. Third, you must use the correct dosage that does not produce side-effects. Otherwise, yes, it is possible to become "addicted" (reset neuron receptors) to a prescribed medication.

12.5 Myth Number Five: Taking ADD Medications Leads to Addiction Vulnerabilities

There is no convincing evidence that the correct use of ADD medications, as described above, leads to any types of future addiction vulnerabilities. Many studies have been conducted to answer the question "Do 'stimulant' medications for attention-deficit hyperactivity disorder contribute significantly to later substance abuse?" Many of those studies are noted below. Again, I should note that I have relied on many other studies than the ones done by the Biederman group (potential conflicts of interest and biases) to come to the conclusion that restricted medication therapy does not increase the risk for subsequent substance use disorders of any kind.

However, there is one qualification. Those who have poor access to proper medical evaluation and treatment may participate in seeking and using diverted restricted medications to discover whether their self-diagnosis of ADD is correct. In this current age of huge numbers of uninsured and poor access to treatment for ADD (among many other things), the "illegal" sharing, purchasing and use of restricted medications has blossomed. Whether such behaviors are valid indicators of "substance use disorders" is highly debatable.[255 256 257 258 259]

12.5.1 *No Significant Evidence* that Using ADD Medications Leads to Future Addictions

The Biederman group research can be summarized: (1) "The findings revealed no evidence that stimulant treatment increases or decreases the risk for subsequent substance use disorders (SUDs) (2008)[260]; (2) Their earlier review of the literature in 2003[261] concluded "stimulant therapy in childhood is associated with a reduction in the risk of subsequent drug and alcohol use disorders"; (3) "Stimulant therapy does not increase but rather reduces the risk for cigarette smoking SUDs in adolescents with ADHD" [262]; and (4) "ADHD symptom control may be important to protect against increased risk of substance abuse." [263]

The non-Biederman research can be summarized: (1) "Early age at initiation of methylphenidate treatment in children with ADHD does not increase the risk for negative outcomes and may have beneficial long-term effects" [264]; (2) Therapeutic interventions aimed at restoring brain dopaminergic tone and activity . . . could improve prefrontal function, enhance inhibitory control and interfere with impulsivity and compulsive drug administration" [265], and (3) "This study concurs with 11 previous studies in finding no compelling evidence that stimulant treatment of children with attention-deficit/hyperactivity disorder leads to an increased risk for substance experimentation, use, dependence, or abuse by adulthood." [266]

12.5.2 Clear Evidence that *Untreated* ADD Leads to Future Addictions of Many Types

On the other hand, there is clear and convincing evidence that *not* treating ADD with appropriate medications sets up such under-treated or untreated ADDers for later addictions of many kinds. [267 268 269 270 271]

12.6 Myth Number Six: Typical ADD Medications Cause Blood Pressure Problems

There have been a number of studies which have been inconclusive or mixed in their results for the question "Do ADD medications adversely affect blood pressure?" [272 273 274]

There is very little good data about the blood pressure effects of ADD medications. The clearest result shows that those who are already being treated for hypertension are not adversely affected by ADD medications.[275] Because of the mixed results of these studies, it is recommended that a certain amount of caution should always be used, and monitoring of blood pressure is often recommended.

However, in my experience, treating ADD with the correct medication generally lowers blood pressure. You might wonder why this has not been studied more extensively. I have tried to find that answer, but with no success, so far. (November 2011)

In addition, there is at least one study that clearly indicates that ADDers have less hypertension than non-ADDers.[276]

There are large amounts of data and research about the relationship between anger, anxiety, depression and increased blood pressure and other adverse cardiovascular events. That research has also resulted in mixed conclusions, but generally the weight of the evidence is that certain kinds of anger and chronic fear, including panic attacks, contribute significantly to increased blood pressure. It makes sense that this would be true, because we know that adrenaline (reaction to fright, and flight-or-fight hormone) increases blood pressure, among other things.

When you are constantly in an overwhelmed, chaotic or worried state of mind, you can expect that the "dread" factor of that mindset will have chronically stimulating effects on the adrenal glands with chronic responsive adrenaline secretion, among other things.

The untreated ADDer's life is often characterized by significant daily anxiety, moodiness, low-frustration tolerance (resulting irritability and anger), and other stressors related to disorganization, poor follow-through, and forgetfulness, among other things.

Often, people with untreated ADD experience panic attacks. When you treat the ADD brain-problem responsible for those symptoms that produce higher levels of stress, the stress goes down (the fear factor, obsessive worrying, irritability, anger, etc.) and, thus, so does blood pressure, and, you would expect, other adverse cardiovascular effects of stress.[277] [278] [279] [280] [281]

13 Myths about ADD

13.1 Myth Number One: ADD is a Myth Diagnosis

There are so many myths about ADD and its treatment, that it is difficult to decide which ones to address first and which ones to address later. This particular myth is also associated with the myth, "ADD is a Fad Diagnosis." That myth is addressed further below in this book.

One of the most prolific and well-known purveyors of the concept that "ADD is a Myth" is Thomas Armstrong, Ph.D. His argument can be summed up as "ADD is in the eyes of the beholder." [282] That is, according to him, making the diagnosis of ADD is so full of inconsistencies and poor explanations that it is too subjective of an assessment to be valid. Well, in the hands of an inexperienced evaluator, that criticism might be correct.

In addition, Dr. Armstrong more-or-less cherry picks his arguments and focuses mostly, if not entirely, on the diagnosis of ADD in children. That, of course, is the easiest place to pick apart the ADD diagnostic process, since children, as I noted above, are very poor at self-reporting and don't have the knowledge base, the language, the experience and the maturity to do even moderately good self-reporting.

13.1.1 Diagnosing ADD in Children is Significantly Unreliable

So, the diagnosis and treatment of ADD in children is full of challenges that should be addressed,[283] [284] [285] but generally aren't, because parents, teachers, and schools don't have the time or resources and there is a huge lack of access to child specialists who could do a better and more thorough job of diagnosis. [286]

Because of the poor access to quality diagnostic and follow-up care, we should be careful about pushing medication treatments — why? — because "treating" a non-ADD brain with ADD medications is wrong. Too much neurotransmitter leads to problems. Also, as noted above, too many "authority" figures in a child's life have too many agendas of their own that may not be appropriate or entirely relevant to making correct treatment decisions.

13.1.2 Diagnosing ADD in Adults is Significantly Reliable

However, making the ADD diagnosis in adults is a whole different ballgame. Yes, you need to still do it right (see above about making the diagnosis). But, in addition to doing it right, adults, by far, are better at answering complex questions about executive functioning and describing the nuances of such difficulties. [287]

In my opinion, the vast majority of children over the age of 12 can usually do fairly good self-reporting and identify details of their experience that helps tremendously in making a correct diagnosis and doing proper follow-up. With respect to children under the ages of 12 or so, I do not particularly support the use of medication strategies for treatment, or, if utilized, utilized only in the most difficult behavioral circumstances or at minimum doses.

As noted above, we know conclusively that the major downsides of ADD are related directly to deficiencies in dopamine (and likely norepinephrine) in the PFC and EB. However, we cannot yet make the diagnosis by utilizing those research techniques that have established that fact — it is very expensive and also somewhat daunting for the research subject, to have to be injected with a radioisotope that identifies dopamine status. In addition, such a procedure cannot actually quantify the individual's dopamine deficiency or give an indication of how much medication or what medication would be correct. The metabolic variables that affect a medication as it travels from oral or skin-patch administration to the PFC and EB are huge.

Even if SPECT scans could make the diagnosis and predict correct medication (and that is still arguable), SPECT scans cost approximately $4,000 and are not covered by insurance for the purpose of diagnosing ADD.

The genotyping procedures that could be helpful in quantifying genetic risk factors for the manifestations of ADD in a particular person are very expensive. Genotyping, instead of clinically diagnosing ADD in young children, has been very helpful in identifying populations that are vulnerable to the development of ADD symptoms and impairments, but, again, such genotyping is very expensive.

Blood tests or measurements using spinal fluid do not correctly measure dopamine and norepinephrine levels in the brain and may actually be more of an indicator of neurotransmitter losses (stranded bridges) that did not get pulled back into the nerve cell after being utilized.

So, the current diagnostic process with adults and older children consists of an experienced evaluator doing his or her job thoroughly.

An experienced evaluator doing their job correctly can come to correct diagnostic conclusions with people who can adequately self-report and are not under pressure to conform answers, guess, or otherwise not be able to self-report very well.

13.2   Myth Number Two: ADD is a Fad Diagnosis

Probably the best recent mainstream article addressing this notion can be found at the New York Times, by Perri Klass, M.D., dated December 13, 2010, *Untangling the Myths About Attention Deficit Disorder.* [288]

The fact is, we do not have the tools to accurately measure the prevalence of ADD in populations, since such a measurement relies on making the diagnosis. Making the diagnosis relies on people defining a problem and seeking a diagnosis. Thus, people's awareness of their own potential for the diagnosis drives the frequency of diagnostic appointments. Fewer people seeking help means fewer diagnoses. More people seeking help means more diagnoses. You can only count what has been measured. Guessing at what has not been measured leads to unreliable prevalence estimates.

There have been rough prevalence assessments made in populations using brief self-report questionnaires, but, as noted above, such questionnaires are not very accurate indicators of the percentage of actual, valid diagnoses. More people are seeking diagnostic help, and more people are being diagnosed because they are seeking diagnostic help.

The short answer to the question "Is it a Fad Diagnosis" is "No." It is a diagnosis that is being made more often every year as people begin to understand what ADD is and that it can be effectively treated.

13.2.1 ADD is Only One of Many Dopamine-Deficiency Conditions Widely Embedded in the Western Hemisphere

What is also clear is that what I call "the dopamine-deficiency syndrome" (of which ADD is a significant player) is so widely genetically embedded in our population that the new complexities of life in the United States have made ADD seem to blossom, when, in fact, it was always lurking. Previously, simpler, less challenging, less chaotic, less multi-tasking lifestyles and demands did not engulf the average ADDer to the extent of producing the feeling of being constantly overwhelmed and unable to keep up.

Why is our new fast, distraction-based, entertainment-driven, consumer-obsessed, multi-tasking, financially-insecure society so challenging for people with ADD? More on that below, under *How Does Serial Single Tasking Produce Typical ADD Symptoms?*

When you fully appreciate the upside of ADD as described more fully in this book in the sections entitled *Risk-Taking, Adventurous, "Sensation-Seeking," and "Adrenaline Junkie" Behaviors* and *ADD: Illness or Condition?* you will begin to understand the characteristics of the majority of people who settled the entire Western Hemisphere during at least two major migrations, one from central Asia (13,000 to 15,000 years ago), and the other from Europe and Africa (most significantly between about 1600 and 1870).

14 Serial Single-Tasking and the ADD Brain

This discussion might cause your brain to hurt a little bit. This is a complex subject, which I will attempt to simplify in a way that does not result in any misrepresentations of what is currently known about the human brain's PFC information processing and working memory.

I have to say that the worst piece of writing that I have ever read related to ADHD and brain processing issues, is found at Psychology Today, entitled *ADHD Brains: The Quintessential Supercomputer.* [289] The writer makes the most unscientific and undocumented claims about the ADD brain that I have seen in a long, long time.

And, he makes those claims for all the wrong reasons — to support the argument that the ADD brain is a different brain, not necessarily a worse brain. Honestly, Dr. Goodman, exaggerated misinformation is not helpful. I have no problem believing the ADD brain is special and not "worse" than any other brain and that the ADD brain, in many situations, can be exactly what the doctor ordered, so to speak. The variation in brains, whether ADD or otherwise, should be respected and you don't have to make exaggerated claims to make it so. That's my rant.

For those people who don't see or experience a significant downside to the way their ADD brain works, great. And, for those who *do* experience a significant downside, give them a chance to choose how they want to deal with that without someone trying to make them feel guilty about *their* assessment of their problems or difficulties. As if, all they have to do is realize how special their brains are, and that will make it all better? Honestly, if your rant, Dr. Goodman, is about how ADD folks are discriminated against and treated with disrespect, then talk about that, and kick some discriminatory butt.

Unlike what Dr. Goodman claims, the ADD brain has some real problems with working memory and with functions similar to what we call RAM (random access memory) in computers. That does not make the ADD brain a supercomputer, anymore than any other brain, but it does make it a different brain.

14.1 IQ and ADD are Significantly Separate Domains of Information Processing

The average person already has a supercomputer brain. Yep. Huge. But each of our supercomputer's operations can be challenged by certain limitations. Intelligence Quotient (IQ) is one of those challenges. The other challenge for the ADD brain, is how much RAM is *not* available without increasing dopamine and norepinephrine levels up to optimal levels.

Dr. Goodman confuses IQ with ADD processing and comes up with exaggerated claims for the ADD brain. There is no evidence that the ADD population, on average, have higher IQs than the non-ADD population. However, there is a large amount of data showing that although IQ and ADD are substantially independent characteristics, there is an interaction between IQ and ADD. [290] [291]

Although testable and substantially understood, IQ (general intelligence), is still very debatable and its neurological underpinnings are not well understood. [292] In fact, the idea of "more brain is better" when it comes to brain mass is being challenged.

Some research has shown decreased brain tissue volume is associated with increasing intelligence. In other words, the "better" brain may be the brain that can minimize the expenditure of energy during the performance of a cognitive task. [293] [294] [295] The human brain, which represents a mere 2% of a human's mass, uses 20% of all oxygen and 25% of all glucose produced in the body. [296]

14.2   The Interaction Between IQ and ADD

General intelligence (IQ) has been clearly understood to have two components — fluid and crystallized intelligence. Fluid intelligence (*Gf*) refers to the ability to reason and to solve new problems independently of previously acquired knowledge.

It includes inductive and deductive reasoning abilities. It is characterized by significant ability to analyze novel problems, identify relationships, and to extrapolate using logic. This ability to connect dots, notice commonalities, and meta-analyze has often been called "intuition," but it is much deeper than that. [297] [298] [299]

Crystallized intelligence (*Gc*) is the ability to use knowledge, training, and experience and is primarily indicated by a person's depth and breadth of general knowledge, vocabulary, and ability to reason. [300] [301] Although there is a significant interaction, it is clear that lower fluid intelligence can lead to less crystallized intelligence.

In addition, high fluid intelligence offers work-arounds (logic, reasoning) for those with ADD in that they may be able to be much better test takers by using those higher-reasoning-powers, even when they don't do their required reading or homework. [302] [303] That multiple-choice test-taking ability, however, is *not* so helpful with tests that require written answers and short essays. Often, high-IQ ADDers find themselves much more challenged by the college-level requirements of large amounts of reading and writing.

14.3 IQ is *Not* the Most Significant Predictor of Future Academic Success

Although people who fit the criteria for ADD who have higher IQs are often better at finding work-arounds for their difficulties, when compared to someone else with the same IQ *without* ADD, the ADD brain cannot outperform the non-ADD brain. [304] [305] [306]

In fact, working memory is a better predictor of future academic success than IQ. [307] [308] [309]

Higher IQ ADDers can often stay out of serious trouble. Because of their high fluid intelligence, they can sense (use reason and logic) that their undiagnosed ADD tendencies could get them into trouble, and they generally become very careful. [310] [311] [312] Higher IQ ADDers are also often protected by their ability to reason from getting in trouble with binge eating, obesity, and substance abuse. [313]

Normal and lower IQ ADDers often get into serious trouble, including criminality, because they do not have the same reasoning power (fluid intelligence) to recognize their vulnerabilities and create strategies to deal with them. [314] [315] [316] [317] [318] [319]

So, exactly what is the comparison between the ADD brain and computer operations that helps us better understand what is going on in the ADD brain that creates challenges to certain kinds of information processing? Well, here it is, as best as I can describe the current understanding.

14.4 Roads, Bridges, Random Access Memory, and Working Memory

As I noted earlier in this book, I use the "bridges-out" concept to describe the most significant dimension of what we know for sure creates the downsides of the ADD brain — low dopamine and norepinephrine neurotransmitters (bridges) in various parts of the PFC and EB.

If you visualize brain cells as microscopic pieces of road all crammed in together in the form of the human nervous system, and you visualize how those pieces of road cannot really transport information any farther than the extent of that one little piece of road (nerve cell) without utilizing a bridge (a chemical called a neurotransmitter) to get the information to the next piece of road (nerve cell) to send it onward along a particular brain circuit (highway), then you can understand that without an adequate number of bridges available to your roads, the roads are limited in their capacity to transport information.

In other words, when the bridges are out, many roads are rendered relatively useless for transporting information very far or very fast.

In a very real sense, the ADD brain is working with lesser amounts of Random Access Memory (RAM) than a brain with more optimal levels of dopamine and norepinephrine in the PFC.

Less RAM, as you probably know, means less "multitasking," and certainly less ability to hold a set of data in a cache for further rapid processing at a near-future point.[320][321]

People with more working memory are not easily distracted according to research done at University of Oregon where investigator Edward Vogel compares working memory to RAM.[322]

14.5   The Human Brain's "Spam Filter"

In addition, a team of investigators in Sweden have identified the parts of the brain which are its "spam" filters.[323] Their work not only showed that a good working memory depends on how well irrelevant data is screened out, but it also showed what parts of the human brain are involved in such screening activities ("spam filters"). Turns out screening out relatively "irrelevant" data (less distractibility) depends on prompt and coordinated efforts between the PFC and the basal ganglia.[324]

The jump in brain activity in these areas was greatest for so-called "high working memory capacity performers" and much smaller for "low working memory capacity performers." It seems clear that one of the functions of higher RAM (higher dopamine and norepinephrine bridge availability) is the ability to deal with increases in data without being overwhelmed by the data.[325] You could say that more RAM allows for more screening, and, thus, more efficiency in processing "important" data. Just what the ADD brain lacks, and wants.[326]

14.6 The Primed and Persistent Prefrontal Cortex Network (The "Cache" and "Data Buffer")

One other very important finding cannot be overlooked — there are *two types* of dopamine bridge processes going on in the PFC related to working memory functions: *tonic* and *phasic*. There are D1 (dopamine 1) receptors that mediate what is called "tonic" dopamine bridge function which allows *longer bridge presence* (think of a draw bridge that gets to stay down for a longer period of time) and, thus, creates a baseline, primed network of roads and bridges for holding information (a volatile cache and data buffer) rather than just transmitting information. The shorter-acting dopamine bridges work only as very temporary or "phasic" bridges to transport, but not necessarily "hold," data.[327] [328]

Another way of saying this is extracellular dopamine is modulated by two mechanisms, tonic and phasic dopamine transmission. *Tonic* dopamine transmission occurs when small amounts of dopamine are released *independently* of neuronal data spike activity, and is regulated by the activity of other neurons and dopamine reuptake. *Phasic* dopamine release results from the activity of the dopamine-containing cells themselves in response to task-related data loads. This task-related activity is characterized by irregular activity of single spikes, and rapid bursts of typically 2-6 spikes in quick succession.

The prefrontal cortical persistent (*tonic*) dopamine-induced D1 receptor connectivity is thought to be one of the major contributors to good working memory.[329] It can be conceptualized as DRAM.[330]

Such persistent (*tonic*) activity can be significantly reduced by at least three variables: (1) lower than optimal number of D1 receptors; (2) higher than optimal number of dopamine transporters, which drain dopamine from the synapses too quickly and too well, thus reducing the tonic, longer-lasting dopamine bridges needed for good working memory function, and (3) over-activity of three different enzymes that are present in the brain that break down (metabolize) dopamine — monoamine oxidases (MAO-A and MAO-B) and catechol-*O*-methyl transferase (COMT).[331] [332]

The over-activity of the enzyme systems have been shown to have an adverse effect on tonic dopamine and working memory.[333] [334]

Although not conclusively proven, when you have to borrow from Peter (the tonic dopamine bank) to pay Paul (the phasic dopamine bank) because Paul doesn't have enough dopamine to properly conduct phasic needs, Peter's bank suffers and can't adequately maintain the tonic dopamine required for good working memory.

14.7   The Human "Attentional Network" is More Than Just the Prefrontal Cortex

Even though the PFC is clearly one of the central players in the proper functioning of the attentional network, other parts to which it is significantly connected and which also depend extensively on dopamine bridges are the basal ganglia (striatum), dorsal anterior cingulate cortex, nucleus accumbuns, thalamus, caudate nucleus, putamen, and cerebellum. In addition, as more completely discussed in Section 15, the EB (insula, cingulate gyrus, amygdala, etc.) has extensive and powerful influences on processes taking place in the PFC.

Other important players in the attentional network are not directly dependent on dopamine as much as the prefrontal cortical network, but the limiting variable for *throughput* to those areas is the availability and reliability of optimal levels of tonic and phasic dopamine bridges.[335]

Since the dopamine-dependent attentional network involves more than the PFC, other names have been invented, such as the cingulo-fronto-parietal cognitive-attention network or the frontostriatal and mesocorticolimbic networks.[336 337 338]

In this book, I will use the term "PFC" to stand for the dopamine-dependent circuits and parts of the attentional network. All other parts that are significant players or feedback operators that are not dopamine-dependent, will be referred to as the "peripheral connections."

Putting more dopamine into the PFC through all the various ways noted in Section 9.1 or through appropriate ADD medications clearly powers up the tonic dopamine-bridge network, along with increasing resources for phasic dopamine operations, without reducing the tonic network (cache and data buffer functions) needed for good working memory.[339 340 341]

Finally, just a few more words about cortical connectivity issues in the cognitive-attention network. Many studies have been done that document what could be called "resting brain activity." However, as you might expect, the brain actually never "rests." So, the current popular name for the relatively unchallenged brain state is "default mode network." A more accurate term is "spontaneous task-unrelated brain activity."

Although the names are different, the researchers are all essentially trying to document what the non-sleeping brain is doing when it is not being presented with a particular task challenge or new data challenge.

The so-called default mode in the PFC is very important. Several studies have shown that *default PFC activity in the*

ADD brain is not suppressed like it is in the non-ADD brain when brains are presented with working memory and visual attention tasks.[342][343] How the default mode network relates to tonic and phasic dopamine is not clearly understood. They may be completely separate operations, or not. However, what is clear about the so-called resting state or default mode in the ADD brain is that it does not shut-down like it does in the non-ADD brain when new data loads are experienced. This is likely one of the additional cumulative variables that works against focused attention due to the "background noise" of a "resting state network" that won't "shut up."

14.8 One Last Paragraph About Dopamine (I'm Kidding!)

There is a book out called *The Dopaminergic Mind in Human Evolution and History*, written by Fred H. Previc, published in 2009,[344] which claims that the *hyper*dopaminergic human brain is the brain that led to adventure, migrations, and, in general, to the advancement of humans. Although, Previc's *hyper*dopaminergic premise is clearly way off target, he does write fluently about the highly-probable significance of dopamine to the development and/or functions of the distinctive human brain. Dopamine is clearly a bigger player in the human brain in so many different ways than it is in non-human brains, that it would be difficult to believe otherwise.[345]

For instance, even the human trait of "fairness" (as opposed to outright kill-or-be-killed motivations) has been shown to be related to the D4 (dopamine 4) receptor gene.[346] That's just one "for instance." Otherwise, it is beyond the scope of this book to comprehensively discuss the data that contributes to our understanding of the evolution of human dopamine functions.

14.9   Neuroanatomy Differences in the ADD Brain

Although the only significant method for fixing most of the downside symptoms of ADD is with certain medications, there is more to the ADD brain than neurotransmitter deficiencies.

There are clearly-established macro and micro-structural differences in the ADD brain, some of which correlate with the same dopamine genes that control dopamine receptors (D1 to D5) and the dopamine transporter (DAT).

For instance, the DRD4 7R/7R repeat gene allele (associated with higher risk for ADD, especially in combination with other genetic DR, DAT or enzyme variations) is associated with cortical thinning in regions of the brain important to attentional control and significantly smaller mean volume in the superior frontal cortex and cerebellum cortex.[347 348]

In several other ADD-related studies, various other white matter and grey matter abnormalities were discovered in the ADD brain.[349 350 351 352 353 354 355] However, these studies did not genotype their participants.

The very best comprehensive article on the significant neuroanatomical discoveries that have taken place up to January 2010 with respect to the ADD brain and normal cognition and attention is *Attention-deficit/hyperactivity disorder and attention networks*.[356] It is a great resource if you wish to know the details of cognitive function neuroanatomy and ADD.   However, as noted below, anatomical differences in the ADD brain are helpful pointers, but they are not the controlling variables in the manifestation of ADD characteristics.

The only reason I bring this up is because neuroanatomical variations are important to note, even if the functional significance of those anatomical differences are not yet completely clear.   It is widely accepted that the ADD neuroanatomical differences are *not* the significant controlling variables in the expression of symptoms and impairments related to the diagnosis of ADD.[357]

However, the fact that a gene type can affect not only the number, density and function of a particular dopamine receptor but *also* be responsible for other structural differences makes for a more convincing set of data with respect to the power of the various dopamine genes (D1-D5 and DAT).

Thus, although there are detectable neuroanatomical differences in the ADD brain and we don't know specifically how they relate to dopamine and norepinephrine malfunctioning, we do know *for sure* that the downside of the neurotransmitter problems can be addressed with medication. As such, the anatomical differences are currently significantly irrelevant from a treatment standpoint.

It is very fortunate that ADD-brain anatomical differences don't control outcomes nearly as much as do neurotransmitter levels and functions.

Many brain illnesses, like Alzheimer's,[358] Parkinson's,[359] tumors, strokes, injuries, and various missing parts are almost entirely anatomically-dependent problems and generally cannot be fixed in any significant way by medications.

Clearly, science is not at a place where techniques have been developed to replace particular damaged nerve cells, tracts, circuits, and other parts of the brain with better parts, except, as you may know, in Parkinson's Disease.[360]

14.10 Under-Powered Cache and Data Buffer: *In One Ear and Out the Other*

The ADD PFC is essentially limited to serial single-tasking much like older computers that had limited amounts of RAM. It was difficult, if not impossible, to open more than one program at a time.

Serial-single tasking means that one thought, one image, one sound, one sensation (one piece of data) is open at a time.

To open (notice) a new data point and pay attention to it, the current data point has to be closed. Since the old data point was closed, and cannot be held in a cache or data buffer (holding area) somewhere, it may just disappear and never get a second chance.[361]

Lack of a significant holding area (tonic dopamine function) for data in the PFC of the ADD brain leads to "significantly unprocessed, streaming data." A 2008 study entitled *Working memory capacity predicts dopamine synthesis capacity in the human striatum,*[362] which has stood the test of time, showed clearly that low dopamine synthesis rates produced low working memory.[363]

In addition, lack of adequate phasic dopamine leads to under-powered concurrent processing which adds to the low processing speeds in the PFC.[364 365 366]

As detailed below, almost all of the significant downsides of ADD brain relate to low working memory.

14.11 Fidgeting Increases Working Memory in the ADD Brain

In 2009, Time Magazine published a catchy article called *Kids with ADHD May Learn Better by Fidgeting*[367 368] in which Mark Rapport, a long-time ADD researcher is quoted:

> "Don't overly tax their [ADHD students] working memory. The average teacher doesn't understand how ADHD kids process information. You might hear something like this in the typical classroom, 'Take out the book, turn to page 23, do items 1 through 8, but don't do number 5.' They have given four directions at once and the child with ADHD and working memory problems has lost several of them, so it's like 'I am at page 23, what am I supposed to do now?'"

The fact is both kids *and* adults with ADD learn better while "fidgeting." Fidgeting is not perfect, but it does have arousal and priming effects on neural transmission in the PFC, probably by increasing available dopamine and norepineprhine.[369] [370]

14.12 What is Good Working Memory? Can Working Memory be Trained?

You can read some of the best writing about working memory in the 2009 book *The Overflowing Brain* by Torkel Klinberg[371] (yep, the guy who discovered the brain's "spam filter"[372]). I don't want to repeat everything that Klinberg covers in his book, but I am going to have to discuss his "enthusiasm" for training working memory — that is, for increasing working memory abilities even in those children and adults who fit the criteria for ADD through the use of specific mental "exercises."

You might think that if there is a strong limiting factor to working memory abilities, such as the level of dopamine in the crucial parts and connectors within the attentional network, that no matter what you did to "train" your working memory, it could not be altered very much, unless you also altered your dopamine levels. In my opinion, you would be mostly correct.

I think it is significant that Klinberg was able to show how certain very targeted brain exercises his team developed could increase working memory by up to 18% ("RoboMemo" computerized training) in ADD populations. The brain is clearly dynamic and capable of a certain amount of rewiring and more efficient wiring. However, there are limits, even to the best training methods for working memory and its fairly distant cousins, fluid intelligence, general intelligence, impatience and impulsivity (delay aversion).

As you might expect, the idea of increasing cognitive-related functioning, including IQ, through training is a *very hot issue*, fired up by the strong hopes for such possibilities. That is, many of us wish we could improve our working memory or IQ through training. Obviously, the more we know about these connections, the more we can structure educational systems and personal educational efforts to give our children and ourselves the best tools possible for brain health and function. So, there have been a relative glut of such cognitive-training studies.[373 374 375 376 377] Not unexpectedly, there are no absolute, slam-dunk, positive conclusions.[378 379]

In addition, there have been studies conducted to attempt to determine dopamine system changes related to cognitive training or working memory training. Some evidence exists for changes in D1 receptor binding,[380] which may have some positive impact on tonic dopamine function (cache and data buffer resources) in the PFC. However, most other studies have shown the clear involvement of the D2 and dopamine transporter (DAT) system with working memory.[381 382]

As noted in my earlier discussions of IQ and ADD, the major controlling mechanisms of human IQ are not understood. We know that there is very little connection between improving the symptoms of ADD, including working memory, and IQ improvements using medications that increase dopamine and norepinephrine levels in the ADD brain.[383] Thus, it is very unlikely that the dopamine-dependent attentional network and its working memory functions have much to do with IQ.

In my professional opinion, high fluid intelligence will be found to be related to some kind of brain structure that is highly genetically influenced. The high-fluid-IQ candidate brain structure will likely consist of an actual, physical set of some type of meta-level, data-processing connections.

We know that gap junctions, which are direct electrical connections between nerve cells, allow for very fast data processing compared to chemical neurotransmitter processes. It is likely that the distribution and number of gap junctions are responsible for creating high-speed meta-connectivity that significantly accelerates associative processing speeds and results in higher fluid intelligence.

It makes sense that since working memory has been shown to be highly dependent on optimal levels of dopamine and norepinephrine in the various connectors and parts of the attentional brain network, that it would be difficult, if not impossible, to raise such neurotransmitter levels through "training" alone.

There are clear indicators that such neurotransmitter levels *can* be elevated by certain behaviors and thoughts/actions involving threat, fear, conflict, risk, and/or pain *and* a number of non-medications, including eating food. It is also very clear that working memory and other executive function deficits in those who fit the criteria for ADD can be reliably increased and relatively normalized with many typical ADD medications.[384 385 386 387 388 389 390 391]

So, the short answer to the question "Can working memory or IQ be significantly increased through cognitive exercises in those who fit the criteria for ADD? is, "not really."

14.13 The Myth of "Neuroenhancement" for the Already Optimal Non-ADD Brain

As I noted earlier, the goal of medications in the ADD brain is to increase dopamine and norepinephrine up to optimal but *not above* optimal. Above-optimal levels of these neurotransmitters do not produce any advantages to learning other than possibly staying up longer which, in, and of itself, can negatively impact long-term memory. I suppose if you have to cram you have to cram, but it does not really constitute learning.

Please note: Students who do *not* fit the criteria for ADD who try typical ADD medications to see if such medications can "enhance" their test-taking, studying, or writing abilities generally find out fairly quickly how much it does *not* work. That is, when they review their essays after an Adderall-enhanced essay test, for instance, they almost always are shocked by how verbose, redundant, and otherwise sloppy their essays are in such an "enhanced" condition.

"Typical" discussions about so-called neuroenhancement can be found on the Internet and at the New York Times.[392] [393] In my opinion, those discussions take a much too casual and unscientific view of the practices of such so-called neuroenhancement.

There are several excellent studies which clearly indicate the *non-usefulness* of typical ADD medications for those who do not fit the criteria for ADD. There is no solid case that can be made for so-called "neuroenhancement," and the neurologists should be spanked for declaring in 2009 that "it is ethical." [394]

These quotes from their report in Neurology (the Journal of the American Academy of Neurology) say it all —

> "It is ethically permissible for neurologists to prescribe such therapies, provided that they adhere to well-known bioethical principles of respect for autonomy, beneficence, and nonmaleficence," and ". . . the risks of the long-term use of off-label medications for neuroenhancement in normal patients without a medical or mental health condition are not known and may not be known for many years."

Really? I guess the term "many years" is open to definition, but it appears to me that not only before,[395] but, also, after the 2009 "neuroenhancement-is-ethically-permissible" report,[396] there has been clear evidence of the downside of above-optimal neurotransmitters.[397] [398] [399] [400] That is exactly what some of the most addictive and powerful illicit drugs do (cocaine, bathtub methamphetamine) — they increase levels of dopamine and norepinephrine to way above optimal. I am waiting, not-so-patiently, for the neurologists to update their 2009 views to current well-known science.

14.14 "Non-Medical" Use of Typical ADD Medications

There are also many good studies regarding the "non-medical" use of "stimulants" by college students and how such behaviors are more-likely-than-not misguided attempts to treat undiagnosed ADD symptoms. In other words, there are a large number of undiagnosed ADDers in college.[401 402 403]

Most, if not all, of the more recent and more valid studies have confirmed that there are *reductions* in cognitive performance for those who are baseline high performers. This conclusion clearly indicates that in the population with the most "optimized" brains, putting more than optimal neurotransmitter into the mix *reduces* performance. Why?

If you can visualize too many bridges in a system of roads, you might also see how that over-abundance of bridges would likely confuse drivers (information flow) and reduce the efficiency of getting from one place to another (processing). The fact that previously "low performers" experienced increased performance using ADD medications is further proof of a spectrum of PFC "processing limitations" from the more subtle (low working memory performance *without* clear-cut ADD) to the more obvious (low working memory performance *with* clear-cut ADD).[404]

14.15 The Inverted U-Shaped Curve (or, the Law of Diminishing Returns)

With respect to the human brain, it appears that there is an optimum level of norepinephrine and dopamine bridges (RAM) below which and above which the brain does not operate at a data-processing optimum. This is often called an inverted U-shaped curve of neurotransmitter effectiveness — too little is not optimal and too much is also not optimal (the descending part of the inverted U-shaped curve). Visualize the vertical axis of a graph as the effectiveness rating and the horizontal axis of the graph as the increasing amounts of dosages.[405 406 407 408 409 410]

Unlike computers, which can be outfitted with increasingly complex hardware that can allow huge amounts of RAM to be utilized, the human brain has a limited number of neurons (capacitors/processors/pieces of road). To optimize those processors (pieces of road) you need just the right amount of RAM (bridges). Too few or too many bridges produces non-optimal performance.

This is likely true of all the neurotransmitters in the brain. There are many of them, including some ions which can be neurotransmitters. Different neurotransmitters are specialized in different systems, regions, and pathways. *Neurotransmission Basics at CNS Forum* is a good place to learn more about the brain's neurotransmitters.[411]

Not all neurotransmitters act like RAM to optimize working memory in the general region of the brain called the PFC. Other neurotransmitters have other functions.

15 How Does the Serial Single-Tasking of the ADD Brain Produce Typical ADD Symptoms?

As I have noted above, I use the "bridges-out" concept for explaining one of the most significant deficits in the ADD brain, the low levels of dopamine activity (completely proven) and the low levels of norepinephrine activity (mostly proven).

Many studies have clearly proven that one of the major contributors to the downside of the ADD brain are deficits in working memory in at least the PFC, but also, possibly located in slow-processing links between the PFC and other brain areas.

I have compared the ADD brain to a computer with less-than-normal RAM to the extent that, as described in several studies, the low dopamine and norepinephrine levels cause clear deficits in working memory and processing speed.

Working memory is the term used for the brain's RAM. More RAM (up to optimum levels of neurotransmitters) allows for more ability to hold data temporarily while, among other things, making decisions about what to process first or later, without losing the data during the time interval that is required for those decisions to be made.

Brain processing operations are more concurrent than parallel. More concurrent processing can take place when there are more circuits available for processing data. Less bridges than optimal means less available circuits and, thus, less concurrent processing. This deficiency in available circuits produces slower overall processing speed. In addition, the relative lack of concurrent processing resources in the ADD PFC and basal ganglia lead to difficulty screening out "noise."

Although we are all pretty much forced to pay attention to the next piece of data, when you have less RAM, you may not be able to put anything on hold for later processing and then data just becomes overwhelming with the next piece replacing the first piece and so on (limited cache and data buffer functions).

What looks like distractibility is, in fact, data streaming relentlessly without much processing. Endless serial attention without a holding area results in constantly streaming thoughts, images, and sensations. And you wonder why one of the major downsides of the ADD brain is distractibility and one of the major experiences of ADDers is feeling overwhelmed most of the time?

Major indicators of the diagnosis of ADD are (1) easy distractibility, (2) relatively uncontrollable moodiness throughout the day, (3) low frustration tolerance — easily angered, irritable, (4) moderate to severe daily anxiety, (5) impatience, (6) impulsivity, (7) hyperactivity — fidgeting, compulsion to move, (9) non-empathic, (10) "hyperfocus", (10) risk-taking or "sensation-seeking" behaviors, and (12) self-injury.

I will explain how the low dopamine and low working memory of the ADD brain facilitates the manifestations of these symptoms, indicators, and impairments.

15.1 Easy Distractibility

"Easy distractibility" manifests itself in several different behavioral and information-processing ways. The signs that distractibility produce include (1) difficulty staying on task, (2) hypersensitivity to sound and touch, (3) difficulty reading, with a typical ADD scenario of read a couple of paragraphs, get distracted by some other thought (or noise), forget what was read, have to re-read a lot; (4) forgetfulness, poor follow-through, disorganization, lose track of time, (5) indecision, procrastination, (6) sleep-onset insomnia and difficulty returning to sleep when awakened, and (7) social "phobia" or anxiety, among other things.

My theory is that the distractibility of ADD is primarily related to the lower processing power and low RAM of the ADD brain (underpowered cache and data buffer functions). This sets up the ADD brain to primarily serial single-task, which only allows for brief, cursory, and sometimes no processing or prioritizing of data received — producing a stream of relatively uncontrollable data.

Working memory deficits have been clearly implicated in distractibility which makes it difficult to screen out "irrelevant" data and to have the capability to choose data to focus on. The phrase I use to describe this process in the ADD brain is "the data chooses you, you do not choose the data — in that regard, you are not in control of the data, it is in control of you."

Although it should be fairly clear how distractibility relates to the ADD brain's deficiency in working memory (low RAM), let me run through each distractibility sign again:

> (1) Difficulty staying on task — focus and choice are relatively absent due to the limitations of serial single-tasking (one task at a time and literally hundreds of data points presenting themselves for processing);
>
> (2) Hypersensitivity to sound and touch — environmental data that can't be screened out

while choosing some other data to focus on —
all data "claiming" equal attention;

(3) Difficulty reading, with typical ADD
scenarios of (a) read a couple of paragraphs,
get distracted by some other thought,
sensation, or noise; (b) difficulty focusing on
words and sentences within all the other words
and lines (distractors) on a page of text; and
(c) forgetting the beginning of a sentence when
reaching the end of the sentence;

(4) Forgetfulness, poor follow-through,
disorganization, poor sense of time — if you
can't choose thoughts due to resource
limitations, then you can't choose actions
either, or prioritize very well, or note the
passing of time. With respect to being able to
be aware of the passing of time, you must be
able to have your "time program" open while
you are working on other things (have other
programs open). The ADD brain has real
difficulty with having two or more programs
open at the same time. It would be like a
computer with such low RAM that it cannot
have a clock program open at the same time as
a word-processing program;

(5) Indecision, procrastination — can't make
a choice, can't narrow down data points or set
priorities (all data gets equal attention), can't
get past the inertia of the weight of too many
thoughts and choices. What appears to be
procrastination is really more about distraction
(indecision, lack of direction) until a deadline
gets close enough to produce enough fear to
increase EB dopamine and norepineprhine to
levels that positively affect working memory,
focus, and follow-through which allow for that
last-minute surge of directed activity;

(6) Sleep-onset insomnia and difficulty
returning to sleep when awakened — can't shut

off or screen out streaming data (sensations, sounds, thoughts and images) and focus on sleep; and

(7) Social "phobia" or anxiety — too much input in "party" situations with so many data points converging from different sources at the same time that the ADDer just wants to escape (get drunk, do drugs, or just leave or withdraw).

People (including professionals) observing these behaviors will often conclude that the undiagnosed ADDer is lacking discipline or will power, is lazy, stupid, unreliable, dyslexic, unmotivated, shy, rebellious, uncooperative, passive-aggressive, dishonest (embellishing or lying), having racing thoughts or grandiose (bipolar), a loner, or autistic, alcoholic, or addiction-prone, among other things.

15.1.1   Reading Impairments (Dyslexia?)

I created "Reading Impairments" as a separate category to make sure that it gets your full attention. As noted above, significant reading impairment is almost always part of the ADDer's life. It is generally *not* an IQ, language or knowledge problem.

The three most common distractibility-related reading impairment scenarios are (1) read a couple of paragraphs, get distracted by some other thought (or noise), forget what was read, and have to frequently re-read, (2) since words and sentences on a page are surrounded closely by other words and sentences above, below, and along side of what a person is attempting to read, the distractibility quotient of any typical page of text is very high and ADDers often find it difficult to focus in on the word or the sentence they are attempting to read without being distracted by the surrounding words, and (3) forget the beginning of a sentence when reaching the end of the sentence (you have to be able to hold a complete sentence in your working memory to understand the meaning of a sentence — similarly, with paragraphs).

The work-arounds that are often used by ADDers are to highlight every sentence, take copious notes, or use a ruler, a pointer, or a finger to stay focused on one word or one line of words at a time. The following quotes are from five different studies done between 2008 to 2011:

2011[412] — "The encoding of information from one event into working memory can delay high-level, central decision-making processes for subsequent events. It is, therefore, possible that, in addition to delaying central processes, the engagement of working memory encoding (WME) also postpones perceptual processing as well. We conclude that encoding of a stimulus into working memory *delays* the deployment of attention to subsequent target representations in visual cortex."

2010[413] — "We found that attentional mechanisms controlled by the dorsal visual stream help in *serial scanning of letters* and any deficits in this process will cause a cascade of effects, including impairments in visual processing of graphemes, their translation into phonemes and the development of phonemic awareness."

2010[414] — "Cumulative incidence of reading disability (RD) by the age of 19 years was significantly higher in children *with* ADHD (51% in boys, 46.7% in girls) compared with those *without* ADHD (14.5% in boys, 7.7% in girls)."

2010[415] — "Individual differences in processing speed are influenced by genes that also increase risk for reading disability (RD), ADHD, and their comorbidity. These results suggest that *processing speed measures* may be useful for future molecular genetic studies of the etiology of comorbidity between RD and ADHD."

2008[416] — "Recognition of the role of attentional mechanisms in reading offers potentially new strategies for interventions in dyslexia. In particular, the use of pharmacotherapeutic agents affecting attentional mechanisms may not only provide a window into the neurochemical mechanisms underlying dyslexia but also may offer a potential adjunct treatment for facilitating dyslexic readers to read fluently and automatically. *Preliminary studies suggest that agents traditionally used to treat disorders of attention, particularly attention deficit hyperactivity disorder, may prove to be effective in improving reading in dyslexic students.*" (all emphasis mine)

15.1.2   Sleep Difficulties

As noted above in Section 12.2 *The Number Two Myth: ADD Medications Cause Sleep Problems*, around 80% of people with ADD have sleep onset insomnia — difficulty getting to sleep — often at both bedtime and later in the night when they wake up.

A large number of people with untreated ADD develop habits of going to bed really late when they "feel really exhausted" because they know that they will have difficulty getting to sleep if they go to bed "too early." The may also utilize "white noise" such as a radio, television, or fan to create a low-volume background noise. Such consistent background sounds can be a "magnet" for the ADD brain and allow it to more-or-less "lock-out" other intrusive or streaming data and set-up the ADD brain for sleep. [417]

Of course, in addition to the "non-medication" strategies noted above for "treating" sleep difficulties, ADDers often resort to over-the-counter and prescribed sleep medications, illicit drugs, and alcohol for sleep. The major reason for this sleep onset difficulty is that data (thoughts, images, sounds, sensations) which is always flooding the ADD consciousness is even more intrusive in a quiet atmosphere and it takes control of the ADD brain (poor "spam filter" as noted above).

There are two excellent studies of ADD sleep problems.

The first study entitled *Association between attention-deficit/hyperactivity disorder and sleep impairment in adulthood: evidence from a large controlled study* out of Massachusetts General Hospital,[418] showed that

> "Adults with ADHD went to bed later than control subjects and had a wider range of bedtimes, were more likely to take over an hour to fall asleep, and were more likely to experience difficulty going to bed, going to sleep, sleeping restfully, or waking in the morning. Adults with ADHD experienced daytime sleepiness more often and reported more sleep problems than controls."

The second study entitled *Sleep problems and disorders among adolescents with persistent and subthreshold attention-deficit/hyperactivity disorders* [419] out of the National Taiwan University Hospital & College of Medicine, Taipei, showed that

> "Adolescents with a childhood diagnosis of ADHD according to DSM-IV criteria, regardless of whether they had persistent ADHD, were more likely to have current and lifetime sleep problems and sleep disorders according to DSM-IV (insomnia, sleep terrors, nightmares, bruxism, and snoring)."

With respect to research done to discover whether typical medications for the treatment of ADD symptoms also improve sleep, the results are mostly positive. One would expect that if you go to bed with an "ADD brain," you are going to be highly distractible and have a difficult time focusing on sleep. One would expect that if you went to bed with more optimal levels of dopamine and norepinephrine that you would be better at choosing what to focus on and better at screening out irrelevant data. And, that is precisely what happens.

Studies showing the positive effects of Ritalin (methylphenidate) for sleep normalization in ADDers include the following:

2010[420] — "According to our results we can say that the MPH not only does not make sleep worse, but that *it improves the quality of the sleep* in those patients with sleep disorders."

2008[421] — "Compared to controls untreated patients showed increased nocturnal activity, reduced sleep efficiency, more nocturnal awakenings and reduced percentage of REM sleep. Treatment with methylphenidate resulted in *increased sleep efficiency* as well as a subjective feeling of improved restorative value of sleep."

2007[422] — "Our data suggest that sleep problems are inherent in adults with ADHD and that methylphenidate reduced total sleep time but *improved sleep quality* by consolidating sleep." (all emphasis mine)

Again, as noted above, in my experience, 80% of adults who fit the criteria for ADD have significant sleep difficulties. When the correct medication is used, it has significant positive effects on normalizing both the ability to get to sleep and sleep quality. A 2004 article at ADDitudeMag.com,[423] gets most of it right about ADD sleep problems. As Dr. Dodson says "About two-thirds of my adult patients take a full dose of their ADHD medication every night to fall asleep."

15.1.3 Time Estimation and Perception Difficulties

At least 80% of adults who fit the criteria for ADD have time estimation and time perception difficulties.

It is almost classic how impossible it is for ADDers to keep track of time while they are doing just about anything else. The awareness of the passing of time requires a kind of "dual-tasking" — notice time while you do other things. Time estimation errors are clearly related to the insufficient RAM of the PFC (poor working memory) of the ADD brain. Several studies have reported that compared to a control group of non-ADDers, adults with ADD showed greater deviation in time estimation and that the magnitude of the time-estimation errors was clearly affected by allocation load of working memory.[424 425 426 427 428]

15.2 Relatively Uncontrollable Moodiness Throughout the Day

As noted above under "Easy Distractibility," due to the RAM limitations found in the ADD brain, incoming data overwhelms system resources and each data point more-or-less *simultaneously* claims attention because of the significant working memory limitations.

As I mentioned earlier, in the ADD brain, "the data is in control of you, you are not in control of the data." You are on what I call a "data roller coaster" — more or less at the mercy of streaming thoughts, images, and sensations, and unable to screen out what you don't want to think about (as if you thought that could happen). So, mixtures of "good" and "bad" thoughts take you up and down throughout the day without you being able to screen out one or the other and choose a set of data to focus on (stability). Since almost all images, memories and thoughts have emotional meaning attached to them, when you are on a *data roller coaster* you are also on a *mood roller coaster*.

The opposite, "positive emotionality (PEM)," is clearly correlated to striatal dopamine 2 receptor availability and the operations of the orbitofrontal cortex and cingulate gyrus. Not only good dopamine function in those areas protects against the development of substance use disorders, but high baseline dopamine-dependent metabolism is clearly associated with high PEM.

Individuals with high scores on PEM have high reward sensitivity, are motivated and have a propensity to experience positive moods (joy, enthusiasm).[429]

People (including professionals) observing this often classify this ADD behavior as temperamental, moody, unpredictable, dysthymic, clinically depressed, bipolar, manic-depressive, borderline personality disorder, flighty, or overly-sensitive, among other things.

15.3 Low Frustration Tolerance - Often Irritable and Easily Angered

When data processing resources are overwhelmed by data due to limited ADD brain RAM, guess what? People feel overwhelmed. Or, as I put it, "the barbarians are always at the gates." The condition of being and feeling overwhelmed by baseline levels of data leads to a sense of dread and irritability ("leave me alone"), and often to easily-triggered anger ("didn't I say, leave me alone?").

In addition to the ADDer feeling that there is always too much baseline data compared to the limited resources available to deal with it (low working memory), when additional data loads are experienced, that feeling escalates to "totally overwhelmed."

If not spoken out-loud, the untreated ADDer feels it at some level. They are often puzzled and angry about the unexplained hypersensitivity, irritability, dread, and panic they keep encountering. Often, the ADDer who knows this about themselves, will find a work-around such as withdrawing, hunkering down, or "escaping" in some way, rather than lashing out.

A 2010 study of "impulsive aggression" in adults with ADD recommended that features such as hot temper/short fuse be included in the list of symptoms characteristic of ADD in adults.[430]

However, as much as I wish a discussion of ADD-related "anger" could be simple, "anger" is not a simple word. There are many types of anger and there are many behaviors that can be interpreted as anger, from protective to overly-aggressive and out-of-control, and from mildly impatient to punitive and intentionally hurtful (power-mongering).

The types of "anger" that are generally displayed by ADDers is the type that is mostly related to "protective" behavior when feeling overwhelmed (which is quite often). In a close second-place are behaviors that are related to not censoring very well, which can feel rude and mean. In third place are "angry" responses triggered by impatience (parking lot, standing-in-line, and road "rage"). Although "victims" of such angry impatience and "mean" behaviors might not agree with me, these ADD behaviors are almost always *not* the kind of "real" rage you might experience coming from an over-amped non-ADDer.

Although, as you will note in this book, I hypothesize that there are not that many people with optimal dopamine, there are, believe it or not, documented downsides to the dopamine-optimized brain. One of the significant ones is how they can get over-amped and seriously enraged and out of control when their dopamine levels in their EB ("EB") shoot up to way above optimal. More information about the downsides of the dopamine-optimized brain can be found in Section 15.10.9.

People (including professionals) observing such behaviors in undiagnosed ADDers often classify them as mean, rude, selfish, quick-tempered, overly-aggressive, borderline personality disorder, detached, or passive-aggressive, among other things.

15.4 Moderate to Severe Daily Anxiety (Often Feeling Overwhelmed)

If you sense that you are being "attacked" by overwhelming amounts of data, wouldn't you be a little fearful? Organisms, including humans, have the "uncanny" ability to sense things.

The main sense that most ADDers will report to you if you ask them is "I can't handle it all." That would be strike number one. What they are noticing is that life (all that data) is too much for them, and the more complex or distracting elements that are introduced into their lives means even more "dreadful" data. Well, any data can be dreadful when it overwhelms system resources and produces a sense of panic. And, you wonder why so many ADDers get diagnosed with anxiety disorders or have panic attacks? Or, why driving a vehicle might be somewhat distressing?

Then there is the whole thing about "forgetfulness." ADDers almost always know they are forgetting something. They know it, but they cannot completely control it. Higher IQ ADDers often figure out work-arounds, like certain kinds of "routines" (sometimes interpreted as "rituals") such as always putting their keys, cell phones, wallets, or purses in a specific place, no matter what. Or, triple-checking doors to make sure they are locked, etc., etc., etc., because they can't remember if they just did that. And you wonder why some ADDers get classified as having an obsessive compulsive disorder?

Well, constant fear of forgetting and worry about it makes for a very anxious feeling. That would be strike number two.

Strike number three for most adult ADDers when it comes to the experience of anxiety is "more worry" — as if worrying about forgetting is not enough. As if worrying about forgetting is not enough, adult ADDers often do "negative day-dreaming." In other words, they aren't doing positive day-dreaming.

What appears very clear to me is that the "pool" of possible distracting negative events in a person's history gets bigger every year (I know, so does the pool of possible distracting positive events in person's history). That pool of negative experiences becomes fodder for distractions and often "plagues" the ADD brain, much more than the pool of positive experiences. Adult ADDers have this sense that they are always on the verge of failure and their "day-dreaming" is more often than not, negative, harking back to bad things that happened before. (A classic ADD sign is the guy or girl who at age 40 is still obsessing about the girlfriend or boyfriend they lost in high school.)

One recent study published in 2008,[431] found that 33% of 97 consecutive adult patients seen in an anxiety disorder specialty clinic fit the criteria for the diagnosis of ADD and were not referred to the clinic for ADD symptoms or evaluation. Only nine of those who had been referred to the clinic for treatment for anxiety had been previously identified as fitting the criteria for ADD.

Some untreated ADDers figure out their limitations and don't push themselves too hard or do not give in to being pushed by others for "more success." They may stubbornly simplify their lives by sticking to one job most of their life, not marrying, not having kids, and keeping their life as structured and simple as possible.

As much as I wish this discussion of "anxiety" could be simple, the word "anxiety" has many meanings. Anxiety can range from a more "free-floating" type, as in a relatively constant feeling of dread and always expecting the worst, to something that is very specifically triggered by a distinct thought or experience similar to a previous traumatic experience that was particularly hurtful or fearful, as in posttraumatic stress disorders ("PTSD") or phobias. In addition, there are panic disorders and panic "attacks" that are often confused with anxiety disorders but which have turned out to be much different than generalized anxiety and phobias.[432]

Not all ADDers are the same. The common denominators are huge, but there are differences that are still not completely understood.

One of those differences is types of anxiety. Due to poor working memory and lack of a significant data buffering process, almost all ADDers experience chronic dread (anxiety) from constant relative data-overload. When a new data challenge shows up on top of the baseline data burden, it can often be very overwhelming, as in multiple-data-point group gatherings.

In addition to that constant marginal baseline data processing "anxiety," some ADDers have the further burden of sensory over-responsivity ("SOR").[433] Panic attacks or panic disorder symptoms are much more common in ADDers than in non-ADDers.[434]

Almost always, the ADD-related data-overload anxiety is extinguished entirely by enhancing working memory by increasing dopamine and norepinephrine levels with appropriate ADD medication (not benzodiazepines or other "tranquilizers").

However, other types of ADD-related anxiety, such as triggered by sensory over-responsivity or panic attacks may require more gaba-ergic medications such as clonidine (Catapres) rather than just straight-forward dopamine and norepinephrine enhancers.

Generalized anxiety disorder, PTSD and phobias are clearly more prevalent in *non-ADDers*. Much more information about the downsides of the non-ADD brain can be found in Section 15.10.9.

People (including professionals) observing this often conclude that undiagnosed ADDers are depressed, pessimistic, worry-warts, compulsive, obsessive, inflexible, afraid of change, agoraphobic, have anxiety disorders, have clinical depression, have panic disorder, or have obsessive-compulsive disorder.

15.5 Impatience

I created impatience as a separate category to make sure that it gets your full attention. Significant and problematic impatience is almost always part of the ADDer's life.

Impatience is really associated with the low-frustration tolerance (easily overwhelmed) of the ADD brain. So, the earlier discussion about low-frustration tolerance applies here.

Waiting for just about anything requires fairly good working memory, in the sense that thoughts and actions must be put on hold during the waiting process. Thus, waiting, in and of itself, produces increased distractibility and unanticipated data.

ADDers will often interrupt others in conversations because they are not in control of their thoughts and "can't put them on hold." If they attempt to put them on hold, they may lose the thought completely.

ADDers usually talk just like they process information — scattered, tangential, often losing track of the previous thought or train of thought or the thread of the conversation. They may blurt out opinions, judgments, criticisms and compliments at totally or relatively inappropriate moments in a conversation and have real trouble modulating language (that is, modifying it to match the tone of the conversation) to stay within the conversation's tonal or emotional range.

There has been some theorizing about the ADD brain's difficulty with inhibition and some research done in the last few years has indicated that possibly inhibitory pathways in the ADD brain are malfunctioning. Research based on tests utilizing "stop-signal tasks" and go-no-go tasks have had mixed results.

However, a 2010 study entitled *Do working memory deficiencies underlie behavioral inhibition deficits?* concluded that working memory deficits clearly underlie the difficulties with the inhibition of behavior often seen in ADD.[435] With low working memory it is very difficult to have a thought and decide what to do with the thought at the same time.

People (including professionals) often interpret such undiagnosed ADD behaviors as rude, self-centered, narcissistic, unsympathetic, dishonest, narcissistic personality disorder, or borderline personality disorder, among other things.

15.6 Impulsivity

Again, ADDers behave pretty much just like how they process information. In other words, streaming data equals streaming behavior — not much thought processing, holding a thought and examining it, or thinking about long-term consequences takes place in the ADD brain.[436][437] Increased impulsive behavior and risk proneness are attributed to decreased dopaminergic tone.[438][439]

15.6.1 Short-Term Thinking, Delay Aversion

Short-term thinking, often called "delay discounting" has been studied over and over again, and it is clearly related to dopamine deficiency.[440][441][442][443] ADDers consistently prefer smaller-immediate over larger-delayed rewards.[444][445]

Without good working memory, it is relatively impossible to actually modify an action or reaction while moving toward an action or reaction because both processes cannot go on at the same time without more RAM (a well-functioning data buffer). It can be thought of as a lack of inhibition, but the actual process is *not* about neurons having a deficit in inhibitory feedback. A better explanation is that without good working memory (a good data buffer), thoughts, images, and sensations are pretty much in control of the ADD brain. Processing is limited, so evaluation and holding back, delay and thinking through ("mindfulness"), do not happen before action takes place.[446][447][448][449]

The claim that impulsive behavior is more frequently a part of the so-called "hyperactive" type of ADD is losing validity as more studies utilizing the UPPS Impulsive Behavior Scale (UPPS) are published.[450] The UPPS scale measures four traits: positive urgency, negative urgency, sensation seeking, lack of premeditation, and lack of perseverance.[451]

The UPSS scale has been utilized to study several ADD-related behaviors, including insomnia[452], obesity.[453], and self-injury.[454] It is very significant that ADD UPSS results and the results found in those other studies are very similar, suggesting that the common traits found therein may have common causes.

15.6.2 Suicidality

With respect to suicide attempts and successes in those who fit the criteria for ADD, the research is mostly clear — the combination of low working memory (not able to think before acting), low stress tolerance, impulsivity, impatience and reduced fear-responsiveness, clearly sets up the ADDer for more frequent suicide attempts and successes.[455] [456]

There is substantial evidence that males with childhood hyperactivity-inattention symptoms are at far higher risk for suicidal behaviors than females.[457] [458]

In addition, the functioning of the fear-response (emotional/brain-hypothalamic-pituitary-adrenal axis and cortisol response) in those who are at risk for suicide is blunted similarly to the blunted cortisol response in those who fit the criteria for ADD [459] (noted in two other sections of this book about risk-taking and self-injury). It is "blunted" because the switch for turning cortisol on and for keeping it on is found in "circuit boards" in the brain collectively called the "EB" which depend on dopamine and norepinephrine to function properly.

The cortisol that is released from the adrenal glands in response to signals from the EB attempts to shut-down (tries to calm down) the dopamine and norepinephrine signaling in the EB.

Because of the lower baseline dopamine and norepinephrine in the EB of ADDers, the ADD brain can "handle" larger amounts of "fear" before the EB reaches the dopamine/norepinephrine threshold for switching on adrenal gland hormones. Similar to how the untreated ADDer will almost always be better at jumping out of planes than the non-ADDer, the untreated ADDer will also almost always be "better" at suicide.

People (including professionals) often interpret such undiagnosed ADD impulsivity as poor self-control, poor discipline, short-sighted, selfish, flighty, risk-taking, lack of planning, attention seeking, dramatic, excitable, entertaining, energetic, addicted to gambling or pornography, or bipolar, or borderline personality disorder,[460] among other things.

15.7 Hyperactivity - Fidgeting, Restlessness, "Driven by a Motor"

The "compulsion to move" found among many ADDers has had many explanations, from inability to inhibit actions, to reward deficiency syndrome, to being an "adrenaline junkie." There have been theories that explain such ADD hyperactivity as a way of "arousing" the PFC to improve working memory.

A study done by Rapport and associates became the focus of a May 2009 Time magazine article entitled *Kids with ADHD Learn Better by Fidgeting.*[461] What Rapport discovered is that during working memory tasks, kids who fit the criteria for ADD had higher activity levels ("fidgeting") than a non-ADD population of kids and that the fidgeting could be eliminated by presenting those same fidgeting kids with non-working memory tasks.

The current theory is that fidgeting somehow increases the "arousal" state (possibly dopamine levels) needed in the PFC for working memory to operate properly.[462] [463]

Although this theory makes very good sense, it has not been proven by actual brain imaging of PFC function in children or adults with ADD during "fidgeting" and non-fidgeting periods while doing working memory tasks. I know, it's probably not so easy to do fMRIs of fidgeting people. I think fMRIs are more accurate if body movement is absent.

However, the feeling of restlessness and the "driven by a motor sensation" is a different experience and can easily be viewed as the behavioral manifestation of a stream of ideas and thoughts that are in control of the ADD brain.

The behavioral explanation is a "a restless brain equals a restless body and restless feelings." Why a restless brain translates into restless behavior in some ADDers and not others, is still not completely understood. However, it is clear that many ADDers unknowingly discover how to increase their working memory through movement, and, of course, they think and feel better doing it.

People (including professionals) often interpret such undiagnosed ADD hyperactivity and restlessness as trouble-making, "easily bored," sensation-seeking, risk-taking, rebelliousness, poor discipline, rudeness, or disobedience.

15.8 Non-Empathic

The adult ADDer is often accused of being non-empathic, forgetful of birthdays and important events, relatively unloving (immature, superficial, with problems with intimacy, etc.) and, often, a less than attentive sexual partner.

Don't get me wrong, I am *not* saying that ADDers don't have a good heart. It is just part of the low-working memory condition to have only "flitting" thoughts of sympathy or empathy which may not get any follow-up behavior.

This may not seem so obvious, but empathy is more than a feeling. To be seen as empathic, one has to not only display the empathic feeling for longer than a flitting moment, but generally also show some follow-through behavior.[464][465][466] In addition, studies have revealed that visual attention deficits contribute to *impaired facial emotion recognition* in boys with

ADD.[467] [468] If you cannot recognize emotions in others very well, it is not likely that you will respond empathically.

A large amount of recent research has highlighted the role of striatal dopamine levels and other dopamine-dependent brain structures and functions correlating to socially-desirable responding, empathy and altruistic motivation.[469] [470] [471] For more information on the neurobiology of "callousness," "empathy," and "fear-tolerance," see Section 17.6 — *Startle Response, Cortisol Response, "Callousness," Empathy, Criminality, and More About "Speed Bumps."*

Although ADDers have feelings (tons of them) and thoughts (tons of them), those feelings and thoughts often *do not* stick around long enough for someone to actually get to notice them or benefit from them.

The distractibility of the ADD brain leads to problems with follow-through and, thus, forgetfulness (or what appears to be forgetfulness), and distractibility during intimate moments and sexual encounters, which can be more than a little irritating. Such distractibility often leads to chronic or frequent "impotence" or difficulty reaching an orgasm.

Some authors claim that an upside of the ADD brain is being *more* empathic. Certain behaviors of ADDers can come across as empathic, such as saying "yes" often, or over-committing. These behaviors are much more related to the ADDer vulnerability to being distracted (influenced) and over-committing (saying "yes" when they really wanted to say "no").

People (including professionals) often interpret undiagnosed ADDers and these behaviors as narcissistic, unloving, uncaring, unsympathetic, promise-breakers, sociopathic, superficial, immature, and sexually compromised, among other things.

15.9 "Hyperfocus"

To many people, "hyperfocus" is a very puzzling aspect of the behavior of the ADDer. How can it be that a supremely distractible person can all of a sudden be so focused on one thing that you can't get them to stop, slow-down, think of others, think of consequences, or change focus. Why do they make such good video game players who can sit and compete for hours at a time? The answer is in the serial single-tasking that takes place in the ADD brain.

If a thought or a pursuit shows up in the ADD brain that particularly captures its attention, it can become "locked on," very similar to a resource-demanding computer software program that eats up all the available RAM and not only makes it impossible to open up any other program, but also may make it difficult to even close the "stuck" program.

This is the most significant variable in creating the hyperfocus of the ADD brain — the single-tasking locked on focus that allows almost nothing else to be noticed.

The other significant variable that leads to "hyperfocus" behavior is the need for structure and stability. So-called "simpler tasks" that may be more activity-oriented rather than a challenge to working memory may become a comfort zone of activity and a preferred activity due to our human need for less chaos (less distraction). In other words, it is a method of "zoning out."

For the person who is being relatively "tortured" by streaming raw data and the associated feelings of relative chaos and disorganization, an entertaining and engaging activity that helps screen out all that other stuff is a welcome relief (video games, reading fiction).

People (including professionals) interpret this undiagnosed ADD behavior as selfish, narcissistic, loner, disobedient, dedicated, autistic, or withdrawn, among other things.

15.10 "Sensation-Seeking," and "Adrenaline Junkie" Behaviors

I have created this category for the purpose of making sure these frequent behaviors exhibited by those who fit the criteria for ADD get your attention.

15.10.1 Factors that Contribute to Increased Risk-Taking Behavior

You may not have thought about this before, but the term "risk-taking" is a problematic term. As you will note in Section 17.2 in this book, I argue for the term "risk-tolerant" as opposed to "risk-taking." I argue that it is not a motivation, but a capability.

On one hand, risk-taking is important and, without it, there would be no follow-through on curiosity, creativity, or other "adventurous" behaviors that are essential to learning, growing, inventing, and evolving. So, there is a risk-taking scale from zero to ten — a zero rating is as potentially unhealthy and has as many downsides to it as a ten.

Risk-taking in the social sciences encompasses a huge number of possible behaviors from risky driving,[472][473][474] risky sex,[475] risky alcohol use,[476] risky drug use,[477] risky tobacco use,[478] propensity to injuries (burns, etc.)[479][480] to risky gambling.[481]

Research to date (November 2011) has shown that there are at least two sets of very significant variables that account for the large prevalence of adventurous and dangerous "risk-taking" behaviors in the ADD population.

First, such behaviors are clearly related to impulse control problems, impatience, and restlessness ("hyperactivity"). We know that impulse control problems and restlessness (including fidgeting) are related to deficits in working memory which, in turn, is clearly related to lower than optimal dopamine and norepinephrine levels in the region of the brain called the PFC.

Second, in addition to the contribution of low working memory to impulsivity and restlessness, there is likely another major contributor to such risk-taking or "sensation-seeking," and "adrenaline junkie" behaviors (sometimes called "courageous").[482] It is the ability to "tolerate" significant increases in norepinephrine and dopamine in the ADD brain without feeling sick (getting side effects from too much neurotransmitter) during and around times of high threat, conflict, fear, and anticipated or actual pain, such as emergency situations, jumping out of planes, cliff diving, speeding, being threatened, fighting, fleeing, and so on.[483 484 485]

Third, due to lower baseline dopamine and norepineprhine functioning in the circuits of the EB (insula, cingulate gyrus, amydala, etc.), the ADD brain can handle more "stimulus" before it triggers the adrenals by thoughts or actions of threat, fear, uncertainty, conflict, or pain. This is the so-called *hypo*responsiveness of the ADD brain's EB.[486 487 488 489 490]

As you will find out in later sections of this book, the term "adrenaline junkie" is somewhat misleading because what is actually taking place is *not* about adrenaline as much as it is about the ADDer figuring out that they can *not only tolerate higher loads of risk* (fear, uncertainty, conflict, etc.), but they can also *feel better* in the midst of thinking about or doing such things.

It would be more accurate to use the term "Emotional Brain junkies" or "EB junkies."

15.10.2 The "Straight-Arrow" Gene

The dopamine transporter gene, a spectrum of most common risky behaviors, and the legal status of the behaviors[491] published in early 2010 (the "Guo 2010 Study") says it the best:

> Our data have established two empirical findings. The first is a *protective main effect in the DAT1 gene against risky behaviors*. The

second finding is that the protective effect varies over age, with the effect prominent at ages when a behavior is illegal and the effect largely vanished at ages when the behavior becomes legal or more socially tolerated. Both the protective main effect and the gene-lifecourse interaction effect are replicated across a spectrum of most common risky behaviors: delinquency, variety of sexual partners, binge drinking, drinking quantity, smoking quantity, smoking frequency, marijuana use, cocaine use, other illegal drug use, and seatbelt non-wearing. We also compared individuals with the protective genotype and individuals without it in terms of age, physical maturity, verbal IQ, GPA, received popularity, sent popularity, church attendance, two biological parents, and parental education. *These comparisons indicate that the protective effect of DAT1*9R/9R cannot be explained away by these background characteristics.* (emphasis mine)

The DAT1 (dopamine transporter gene) and DRD4 (the dopamine D4 receptor gene) are clearly implicated in producing the very specific characteristics used in the criteria for making the diagnosis of ADD.[492] [493]

So, exactly what is the so-called "protective effect against risky behavior" noted in the Guo 2010 Study? It is this — "the protective effect is a general effect concerning *risk aversion or behavior conservatism.*" (emphasis mine) They go on to further say:

The evidence does not support the argument that *DAT1* is a gene specifically for craving alcohol or tobacco, an appetite for sexual partner variety, or a propensity for violence for three reasons. First, quite different biochemical mechanisms may be at work for alcohol craving, tobacco addiction, sexual preference, or violent inclination. A single genetic variant in *DAT1* is unlikely to be responsible for all the biochemical processes that underlie such a variety of behaviors. Second, the large majority of white males (94%) belong to the "higher risk" group of the Any10R genotype. Although this group scored higher on all of the ten risky behavior measures investigated in this study, it is more appropriate to view this large majority as representative of the *population average. It is the 6% possessing the 9R/9R genotype that stand out as behavioral conservatives or straight arrows.* (emphasis mine) [494]

I am hoping the above phrase "population average" as it applies to those who belong to the higher-risk group, is not lost on you. Just in case — as alleged in other places in this book and which will be a core data point in *The Culture Genes™* — the average brain in the Western Hemisphere *is* the dopamine-deficient brain.

Further evidence supporting the 9R/9R optimizing effect on dopamine functioning in the PFC can be found in a study about stimulant medication side effect factors in 5 to 16 year-olds.[495] The very few children in the study with the DAT1 9R/9R experienced significant worsening of dysphoria (moody, irritable, sad, crying) and emotionality during methylphenidate treatment. This high vulnerability to side effects of methylphenidate in 9R/9R types has also been documented in at least three other studies.[496 497 498]

A study investigating the effects of dextroamphetamine in non-ADD 9R/9R college students found the effects of amphetamine were indistinguishable from placebo.[499] The study concluded that "In the case of *DAT1* and amphetamine, this study supports a view that homozygosity for the nine-repeat allele would likely confer protection from dependence on amphetamine because of a lack of reactivity to the drug."

Of course, the 2010 Guo Study ("Straight Arrow Gene Study") was much later than the other 9R/9R studies noted above, so those earlier studies did not have a chance to discuss the findings of the Straight Arrow Gene Study. Had they had the chance to do so, they would have likely wondered out loud about why any of the 9R/9R types even got diagnosed with ADD, since, in all likelihood, they barely fit the criteria. In addition, none of the pre-Straight Arrow Gene studies came to what I think is the obvious conclusion — the dopamine systems related to the DAT1 gene in those 9R/9R types was optimal and adding more dopamine to the 9R/9R system clearly created side effects from the presence of above-optimal dopamine.

There was some "redeeming" speculation in those studies, however, in which it was proposed that possibly a norepinephrine deficit accounted for the diagnosis of ADD in DAT1 9R/9R types and that they would respond better to a medication that might address norepinephrine deficits. To date (November 2011), I have not been able to find such a follow-up study. In addition, I have not been able to find a study that confirmed the rates of the DAT1 9R/9R in current European populations.

Henceforth, the DAT1 9R/9R gene shall be known as the "straight-arrow" gene.

All this data clearly supports my theory that the major contribution to the characteristics of ADD and many other related dopamine-deficiency conditions is a *dopamine deficiency*. (Please, don't forget, when I say "dopamine deficiency in this book, I also mean "also likely norepinephrine deficiency.")

Just to make sure you are getting this, the mechanism of optimal dopamine transporter genetics that makes for a "straight-arrow" is optimal dopamine function and presence which confers a protection against "risky behaviors" based on the aversive power of the side-effects ("physiological speed bumps") of above-optimal levels of dopamine and norepinephrine. (Explained in even more detail below.)

15.10.3 Your "EB" is Dopamine and Norepinephrine Dependent

Epinephrine from the adrenal gland stimulates the release of the arousal-related neuromodulator norepinephrine in the brain by activating beta-adrenoceptors located on vagal afferents terminating on brain-stem noradrenergic cell groups in the nucleus of the solitary tract and locus coeruleus. (I knew you would want to know that!) Noradrenergic projections originating in these nuclei connect to forebrain and PFC structures involved in learning, modulation of aggressive behavior, hyperactivity and working memory. [500] [501] This could be termed the "bottom-up" effects of epinephrine on the brain.

Very powerful "top-down" influences on adrenal gland processes originate in the very dopamine/norepinephrine-dependent limbic and prefrontal cortical structures which play very important roles in processing threat,[502] fear,[503] conflict,[504] mismatch (data conflict)[505], "disgust," and pain,[506] including related learning,[507] which creates future anticipation and priming effects.

This system of specialized "threat" processors makes up the EB. In a very real sense, these very sensitive, highly-associated, but still significantly specialized circuit boards could be called the "CNS Adrenal Glands" because of how sensitive and powerful they are with respect to processing incoming data for the purposes of defense and survival ("emergency" responsiveness).

The term "affective neuroscience" was coined by Jaak Panksepp.[508] [509] The popularization of the term "Emotional Brain" is generally attributed to Joseph LeDoux.[510]

Very importantly, relatively *all* of the EB signals are routed to and through the brain's executive circuits (mostly PFC) for editorial and management oversight and modification by such judgment systems. As noted earlier, these management systems are very dependent on optimal working memory and dopamine and norepinephrine processes. Such signal-vetting by the executive circuits takes place *almost always before* such EB signaling is allowed to trigger HPA responses. I say "almost always before" because there is a theory that there is such a thing as an "unthinking response" — a reaction to a "threat" by the EB that bypasses executive oversight. Such "unthinking reflexes" clearly take place at the spinal cord level,[511 512] but there is no substantial evidence that *unthinking reflexes* take place at the brain level in neurologically-intact, average adults.[513 514]

The thalamus, a two-lobed specialized circuit board located centrally in the brain, is the conduit for almost all sensory input to the brain. Visualize two small chicken eggs sitting side by side connected by a wide bridge at their middle.[515] It is populated by a large number of dopamine 2 (D2) receptors.[516 517 518]

Not long ago, as noted by LeDoux, the thalamus was thought to be capable of by-passing the prefrontal executive vetting process, but that is no longer held to be completely true.[519] It can begin a *bypass* process, but it has huge feed-forward and feedback circuits to and from executive areas located mostly in the PFC.

Those feedback circuits can quickly modify any "independently" generated "emergency" thalamic output directed to the amygdala without executive oversight by intense feedback to the thalamus, itself, and also to the amygdala. LeDoux's circa 1996 theory of independent "high road" (executive oversight) and "low road" (no executive oversight) thalamic sensory processing and responses [520] has seen a lot of modification since then.[521 522 523 524]

An October 2011 publication[525] reported how methylphenidate (Ritalin) clearly amped-up activation in the thalamus and other sensory processing and working memory areas. A May 2010 study revealed the data "censoring" limitations of low thalamic dopamine D2 receptors.[526]

A number of so-called "CNS-based primitive reflexes" exist in human infants. They all disappear at different times during normal neurological development, with the last one, the plantar reflex, disappearing at about one year.

None of these primitive reflexes are the same as the *startle response* which is measured mostly by two different methods.[527]

Although it has been proposed that the startle response is the closest thing in an average adult to a possible brain-based *unthinking response*, it *can* be modified by cognitive training. I write much more about startle responses in Section 17.6.

The specialized processors of the EB include the insula,[528] anterior cingulate cortex ("ACC"),[529] amygdala,[530] basal ganglia (nucleus accumbens,[531] caudate nucleus,[532] ventral tegmentum[533]), cerebellum,[534] and the pulvinar of the thalamus.[535] Think of them as specialized circuit boards in your brain, just like the dedicated video card in your computer.[536]

This group of EB processors are either part of the brain called the limbic system, very close to it, or highly-connected to it.

The scientific community has not been very successful at finding a more accurate term for this highly connected, but not completely localized system of processors other than the "limbic system."[537] [538] The major circuit boards are:

(1) Insula: Along with the cingulate cortex, the insula is very involved in monitoring pain (perception).[539] The insula is implicated in negative emotional states like disgust, pain and hunger.[540] The insula clearly receives direct nerve tract input from body sensations of all types, including cold, heat, and pain.[541]

Insula activity is correlated with anticipation of aversive stimuli.[542] Insula operates as a relay with the limbic system for pain, as evidenced by several studies that found insula activation during the experience, imitation, or imagination of pain.[543]

(2)   Anterior Cingulate Cortex ("ACC"): This brain area is particularly active during experiences of physical pain and social pain (such as rejection or exclusion).[544] It clearly facilitates autonomic and behavioral responses (flight or fight) to noxious stimuli (not just pain), and coordinates motor responses including avoidance, grimacing, wincing and vocalization.[545] The ACC is clearly involved in detecting the presence of conflict during information processing, and in alerting prefrontal systems to resolve the conflict.[546 547] The cingulate cortex has several divisions and separate sets of specialized cortical connections.[548]

(3)   Amygdala: A very-connected EB processor[549] which is activated in response to fearful emotional and threatening stimuli, including expression, regulation, memory and learning related to threat and fear.[550 551 552 553]

(4)   Thalamus: The thalamus is more than just a glorified sorting machine sending sensory data to correct EB and cortical areas. Its entire front half, the pulvinar,[554] is intensely bi-directionally linked to many cortical and EB areas, meaning it lets prefrontal and cingulate cortex and other cortical areas have a vote in how it triggers the amygdala. It is highly dopamine dependent.[555 556 557]

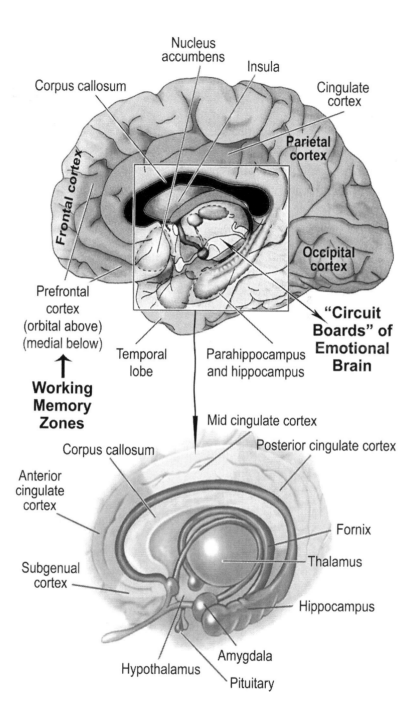

Nucleus
accumbens

Insula

Corpus callosum

Cingulate
cortex

**Parietal
cortex**

Frontal cortex

**Occipital
cortex**

Prefrontal
cortex
(orbital above)
(medial below)

Temporal
lobe

Parahippocampus
and hippocampus

**"Circuit
Boards" of
Emotional
Brain**

**Working
Memory
Zones**

Mid cingulate cortex

Corpus callosum

Posterior cingulate cortex

Anterior
cingulate
cortex

Fornix

Thalamus

Subgenual
cortex

Hippocampus

Hypothalamus

Amygdala

Pituitary

For the *non-ADD* brain and its dopamine-optimized EB, further increases in dopamine activity produce aversive side effects much more quickly and intensely.

It is almost exactly the same aversive responses the *non-ADD* EB and PFC have to smoking a cigarette (a dopamine stimulator). In the *non-ADDer*, the aversive nicotine experience is a consequence of the "sickness" and cognitive decline (side effects) produced by above-optimal dopamine.[558]

The "blunted cortisol response" in ADDers is clearly a result of a *hypo*active ADD EB compared to the non-ADD EB.

That lower baseline ADD EB dopamine produces a very much slower and lower cortisol response to the same set of stimuli that would trigger larger responses in the non-ADDer. Such higher non-ADDer cortisol responsiveness contributes to both an upside and a downside. The more dopamine-optimized brain is likely more vulnerable to developing symptoms of "anxiety" and posttraumatic stress disorders.[559] [560] (More about that in Section 15.10.9)

"Threat" in this book stands for all types of anticipated (imagined) or physically-present threat: aggression, fear for life or limb, pain, data conflict (mismatch), and noxious visual, taste, airway, sensation, and auditory stimuli.

The figure on the next page shows the *differences* between non-ADD and ADD EB dopamine and subsequent cortisol responses.

"Low-DAers" means people with low baseline dopamine and norepinephrine determined by low working memory who may not otherwise significantly fit the criteria for ADD.

The *most important areas* to note are the white areas showing smaller or larger threat tolerance capacity *before* the PFC and HPA are triggered and before side-effects from too much EB dopamine might be experienced.

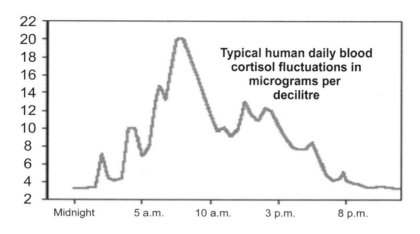

Typical human daily blood cortisol fluctuations in micrograms per decilitre

Evidence-Based, Simplified Representations of Dopamine and Cortisol Responses to "Threat"

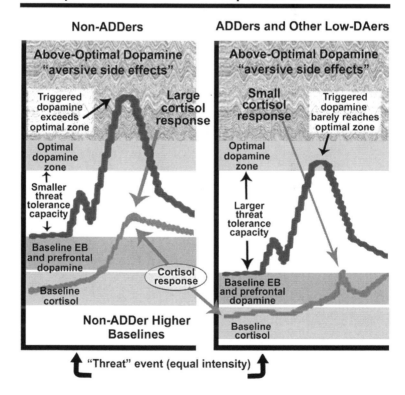

The graphics on the following pages show simplified, but correct information about the processing of sensory data by the thalamo-cortico-emotional-brain-circuits (also known as cortico-striato-thalamic loops[561]) which can lead to triggering of the hypothalamic-pituitary-adrenal circuit.

These circuits, although necessary for properly processing almost all sensory data, have clearly been *very necessary for the survival of humans*, since they are completely responsible for detecting and processing threats of many kinds. They consult with the PFC and each other for decision-making about whether to trigger the adrenal glands through the hypothalamic-pituitary response.

Although highly stimulating data (high threat-rated data) may start the amygdala-hypothalamic-pituitary triggering process, such initial triggering build-up is modified very quickly by PFC oversight to prevent, well, you know, the red phone from actually ringing, if it doesn't need to.

There is a threshold for triggering, and it varies from person to person.

When the pituitary gland is finally triggered by the hypothalamus, it sends (1) fast-traveling nerve stimulation to the adrenal medulla, and (2) slower-traveling blood-borne adrenocortico-tropic hormone (ACTH) to the adrenal cortex.

The adrenal medulla quickly secretes epinephrine (adrenaline) and norepinephrine into blood, which primes the body for threat responses. The adrenal cortex is triggered later by blood-borne ACTH, to secrete cortisol into the bloodstream.

Cortisol (1) calms down the EB, especially the amygdala, hippocampus and hypothalamus — this is a classic closed-system negative-feedback loop for calming down an amped-up process to promote homeostasis; (2) anti-inflammatory and down-modulation of immune systems (anti-auto-immune), and (3) many other immune and metabolic activities.

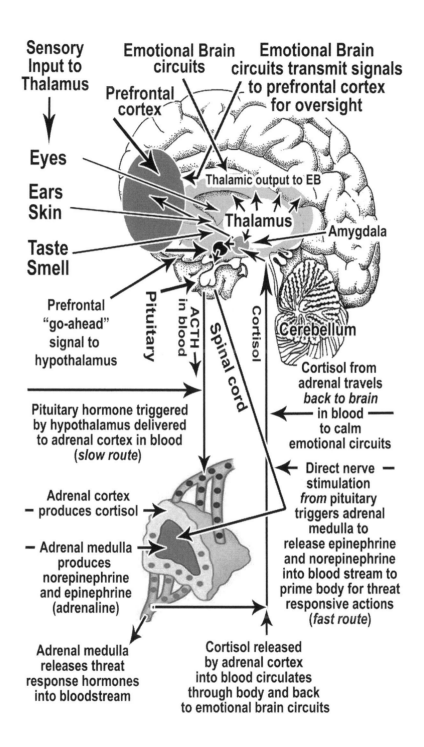

Sensory Input to Thalamus

Emotional Brain circuits

Emotional Brain circuits transmit signals to prefrontal cortex for oversight

Prefrontal cortex

Eyes

Ears
Skin

Taste
Smell

Thalamic output to EB

Thalamus

Amygdala

Prefrontal "go-ahead" signal to hypothalamus

Pituitary

ACTH in blood

Spinal cord

Cortisol

Cerebellum

Cortisol from adrenal travels *back to brain* in blood to calm emotional circuits

Pituitary hormone triggered by hypothalamus delivered to adrenal cortex in blood (*slow route*)

Direct nerve stimulation *from* pituitary triggers adrenal medulla to release epinephrine and norepinephrine into blood stream to prime body for threat responsive actions (*fast route*)

Adrenal cortex – produces cortisol

– Adrenal medulla produces norepinephrine and epinephrine (adrenaline)

Adrenal medulla releases threat response hormones into bloodstream

Cortisol released by adrenal cortex into blood circulates through body and back to emotional brain circuits

The opposite page is a simplified flow-chart of typical events when the brain processes sensory data, except for steps ❼, ❽, ❾, ❿, and ⓫. Those steps are only significantly activated if the threshold for triggering the hypothalamus-❻ is exceeded and it sends enough corticotropin releasing hormone (CRH) to the pituitary-❼ to stimulate (a) ACTH-❽, and (b) neuronal-firing-❾ to the adrenal glands for threat response activities. Other than threat-response functions, the hypothalamus and pituitary have many other duties.[562] [563]

The typical sequence of events in the brain's response to threat are: ❶ Sensory data from eyes, ears, skin, tongue, nose, directed to thalamus (sensory clearinghouse) ➡ ❷ Thalamus has specialized input files for sensation data and it forwards data to (a) relevant specialized EB circuits (amygdala, insula, cingulate cortex, etc.) *and* (b) the PFC and other specialized cortical areas (auditory, visual, motor) ➡ ❸ Many EB circuits feed-forward their votes to PFC (thalamus independently feeds votes to PFC especially through pulvinar) ➡ ❹ the PFC processes the votes from EB and does (a) quick-and-dirty assessments (Is this really a threat? Should we pause for a second or two and reassess?); and (b) follow-up processing to fine tune responses (analyze alternatives, consequences, vet data further) — that is, *if there is enough working memory to do such "fine tuning" and reappraisal*) ➡ ❺ PFC provides its votes to (a) several EB circuits (modifying their influence up or down) and (b) to the hypothalamus after conducting both short and sustained "executive oversight." At the same time, many EB circuits are modifying their "stance" and sending updated votes to the amygdala ➡ ❻ Hypothalamus gathers votes from (a) amygdala, PFC (high-influence voters), and (b) many other brain areas (low-influence voters) and responds appropriately ➡ ❼ The pituitary. If hypothalamus triggering is sufficient, the pituitary takes action through ➡ ❽ Pituitary sends ACTH into blood (slow) ➡ ❾ Pituitary sends nerve signals to adrenal medulla (fast) ➡ ❿ Adrenal (a) medulla quickly dumps adrenaline and norepinephrine into blood, and (b) cortex slowly secretes cortisol into blood ➡ ⓫ cortisol slowly returns to EB areas and calms them down (other actions include anti-inflammatory and pro-immune[564]).

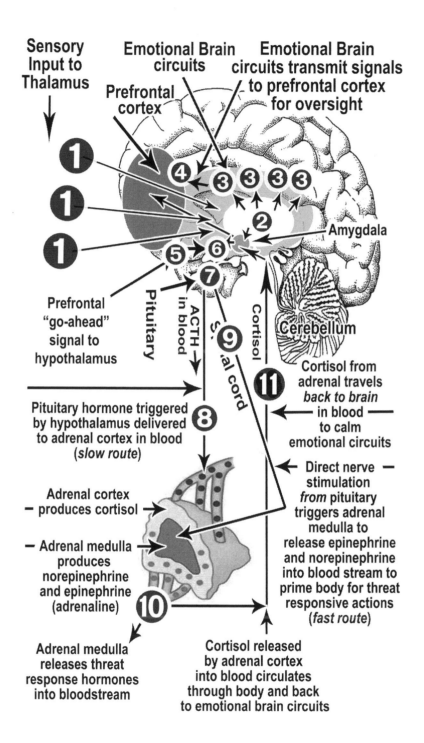

Sensory Input to Thalamus

Emotional Brain circuits

Emotional Brain circuits transmit signals to prefrontal cortex for oversight

Prefrontal cortex

Amygdala

Prefrontal "go-ahead" signal to hypothalamus

Pituitary

ACTH in blood

Spinal cord

Cortisol

Cerebellum

Cortisol from adrenal travels *back to brain* in blood to calm emotional circuits

Pituitary hormone triggered by hypothalamus delivered to adrenal cortex in blood (*slow route*)

Direct nerve stimulation *from* pituitary triggers adrenal medulla to release epinephrine and norepinephrine into blood stream to prime body for threat responsive actions (*fast route*)

Adrenal cortex – produces cortisol

– Adrenal medulla produces norepinephrine and epinephrine (adrenaline)

Adrenal medulla releases threat response hormones into bloodstream

Cortisol released by adrenal cortex into blood circulates through body and back to emotional brain circuits

15.10.4 EB, PFC, and HPA Dopamine "Triggering Thresholds"

There is very little data so far on what processes, thresholds, and criteria control the triggering of EB-circuit threat-related dopamine flooding in order to get PFC attention and action and then what it takes for the PFC "thinking process" to turn on the hypothalamus alarm system and the processes leading to emergency readiness.

Dopamine flooding out of nerve cells and creating increased signaling has generally been thought of as being a continuous operation, that is, just like a volume control on a radio, rather than an on-off switch or an all-or-none threshold — as in, below threshold level, no EB or PFC operations activated at all.

This part of the threat response equation is going to be very difficult to figure out. However, there is significant evidence of CNS triggering mechanisms with respect to (1) the "transition" (triggering) from non-triggering less painful stimuli to significantly-triggering painful stimuli[565]; (2) triggering systems that mediate self-regulatory control in bulimia[566]; and (3) triggering systems (connectivity) with respect to "attitudes" (abilities) about risk tolerance versus risk aversion[567], among many others.

My favorite is a 2011 study (endnote 567) called *Turning on the alarm: The neural mechanisms of the transition from innocuous to painful sensation.* I would have used the words "the transition from non-threatening to threatening pain sensation." That study clearly showed that EB triggering related to painful heat stimuli proceeded in a fashion that was *not* linear, but sigmoidal, which can be characterized as a variation closer to an all-or-nothing threshold response than a process similar to the volume control on a radio.

The other two studies also clearly showed how *higher levels of sensory or other cognitive input* were needed to trigger EB operations in those with bulimia and those who are more risk tolerant.

Again, EB circuit boards are dopamine and norepinephrine dependent, so any triggering that results in dopamine flooding is dependent on the status of dopamine functions in the EB which can be significantly measured by fMRI techniques. So-called "resting connectivity" is actually a measure of baseline neurotransmitter-induced signaling. Higher baseline dopamine-induced signaling (more dopamine bridges working at baseline) results in higher "connectivity" and, thus, earlier threshold triggering than what happens with less "connected" circuitry. The ADD EB with less available dopamine bridges at baseline is less connected at baseline.

15.10.5 Advice to ADDers About Using ADD Medications in "Risk" Situations

My advice to ADDers who are using medication and who wish to excel at scary, risky, defensive, offensive, or emergency-related activities or occupations, *don't do them on ADD medications.* "Normalizing" your dopamine and norepinephrine in your attentional and emotional networks will turn you into someone like me — not so good at jumping out of planes, or doing risky or scary things. In other words, as a medicated ADDer, you would be taking away the very thing that helps you perform better in "threat" situations.

On that note, let me say a few things about the U.S. military's position on the use of so-called "go" pills, which include at least dextroamphetamine (Dexedrine) and modafinil (Provigil).[568] Unless they know something I don't know, or have access to some sound scientific findings to which I do not have access, their protocol of utilizing dopamine and norepinephrine enhancing drugs in either ADDers or non-ADDers for the purposes of doing better in combat situations may be ethically defensible, on balance, but, otherwise clearly scientifically wrong-headed.

You may remember the Tarnak Farm Incident of April 17, 2002 in which U.S. Air National Guard Major, Harry Schmidt, after being ordered to "hold fire" and "exhibiting arrogance and a lack of flight discipline"[569] killed and injured many Canadian soldiers who were conducting night-firing exercises at Tarnak Farms, near Kandahar, Afganistan, by dropping a laser-guided 500-pound bomb on them.[570] The incident set off a firestorm of discussions about not only Major Schmidt's use of dextroamphetamine prior to the incident but, also, the US military's protocols for the use of such medications to "treat" fatigue. It is beyond the scope of this book to revisit all those earlier discussions of the Tarnak Farm incident, or the continuing discussions of the incident to this day in the research literature. If you wish to read a detailed legal discussion of such circa 2002 "go" pill usage, I recommend Matthew Hoffman's *The Military's Need for "Speed": A Case Study on the FDA's Regulation of Off-Label Prescriptions.*[571] Other articles since then include the 2008 *Go pills in combat: prejudice, propriety, and practicality* by John Caldwell, Ph.D.,[572] and the 2010 study, *Fatigue and stimulant use in military fighter aircrew during combat operations.*[573]

However, omitted from all such aviation research are any references to the scientifically established downside of these non-caffeine military-medication strategies for "fighting" fatigue. I guess they have not heard of the "inverted U-shaped curve" or the law of diminishing returns with respect to how above-optimal levels of dopamine and norepinephrine degrade performance (poorer judgment, longer reaction times, decreased cognitive abilities as noted in Sections 14.13 through 14.15).

As noted earlier in this book, caffeine has shown itself to be very useful for treating fatigue, without creating above-optimal dopamine and norepinephrine levels. In that regard, if you wanted to treat fatigue without creating a dopamine or norepinephrine excess in non-ADD pilots, which excesses have been shown to *decrease performance*, you might choose caffeine.[574] With respect to ADD pilots, well, apparently, they don't exist in the military. That's too bad, because they would likely be better in combat and emergency situations than the non-ADDer, especially without such "fatigue-fighting" medications. I'm just saying...

I am hoping these concepts about larger and smaller threat tolerance capacities related to dopamine-deficient and dopamine-optimized brains, respectively, do not get lost on you. It will help you understand so much about why, for instance, self-injury has such positive "healing" effects. (More about that in Section 15.11.) It will also help you understand why close to 60% of prison inmates fit the criteria for ADD. (More about that in Section 17.6.)

15.10.6 The Adrenal Gland's "Split Personality"

The adrenal glands can be thought of as having a split personality — one part of them sets up your body to fight or flee (optimizes survival physiology), and another part of them provides calming feedback to the threat-sensitive EB brain activations through a hormone called cortisol.[575] In addition to calming EB signaling, cortisol also *down-modulates inflammation and immune responses*. There are usually two adrenals, each one sitting on top of a kidney. Their split personalities are manifested in their split anatomy, with each of them having two distinct, very separate parts, the adrenal cortex (on the outside) and the adrenal medulla (more inside).

The adrenal medulla is highly connected to the EB nervous system and, thus, it is very fast at responding to EB nerve signaling to quickly provide the emergency response hormones epinephrine and norepinephrine (adrenaline).

Each cortex of each adrenal dumps their products (corticosteroids, cortisol, aldosterone, and androgens) almost directly into a very large vein called the inferior vena cava giving those products direct but relatively slow distribution through veins and arteries to the whole body and brain.

The adrenal cortex is triggered by blood-borne hormones from the pituitary gland after the pituitary is triggered by prefrontal cortex commands after EB signaling to the prefrontal cortex is "processed." Prefrontal "processing" is dependent on working memory function (available dopamine), and it differs in from person-to-person. The adrenal-cortex-calming-cortisol response is a slower response since it is delivered through relatively slow-moving blood flow to the body and the brain.

So, not only do your adrenal glands get your body ready for "fight or flight," they provide calming feedback to your EB so that it does not stay "threat-stimulated" for too long.

15.10.7 The "Risk-Taking" Trilogy

Remember, from above, the study that showed how higher than optimal levels of such neurotransmitters, in already high-performers, degraded performance rather than enhancing performance. Thus, *low-baseliners* (ADD brains) have three potential variables that contribute to dangerous, risky, or so-called "novelty-seeking" [576] [577] behavior: (1) decreased working memory (Ignorance is bliss? Consequences, what's that?), (2) they *can* do it, and (3) they feel better doing it — calmer, faster, more focused, "alive," and engaged. The threat-fear-pain response (also called the nocioceptive response) treats their ADD by increasing dopamine and norepinephrine levels in their EB (insula, anterior cingulate cortex and amygdala)[578] which has priming effects on the PFC and other attention-related areas.

So, just to make sure you get this very important concept locked into your head, I will repeat it.

The most important thing to remember about the upside of the ADD brain is that those who have the unmedicated ADD brain will almost always be able to jump out of planes or "put out fires of all types" better than those who do not fit the criteria for ADD. The reasons for this are:

> (1) Anticipation and/or actual experience of "threat" increases dopamine and norepinephrine in the human brain through emotion-related neurocircuitry (insula, anterior

cingulate cortex, amygdala, hypothalamus); [579] [580]

(2)   Studies have shown that carriers of one of the well-known ADD risk genes have significantly lower dopamine-mediated cortisol (stress hormone) responses than normal controls to stress,[581] meaning they can tolerate much larger increases in dopamine before stress-regulation mechanisms create higher levels of brain-calming cortisol; [582] [583] [584]

(3)   When you *start with lower* than optimal dopamine and norepinephrine (*the ADD brain*),[585] [586] and you are presented with a "threat" or a situation that activates your EB, your dopamine and norepinephrine levels will move *up towards optimal* which produces the same positive effects that traditional ADD medications produce for the ADD EB. In other words, your ADD brain is being "medicated" by the increased EB output of dopamine and norepinephrine and you feel calmer, more focused, faster, and better. Such a positive "threat" response is often responsible for the last minute focus, concentration, and completion of assignments by the ADDer as the fear factor goes up as a deadline approaches (indecisive until the fear of a quickly approaching deadline kicks neurotransmitters up high enough to produce focus, organization, direction, and follow-through — a process often incorrectly called "procrastination");

(4)   When you *start with optimal* dopamine and norepinephrine (*the non-ADD brain*) and you are presented with a "threat," your dopamine and norepinephrine levels will be kicked up to *above optimal* levels. You might think that "more is always better" and that such higher levels of neurotransmitters would have

an advantage, but they *decidedly do not.* As noted in several earlier sections of this book, above-optimal levels of dopamine and norepinephrine produce, among other things, nervousness, shakiness, queasiness, confusion, and a decrease in performance from the higher baseline. (Too many bridges in a system of roads produces confusion and inefficiencies.) In other words, your non-ADD brain is being "over-medicated" by the above-optimal neurotransmitters and you are experiencing typical "over-stimulation" side effects *as if* you were taking the wrong ADD medication or too much of the right ADD medication.

15.10.8 Who Makes the Best "First Responders"?

Anecdotally, there is much evidence that adults who fit the criteria for ADD are often able to handle high-risk situations (emergencies, threats, risky tasks, risky activities, etc.) with better focus, less confusion and ambivalence or "nervousness" than adults who do not fit the criteria for ADD.

The EB is dopamine-dependent.[587 588 589 590] Uncertainty about potential negative future outcomes clearly stimulates the EB more than does certainty.[591] "Uncertainty" (risk) is clearly more "tolerable" if you start with the ADD-EB's lesser dopamine and norepinephrine functioning. In fact, not only is risk and uncertainty more tolerable, it is "healing."

I have not been able to find any studies on the prevalence of ADD among police, firefighters, emergency medical technicians, and military enlistees. If you know of any, let me know.

Such data would be very important because it would clarify so many things about what I consider to be one of the greatest upsides of the untreated ADD brain — baseline low dopamine and norepinephrine levels in the PFC and the EB which allows the ADD brain to do much better in emergency situations than the non-ADD brain.[592]

The closest I could come to finding relevant research along these lines were the following:

(1) 2009: *A neuroscience approach to optimizing brain resources for human performance in extreme environments.*[593]

(2) 2010: *Differential brain activation to angry faces by elite warfighters: neural processing evidence for enhanced threat detection.*[594]

(3) 2011: *Cortisol Awakening Response Prospectively Predicts Peritraumatic and Acute Stress Reactions in Police Officers* ("2011 Cortisol Study").[595]

(4) 2008 to 2011: Several studies looking at the effects of "pressure" on handgun accuracy and reaction times attempting to generally answer the question "Does first-responder performance decrease under pressure?" Studies came out of the United States, Canada, Israel and The Netherlands.[596 597 598 599 600]

All those studies are notable for their attempts to figure out what traits, physiological markers, and other variables make for the best performing first responders and the least vulnerable to posttraumatic stress disorder.

The 2011 Cortisol Study showed that a greater cortisol awakening response (CAR) was a significant "pre-exposure risk factor for peritraumatic dissociation and acute stress reaction symptoms during police service." In other words, those who started the day with higher baseline cortisol levels due to more active EBs (most likely *non*-ADDers) were more vulnerable to the long-term downsides of such frequent higher EB responsiveness — a non-ADDer amplified response. Pre-exposure cortisol levels were measured in 296 police recruits before critical incident exposure on the job and again at 12, 24, and 36 months following the start of active police service.

It is unfortunate that there is no occupation-related screening in place for identifying those who fit the criteria for ADD. Several benefits of such "dopamine-deficiency" screening in certain occupational populations would be (1) to identify those who would actually be the best on patrol and in emergency situations and screen out those whose performance would actually decrease due to too much neurotransmitter from the stimulation of emergency situations; and (2) to help first responders who clearly fit the criteria for ADD to be able to reduce the domestic violence (and other dopamine-deficiency related behaviors) in their populations by allowing them to utilize appropriate short-acting medications on their way home from work, or at least have the opportunity to learn about the downsides of the ADD brain.

Domestic violence in first-responder families is much higher than in the rest of the population.[601] [602] Undiagnosed and untreated ADD may have upsides for better functioning in emergency situations, but when the EB stops churning at the "end" of the work day, the ADD brain returns to its low working memory baseline — impulsive, impatient, short-tempered, non-empathic, and overwhelmed easily, among many other ADD downsides that can contribute to domestic violence, among other things.

It appears that the scientific community is either very hesitant or it is prohibited from researching the prevalence of ADD in first responders, or, the members of those occupations do not want to know the truth. *I can't say that I blame them since, honestly, who wants to know that they have an "illness."*

This is one of the major reasons I do not brand ADD as an illness but, more rationally, as a condition which has clear-cut upsides in addition to its downsides. Again, it is scientifically irrational to call something a disorder or an illness when it has a clear and significant upside. By unscientifically emphasizing the downside of the ADD condition, we set ourselves up to miss out on the upside of the ADD brain *and* to mismanage the downside of the ADD brain. (More about this in Section 16.)

People (including professionals) observing dangerous risk-taking behaviors may interpret them as careless, irresponsible, illogical, undisciplined, overly aggressive, grandiose, stupid, or courageous, among other things.

15.10.9 The Downsides of the Dopamine-Optimized Brain

Now might be the best time to discuss the downsides of the non-ADD, dopamine-optimized brain, since I have just finished the section in which I cite several cortisol and posttraumatic stress disorder studies. I am proposing that the average or normal brain in the Western Hemisphere is the dopamine/norepinephrine-deficient brain, of which the ADD brain is the current prime example. Significantly dopamine-optimized brains are a small minority.

As noted in the 2011 Cortisol Study a few paragraphs ago, higher within-average-range morning cortisol levels in pre-deployed police candidates predicted higher levels of subsequent peritraumatic dissociation and acute stress reaction symptoms during later active police service (a longitudinal study). That and several other studies confirm that non-ADDer threat-related EB triggering clearly stimulates higher adrenaline and cortisol responses than the same threat stimuli would for the ADDer. The downside of such relative "*hyper*-responsiveness" is what I call "over-amping" (high blood pressure, increased heart rates, too much exposure to above-optimal brain cortisol, rage, and decreased performance in emergency or threat situations).

Although the Guo 2010 Study (the "Straight Arrow Gene Study") showed that the DAT1 9R/9R gene was almost completely protective with respect to risky behaviors, in other studies, the genotype has been clearly associated with angry-impulsive personality traits and a vulnerability to borderline personality style "over-amping" behaviors.[603] This makes perfect sense in light of the non-ADDer EB's very small window for threat tolerance and its vulnerability to creating the above-optimal dopamine, over-amped, decreased-performance-and-judgment, longer-reaction-time condition.

Startle response studies have shown mixed results, but clearly involve "optimal" dopamine and processes affecting dopamine function.[604] Similarly, the highly sensitive personality is clearly associated with the same optimal dopamine processes.[605] Noise sensitivity, which is clearly measured by most startle response research protocols, has not been significantly studied since 1992.[606]

In the final analysis, the ADD and non-ADD brains and bodies have clearly different but somewhat equal upsides and downsides. So, as they say, "pick your poison."

Not Medicated	*ADD*er	*Non-ADD*er
IQ, Creativity	No advantage	No advantage
Working memory	Low	Optimal
Dopamine tolerance	High	Low
Emergency capable	High	Low
"Risk" protection	Low	High
"Threat" tolerance	High	Low
Pain tolerance	Low	High
Disgust tolerance	High	Low
Cortisol response	Low	Optimal
Immune System	Less optimal	More optimal
Anti-Inflammatory	Less optimal	More optimal
Panic "attacks"	More likely	Less likely
PTSD	Less likely	More likely
Anxiety disorder	Less likely	More likely
Startle response	Low	High
Seasickness	Low	High
Withdrawal in general	Variably better	Worse
Empathy	Less likely	More likely
Attachment	High	Low
Addiction	High	Low

15.11 Self-Injury

There are many misunderstandings about self-harm, self-injury, and suicidal inclinations. I have included self-injury as a separate category under the symptoms of ADD because I want to make sure it gets your attention.

Self-harm, deliberate self-harm and self-injury are defined as the intentional, direct injuring of body tissue *without* suicidal intent. The most recent "official" term is "non-suicidal self-injury" (NSSI).[607] These terms are used in more recent literature in an attempt to reach a less pejorative terminology. Older and relatively inaccurate terminology was "self-mutilation." I am adopting the term "self-injury" because it is clearly more scientific and less confusing. An injury is an injury. A "harm" is arguable. The best subcategories of self-injury are *experimental* and *ongoing*.

There is a huge difference between the *experimental* self-injurer and the *ongoing* self-injurer, just like there is a huge difference between the experimental (dopamine-rich) college Adderall user, and the ongoing (dopamine-poor) college Adderall user. Both the experimental self-injurer and the experimental Adderall user *soon* find out that the behaviors are not so helpful, do not make them feel better, and they generally abandon the behavior *because* it makes them "worse" in many ways, rather than better.

The problem with the term "self-harm" is the term "harm." Even though such ongoing behaviors may be judged or experienced as painful, "sickening" or possibly "disfiguring," they almost always lead to feelings of catharsis, relief, "normality," groundedness and/or "euphoria." Such a feeling of "euphoric normalcy" is also often experienced while being tattooed.

Self-mutilation does occur, but it is rare. The subcategory of "self-mutilation" is reserved for behaviors that, when examined and evaluated, were the result of actual motivation to disfigure one's self. An example would be someone so disgusted with some aspect of life or how people are treating them, that they pluck an eye out or cut a tongue off, or cut an ear off. The term self-injury does not include self-poisoning, which is a subcategory of "self-harm" which is rare and more related to suicidal behaviors than to ongoing attempts to "fix" something.

I use the term "euphoric normalcy" to stand for the feeling that ADDers have when they discover the correct dopamine-optimizing experience, street drug, or medication. They experience such a significant cessation of "noise" and confusion, such a better sense of time, presence, quietness, focus, and lack of moodiness or dread, that they often define it as "euphoria." In actuality, it is the feeling that those with optimal dopamine levels are feeling almost all of the time. Such a mindset which results from a "close-to-optimal-dopamine" brain-state is very frequently a shocking experience for the "untreated" ADDer.

The most well-known and practiced form of self-injury is skin-cutting, but "self-injury" also covers a wide range of behaviors including burning, severe scratching, pinching, banging or hitting body parts, interfering with wound healing, hair-pulling, nail-biting, and bone breaking.[608] Substance abuse and eating disorders are not considered "self-injury," but the spectrum of "self-injury" is wide and not perfectly categorical. For instance, adolescent "cutters" and "overdosers" are quite different.[609 610] Extensive tattooing is not considered self-injury, but, that conclusion is clearly arguable.[611 612]

It is unfortunate that there is a glaring lack of research about the association between ADD and self-injuring behaviors, since the combination of the low working memory (Consequences, what's that?), low frustration tolerance, impatience, impulsivity,[613] chronic anxiety and moodiness,[614] and the risk and sensation tolerance of ADDers contribute fiercely and directly to self-injury behaviors. One of the only resources I found about self-injury and ADD can be found at a United Kingdom website, *Why Do Some Teenagers With*

ADHD Self Harm?[615] Otherwise, pubmed.com had no significant search results for terms such as "ADHD and self-harm or self-injury."

In October 2011, CNN.com published an article entitled *Self-Injury: A Silent Epidemic*,[616] in which the authors do not even mention that such behaviors may have a connection to the upside or the downside of ADD. In fact, they don't even mention the terms ADHD or ADD. However, they allege the following:

> "In fact, our longitudinal data show that many people who struggle with self-injury during their formative years, like those who try drugs, eating disorders, or delinquency, grow out of it to live fully functioning productive lives as professionals, parents, spouses, without further problems."

I suppose the conclusion "many. . . grow out of it" means "many." I assume the authors are not using the term to stand for "a majority." "Many," of course, is a very vague term, and, in the context of the CNN article, comes across as an attempt to reassure us that "it's okay — no long-term harm, no foul." In addition, the authors do not define what "fully functioning" means. That term is also not defined in their book *The Tender Cut: Inside the Hidden World of Self-Injury*, by Patricia and Peter Adler.[617]

Although it is beyond the scope of this book to engage in a longer critique of *The Tender Cut*, it is impossible to ignore its outdated and superficial treatment of "causes." Unlike *The Tender Cut*, Matthew Nock's 2010 detailed review article *Self-Injury* ("Nock 2010 Review") covers self-injury literature and causation variables in a very comprehensive manner.[618]

The terms *neuroscience, neurology* or *neuropsychology* are never used by the Adlers. The term *neurotransmitter* appears in their book once. I cannot find any significant evidence that the Adlers cared enough about scientific truth to more deeply investigate what psychiatrists really believe these days about self-injury, or what the scientific community has discovered. Instead, for their 2011 book, the most current literature they quote from for the purpose of mentioning dopamine (almost as an after-thought), is a single 2003 source, which is a book about drugs — a 2003 book which was updated in 2008, entitled *Buzzed: The Straight Facts about the Most Used and Abused Drugs from Alcohol to Ecstasy.*[619] In addition, the word "norepinephrine" never appears, and the word "adrenaline" appears five times, used by self-injurers, but not by the authors.

In other words, the Adlers do a very good job of not only under-powering their only reference to dopamine, but also do an excellent job of ignoring all the evidence gathered since 2003 with respect to the significant contribution that dopamine deficiency makes to cutting and practically all other "self-injury" behaviors.

On the upside, the Adlers' book is a treasure of hard work, good intentions, and aching truth. It is also highly intellectual. For such a highly intellectual work, however, it is dismally out-dated as to its descriptions of psychology, psychiatry, psychiatrists, and the so-called "medicalization" of America. A better and more accurate term would be the global *physicalization* of brain and mind processes. Medicalization is an inaccurate and pejorative term and seems rather quaint and petty as used in *The Tender Touch.*

On the upside, the Adlers do an excellent job of documenting the wide range of experiences of self-injurers and the social-environmental variables likely contributing to the alleged increased prevalence of self-injury. However, their allegation that "Self-injury. . . [has changed] from being primarily a mental disorder, or a disease, into a social trend" is way off the mark. It all depends on whether the behavior is more experimental or more ongoing. The terms mental disorder and disease are quite out of date, but the idea that self-injury has no significant downside is insupportable.

What is clear is that self-injury has a history of being well-hidden, but it is *not* so hidden now (thankfully). To allege that any form of self-injury is a social trend or that the actual prevalence of self-injury has increased over recent years, one would have to have data on the previously hidden behavior to make a valid comparison. Obviously, counting hidden behavior is difficult, so you can't say, for sure, that the prevalence has increased. You can say *for sure* that self-injury has come out of hiding.[620] The only way you could try to assess the previous "hidden" prevalence of self-injury would be to do some significantly broad surveys of older adults regarding their earlier, "hidden" behaviors. I am not aware of any such studies.

One could hypothesize that "self-injury" for the purpose of feeling better has also been forced into a higher prevalence over the last 300 years, based on the stigma, criminality, and pressures against "other-injury" dopamine-fixes. Fighting, lashing out, loud arguing, "drama," and violence of many types have become rather well-regulated. The "Wild West" is gone. Those kind of "gunslinger" dopamine-fixes will get you jail time.

Just like any proven effective treatment of a condition becomes "popular," culturally or subculturally sanctioned effective "treatments" for low dopamine levels have and will continue to spread like wildfire, especially through dopamine-deficient populations. As noted in Section 19 of this book, dopamine deficiencies significantly contribute to high vulnerabilities to suggestion — in other words, such an effective treatment as cutting for feeling better, can be expected to become even more popular in a population who is scientifically known to be more vulnerable to peer pressure, fads, trends, and group belongingness.

Self-defined "deviancy" is clearly a way of solidifying an identity. Identities are very important. I genuinely honor and respect a person's self-defined identity. However, my scientific self knows that if you self-define your behavior as deviant, well, believe me, the dopamine enhancing effects of that behavior will be turbocharged. In that regard, when so-called "deviant" behavior becomes more "mainstream," it has the potential to lose its dopamine punch.

Undoubtedly, when it comes to inducing physical pain or "system shock" for the purposes of increasing dopamine and norepinephrine levels towards optimal (calmer, less noise in your head, grounded), *that* behavior will *not* likely lose its punch, whether it is branded as average or deviant.

Such Emotional-Brain stimulating, self-injury behavior can be said to have biologically intrinsic value and does not actually have to be learned, unlike the dopamine punch of binge shopping, which is a less intrinsic, but clearly powerful dopamine stimulator. In that sense, one could rationally propose that the self-injurer has found a less dysfunctional (in the long run), less damaging, and more powerful method for increasing dopamine than let's say, the tobacco smoker, the alcoholic or the over-eater, that is, if the self-injurer is *not* also utilizing those "treatment" strategies. (If, only....)[621]

Most, if not all, on-going "self-injury" should be viewed as genuine attempts to fix dopamine-deficiency conditions. Again, when there are *so few* resources available for accessible, informed and effective help, in a world where peers, family, and wise elders are so distracted as to be mostly unavailable, and healthcare is third-rate, just what is a person supposed to do? In fact, in Nock's 2010 Review, he specifically refers to this phenomena as the "pragmatic hypothesis."

The fact is that such self-injury and self-damaging behaviors are *not* limited to teenagers and they take place in many adults with ADD (and other diagnoses), and, of course, in many people who are "undiagnosed."[622]

What ongoing self-injurers may grow out of is the more obvious self-injury behaviors, not unlike how many ADDers grow out of their more obvious fidgeting behaviors. What self-injurers generally *do not grow out of* is the less obvious, but possibly even more destructive, other forms of self-damage, such as smoking cigarettes, over-using alcohol and drugs, and participating in physically or financially dangerous, adrenaline-inducing behavior of many kinds. It's a process of substituting a more "acceptable" self-damaging behavior for the more developmentally "appropriate," earlier, self-injury behaviors. The common achievement that almost all such behaviors share, whether they are "sanctioned" self-damaging types or alleged "less sanctioned" self-injury, is to increase dopamine and norepinephrine levels.

In that regard, and with all due respect to the Adlers, the name of their book should be *The Healing Cut*. There is nothing "tender" about cutting to feel better. If it was "tender," it would not likely work.

In Nock's 2010 Review, he states that the "role of pain and endorphins in self-injury represents one of the most intriguing, but as yet understudied, aspects of self-injury." He cites one study.[623] There are others.[624 625] Unfortunately, Nock did not cite any studies regarding the key roles of dopamine, norepinephrine and prefrontal cortical attentional domains on experiences related to pain.

"Pain tolerance" is at least a dual-domain variable in that there are at least two very important physiological responses to pain (1) the emotional-brain response that starts with just the thought of impending pain (which results in adrenal gland stimulation creating muscle tension, nausea, and increased glucose metabolism, heart rate, cortisol, norepinephrine and dopamine levels) is more tolerated by the ADD brain, and (2) pre-pain dopamine is much lower in ADDers, and is increased by the anticipation of pain and the pain, itself.

Pain, itself, and the stress experience related to it significantly activate dorsal and basal ganglia dopamine activity.[626] In addition, dopamine D2/D3 receptor availability correlates with individual response characteristics to pain in what appears to be an inverse relationship to receptor availability and extracellular dopamine — less extracellular dopamine, more pain; more extracellular dopamine, less pain.[627][628]

In that regard, at least at one level of dopamine processing, the activity of self-injury, although clearly painful to begin with, results in not only higher levels of tonic dopamine which "treats" the ADD brain but, also, less end-point pain. End-point pain "relief" and a sense of "normalcy" brought about by pain induction, are more than enough reward for an ADDer to repeat self-injury behavior frequently. The higher pain threshold in the *non-ADDer does not* facilitate "pain-targeted" behavior, since there is no known physiological or cognitive advantage to thinking about or inducing pain for the non-ADDer.

And, finally, there is the highly-dopamine dependent basal ganglia (striatum with its caudate, putamen, globus pallidus, substantia nigra, and subthalamic nucleus). The basal ganglia have a limbic sector including the nucleus accumbuns, ventral pallidum, and ventral tegmental area. (I know. Way too much information. But, I have to go there when it comes to pain processing.)

The basal ganglia play a key role in pain processing.[629] In fact, in fibromyalgia patients who often have a clear history of fitting the criteria for ADD from childhood,[630] the basal ganglia dopamine processes are so extremely depleted as to give practically no dopamine response to pain compared to controls.[631]

One of my favorite articles on pain and disgust tolerance is *Does it look painful or disgusting? Ask your parietal and cingulate cortex.*[632] That article was followed-up a year later with *Brain networks responsive to aversive visual stimuli in humans.*[633] As far as I can tell, and you can correct me on this if you want to, but clearly, those who fit the criteria for ADD have a lot more fun and less aversive reactions (illness) with disgusting aspects of *Beavis and Butt-head*, *South Park*, *Dirty Jobs*, and the list could go on.

In my professional experience, proper treatment of ADD almost always significantly reduces or eliminates such self-injury behaviors in those with ADD. Self-injury behaviors associated with other psychiatric disorders generally *cannot* be treated the same way as ADD is treated, and may be more difficult to modify.

People (including professionals) may diagnose such self-injury behavior as clinical depression, suicidal behavior, borderline personality disorder, bipolar disorder, or psychosis, among other things.

15.12 Fibromyalgia and "Allergies"

15.12.1 Fibromyalgia

As noted just a few paragraphs ago, fibromyalgia has been shown to be clearly associated with early-life and current diagnoses of ADD — *High frequency of childhood ADHD history in women with fibromyalgia* (2010) ("2010 Madrid Study").[634] Of 201 patients attending at a Rheumatology Service at the University of Madrid, Spain, 32.5% fit the criteria for ADHD compared to 2.52% in a matched control group.

Many other studies have discovered such correlations between ADD and fibromyalgia with positive treatment results for both of them with typical ADD medications.[635] In my own practice, I have seen it from the other side, that is, people who come to me for their ADD evaluations, but who also clearly fit the criteria for fibromyalgia, who, when treated correctly for their ADD (and sometimes for co-existing clinical depression) are often astounded by how the fibromyalgia symptoms clear up.[636] This is not just true of women, but also very true in men who often have a different set of "paresthesias" from women than the classic fibromyalgia symptoms. Nonetheless, those male fibromyalgia pain symptoms disappear when the ADD is treated correctly.

In my practice, ADDers who also fit the criteria for fibromyalgia, were clearly highly motivated, very driven, generally high IQ types who would not let anything get in the way of success, even if it meant 80 hours of work a week to keep up with colleagues who could do the same work in 40 hours. In other words, their low working memory, distractibility, disorganization, and other ADD-related processing obstacles got in the way, but they were "willing" to "burn themselves out" to reach their goals. In my world, at this point in time, I classify much of what I have seen with respect to fibromyalgia as "end-stage untreated ADD" in someone who is highly driven and just won't be stopped. Well, until they hit their physiological limits.

What I find somewhat disturbingly interesting is that some researchers have been studying both the pre-morbid and post-morbid cognitive difficulties associated with fibromyalgia since at least 2001, but did not, until as recently as 2008, link those ADD-like characteristics to fitting the criteria for ADD.[637 638] Did I say unfortunate? Should have.

Even more unfortunate is the recent, *October 2011, Drug Class Review: Drugs for Fibromyalgia Final Original Report*, an 86-page review out of Oregon Health and Science University ("2011 Oregon Fibromyalgia Drugs Report").[639] It makes no mention of any of the typical ADD medications for treating fibromyalgia, but includes reviews of 32 other medications. In all fairness, however, it must be said that the mission of the Oregon report was to utilize studies that fit somewhat stringent criteria. Apparently, although there are a number of clinical reports of the efficacy of ADD medications for treating fibromyalgia, there have been no large, controlled studies.

15.12.2 "Allergies"

Anecdotally, there is reliable and extensive evidence that ADDers experience much higher rates of difficulties with asthma, certain allergies, eczema, and autoimmune conditions. Often, those symptoms *will* significantly disappear with appropriate ADD medications — maybe not immediately, but clearly, over time, treating dopamine and norepinephrine deficiencies changes stress reactions and immune system dynamics, among other things.

A significant amount of research has been done with respect to the correlation or association between dopamine and cortisol responses and ADD, allergies, asthma, and immune response processes. Both cortisol and dopamine have been clearly implicated in inflammation-control processes. Cortisol, dopamine, and norepinephrine dysfunction have all been clearly and convincingly implicated as major contributors to low working memory, hypofunction of the EB, and other neurophysiological processes significantly related to ADD downsides and upsides.

Often the question has been "Which came first the ADD or the allergy?" Although much research has been devoted to attempting to discover whether the symptoms and impairments of ADD might be caused by allergies, toxins, and nutritional variations, no firm conclusions have been made.[640 641 642] When you add in the upside of ADD (it creates the best defenders and other types of emergency-capable humans), there is really no adequate explanation for a "selection pressure" for such innately emergency-capable humans based on a nutritional, immunological, or any conceivable non-genetic or long-past epigenetic origin for such humans.

In essence, such emergency-capable humans (ADDers) are precisely why we are still here. It is more than relatively unlikely that dopamine-optimized individuals would have assured such an outcome for humans. And, that is very likely why there are so *few* dopamine-optimized humans in general, but clearly, even fewer in the Western Hemisphere.

When research has been directed to the association between ADD and eczema, rhinitis and/or asthma, several studies have shown positive connections. In almost every such study, there was a high correlation between atopic eczema and ADD in children with sleeping problems.[643 644] A small but very good 1999 Israeli study revealed that such alleged eczema-related sleep disturbances very significantly *also took place while the eczema was in remission.*[645] One more time — *in remission.*

As noted in several sections of this book, about 80% of children and adults who fit the criteria for ADD have substantial sleep disturbances (almost always fixed by correct ADD medication). Thus, if you subtract the sleep difficulty from the equation set forth in those studies of atopic eczema, it is clear that the major correlation is between *eczema and ADD*, not eczema and sleep problems. Although, without a doubt, rhinitis and eczema can be significant "distractors" which can add to the sleep difficulties of ADDers, they are *not* likely the root "cause" of those sleep problems and, thus, *also not* the root causes of the subsequent daytime "ADD-like symptoms." *ADD is the cause of the daytime ADD-like symptoms.* Some other mechanism *other than* sleep disturbances likely causes both the atopic and ADD disorders. That likely-candidate common-denominator is dopamine, which has clearly been shown to be a significant player in autoimmune processes.[646 647 648]

It is unfortunate that, even though much has been discovered about the association between ADD, atopic disorders, and sleep disturbances since as early as 1999, a 2010 study does *not* even mention the proven sleeping disturbances clearly associated with ADD in both children and adults.[649] (See Sections 12.2 and 15.1.2 for details on ADD and sleep impairments and treatment.) The authors declare "The cause of awakenings during [atopic dermatitis] *disease remission* is not known, but it is hypothesized that the sleep abnormality induced by the pruritis may become a *learned sleep pattern.*" (emphasis mine)

Actually, had the authors of the 2010 report wanted to be truly scientific, they would have said, "At least two possible hypotheses can be forwarded based on previous research:

(1) active atopic dermatitis fragmented-sleep habits spill over into non-active, non-itchy remission periods (habit hypothesis), and (2) there is a strong association between ADD, sleep disturbances and eczema, and such non-itchy remission-period awakenings could be attributed to an underlying mechanism that contributes to both frequency of eczema and the disturbed sleep (ADD hypothesis).

I know, you are thinking, well, "What about a third hypothesis — all three difficulties, ADD, eczema, and sleep disturbances are all related to an underlying allergy-related, non-dopamine/norepinephrine cause?" It's a good hypothesis which, as noted in the second paragraph of this section, has been repeatedly tested and which has not found any significant supporting data.

Such a flawed scientific analysis of similar findings can be found in two other 2010 studies in which the authors, although alleging that (to paraphrase) "eczema caused sleep problems which, in turn, caused subsequent daytime ADD-like behaviors," do not even cite a single source for what else might link eczema and sleep disturbances — ADD! Are those researchers completely unaware of the large number of studies that show consistent and very prevalent sleep disturbances in those who fit the criteria for ADD who *don't* have eczema symptoms?

Two other notable studies are: (1) A 2011 study showed a clear association between allergic sensitization and ADD[650]; and, (2) Another 2011 study confirmed the "marked" comorbidity between asthma and ADD.[651]

With respect to cortisol and allergies, a series of studies starting around 2003, demonstrated that a "blunted cortisol response" is clearly associated with asthmatic children and with atopic diseases of other types.[652 653 654 655] An *under*active cortisol response to threat, fear, and/or pain as consistently found in ADDers (see Section 15.10.3) would clearly compromise adequate cortisol response to inflammations generated by all types of noxious stressors, such as toxins present in industrial outdoor and indoor pollution, poisons, etc.

Inhaled dopamine clearly *reverses* existing bronchospasm, but may not *prevent* asthma-related bronchospasm or assist in maintaining healthy, open airways[656][657][658][659] — the exact same function of traditional "reliever" inhalers noted below. Benzedrine inhalers (mixture of dextro and levo amphetamines) were widely prescribed as bronchodilators between about 1928 and 1950. They also became popular for recreational "stimulant" use which was done by extracting the inhalant strip from the container and swallowing it or finding other "creative" ways to ingest it.[660] Clearly, inhaling such an amphetamine mixture produced the release of dopamine in airway walls, which was then responsible for bronchodilation. The untested question that remains is whether oral ingestion of amphetamines or methylphenidate can cause a similar, but more delayed dilation of airways.

The other very effective bronchodilators for use in asthma-related bronchospasm and for treating the bronchial inflammation that contributes to such airway constriction are, guess what, corticosteroid inhalers.[661] Corticosteroid inhalers and their cousins all mimic natural, *endogenous cortisol* and its actions: anti-inflammatory properties, reducing histamine secretion and stabilizing lysosomal membranes and damping down immune system over-reactivity.[662]

I hope those cortisol facts are not lost on you. But, just in case — since a significant majority of ADDers have reduced EB-HPA responsiveness and consequent lower cumulative cortisol activity, it is likely that they would have decreased cortisol resources for damping down possible inflammations in their airways due to airway surfaces (sensitive mucous membranes) reacting to noxious inhalants (pollen, pollution, etc.).

The actual treatment of asthma involves the use of both a "reliever" inhaler, and, if needed, a "controller" inhaler. Reliever inhalers are for quick symptomatic relief of airway blockage due to over-stimulated and constricting airways (airways constrict in response to toxic threats) and are usually beta-2 adrenoreceptor agonists (think of an agonist as a trigger device). You may recognize that the "adreno" in adrenoreceptor sounds like "adrenal." It should. Adrenoreceptors in the smooth muscle of your bronchus react to the presence of noradrenaline and adrenaline (epinephrine) (your own, or from inhaling something that mimics them) by making the smooth muscle relax (unconstrict). As noted above, so does inhaling amphetamine (or dopamine) unconstrict constricted airways.

However, both noradrenaline and adrenaline trigger *all* adrenergic receptors, including α_1, α_2, β_1, β_2, and β_3 receptors, so they aren't very selective. That's why, after discovering that β_2 types densely populate bronchial smooth muscle, and that they are responsible for relaxing that smooth muscle (unconstricting airways) researchers created very targeted β_2 triggering medications for the specific use of de-constricting and opening-up constricted asthmatic airways. (Mostly, acetylcholine receptors are responsible for the original airway constriction.) There are huge reserves of β_2 adrenoreceptors in airway smooth muscle, which likely account for how long it takes, if at all, for chronic asthmatics to become insensitive to β_2-related medications.[663]

I apologize for all the details. I am hoping you are not losing track of the main thread in this allergy section which is that the most powerful variables that contribute to the facilitation of asthma *also* contribute to the turbocharging of ADD — (1) compromised dopamine-function both in bronchodilation and immune response; and (2) compromised cortisol responses due to a hypoactive EB resulting in EB-HPA axis hypoactivity.

In my opinion, it is very unfortunate that we are not aggressively screening for ADD in those with asthma, eczema, and other related autoimmune diseases. You might ask, "So, how would that help?" It would be more than nice to know if appropriate treatment of dopamine-dysfunctions such as those found in the ADD-brain (and body) would make a difference in the progression of asthma and other atopic difficulties. Wouldn't it?

Okay. One last data point. It is more than interesting to note that the prevalence of asthma, even in some countries and provinces which experience high levels of pollutants and other atopy/allergy triggers have low rates of asthma. China, Greece and Russia had the lowest prevalence of asthma as of 2004.[664]

One 2010 Canadian study showed that Chinese ethnicity decreased the risk for asthma and related atopies and allergies among adolescents in five Canadian cities.[665]

Also, interesting to note: Prevalence of ADD in those same low-asthma countries is also very low.[666][667] It can be argued that such a prevalence correlation may be an indicator that the *non-ADD brain and body* may offer signficant protection against the development of atopy, asthma, and certain immune dysfunctions, even in high pollution environments.

15.13 Sex, Porn, Masturbation, Sex Crimes

ADD and sex, pornography, masturbation, sex crimes? What can I say? I guess I could write about dopamine. It is clearly involved in anticipated, imagined, and reality-based sexual behaviors between people and alone. However, it is not the only powerful endogenous chemical involved in the human sexual experience. Sex is neuro-chemically very complicated. Sex between people brings into play "bonding" chemicals such as oxytocin which are not as relevant in masturbation.

Orgasm, but not sexual stimulation without orgasm, triggers prolactin in males and females, which damps down hypothalamic dopamine and decreases libido for a few hours to a few days post-orgasm.[668][669][670] For the most accessible circa-2000 understanding of the neurobiology of sexual function see Archives of General Psychiatry, November 2000.[671] Unfortunately, I could not find any other comprehensive, accessible reviews about the neurobiology of sex-related behaviors and EB processing.

And, then, there is the subject of sexual offenders of many types, including exhibitionists, molesters (frotteurism — paraphilic rubbing against a non-consenting person, etc.), rapists, peeping-toms (criminal voyeurism), and pedophiles. And, then, there are risky sexual behaviors, some rising to the level of criminality — promiscuity, infidelity, incest, sexual harassment, and professional boundary violations. ADDers are more vulnerable to many of these behaviors due to ADD impulsiveness, distractibility, and risk tolerance (lack of speed bumps).[672 673 674 675]

The question of whether over-activity or "addictions" to sex, porn and masturbation can be dopamine-fixes for the low-dopamine ADD brain has not been significantly answered. It appears to be "no." But it is not certain. Clearly, since the ADD EB can tolerate much more dopamine flooding before experiencing aversive or negative feedback to such flooding, the ADD EB low baseline dopamine contributes to a higher tolerance for imagining and participating in risky, deviant, "disgusting," borderline illegal, or outright illegal behaviors.

One could argue that imagination and anticipation of sex or sex-related content could conceivably increase dopamine levels and be helpful in that regard, but not likely so "necessary" for the non-ADD brain with its baseline optimal dopamine levels. One could also argue that "sex-dreaming" would be more powerful for treating low dopamine levels than actual behavior resulting in orgasm, since orgasms have a damping effect on dopamine through prolactin stimulation. Maybe that is why so-called "romance" novels can be so "addictive." They likely increase baseline dopamine for ADDers which results in "better, faster, calmer." For the non-ADDer, too much dopamine would be aversive.

16   ADD: Illness or Condition?

Generally, the term "illness" means unhealthy condition; ailment, affliction or infirmity. In Western medicine, there is virtually no distinction between the terms "illness" and "disease." The term illness does not denote, connote or imply that there is an "upside" to the diagnosis or the causes of the condition. Logically, I find it very difficult to call ADD an illness, disease or disorder, since it clearly has a significant upside. To me it is a well-documented type of brain. And, as you will note in this book, I propose that it is the average Western Hemisphere brain.

16.1   What Significantly Prevents ADD from Being Rationally Labeled an "Illness"?

If you fit the criteria for ADD, it is highly likely that you will always be able to deal with emergency situations, putting out fires, and jumping out of airplanes better than someone who does not fit the criteria for ADD. (I would bet money on it since it is true 90% of the time.) You will be calmer, more organized, more focused, show better judgment, have better performance, with shorter reaction times and less shakiness, among other things, than the non-ADD person, unless you are medicated while doing those activities.

I will also repeat what I said in Section 15.10, right now, to make sure you clearly understand what is *the true upside* of the untreated ADD brain, and not what are so many misunderstandings about the alleged upside of the untreated ADD brain. (Hint: It's *not* that it is a more creative, adventurous, novelty seeking, or higher IQ brain.)

16.2   Lack of "Speed Bumps"

The upside is that those with the untreated ADD brain have relatively few speed bumps (discomfort, ill feelings, side effects) to slow them down from having thoughts or doing things that, in a non-ADD brain, would spike dopamine and norepinephrine to above-optimal levels, providing a reliable and significant disincentive to those with the non-ADD brain. Got it?

The untreated ADD brain can tolerate large increases in dopamine and norepinephrine that the non-ADD brain cannot tolerate without side effects.

That means "ADDers can think it and do it" and *feel better* thinking it and doing it. Non-ADDers generally *cannot* think it and/or do it without subtly or significantly feeling "sick." Believe me, even if the aversive feeling may sometimes be subtle, feeling sick is a clear disincentive for the non-ADDer. It will generally keep them from indulging in many of the behaviors for which untreated ADDers are known.

It is unfortunate that so-called "choking under pressure" studies have not included imaging of dopamine in the EB of those who choke. Guess what? *Only* individuals with a high working memory capacity (dopamine, anyone?), choke under pressure on math problems with high working memory demands.[676][677]

One more time, the reasons for the upside of the ADD brain are:

(1) Threats, fear, and anticipation of or exposure to pain increase dopamine and norepinephrine in the human brain through emotion-related neurocircuitry (insula, anterior cingulate cortex, amygdala, hypothalamus);[678][679]

(2) Studies have shown that carriers of one of the well-known ADD risk genes have significantly lower dopamine-mediated cortisol (stress hormone) responses than normal controls to stress,[680] meaning they can tolerate much larger increases in dopamine before stress-regulation mechanisms create higher levels of brain-calming cortisol;[681][682][683]

(3) When you start with lower than optimal dopamine and norepinephrine (*the ADD*

brain),[684][685] and you are presented with a "threat" or a situation that activates your emotion-related neurocircuitry (insula, cingulate cortex, amygdala, hypothalamus), your dopamine and norepinephrine levels will move *up towards optimal* which produces the same positive effects on working memory that traditional ADD medications produce. In other words, your ADD brain is being "medicated" by the increased emotion-related neurocircuitry output and you feel calmer, more focused, faster, and better. Such a "threat" response can even be responsible for the last minute focus, concentration, and completion of assignments as the fear factor goes up as a deadline approaches. Think of a deadline as a train coming down the tracks toward you. As the train (deadline) gets closer, fear skyrockets. That fear stimulates the ADDer's EB increasing dopamine and norepinephrine and working memory to the point that the ADDer can finally get undistracted (make decisions), focus and follow-through. See *Neural Processing of imminent collision in humans* for a great discussion.[686] This process is incorrectly called procrastination;

(4) When you start with optimal dopamine and norepinephrine (*the non-ADD brain*) and you are presented with a "threat" or potentially adrenaline-activating situation, your dopamine and norepinephrine levels in your EB will be kicked up to *above optimal* levels. You might think that "more is always better" and that such higher levels of neurotransmitters would have an advantage, but they *decidedly do not*. As noted in several earlier sections of this book, above-optimal levels of dopamine and norepinephrine produce, among other things, nervousness, shakiness, queasiness, confusion, and a significant decrease in performance from

the higher baseline. (Too many bridges in a system of roads produces confusion and inefficiencies. Just envision the difference there would be when driving up to an intersection that had one or two bridges to choose from *to* driving up to an intersection that had several bridges to choose from. Engineers call this too-many-bridges scenario "noise.") In other words, your non-ADD brain is being "over-medicated" by the increased dopamine and norepinephrine and you are experiencing typical "over-stimulation" side effects *as if* you were taking the wrong ADD medication or too much of the right ADD medication.

This clear advantage of the untreated ADD brain allows many people in certain occupations to excel — first responders, military, firefighters, most sports, deadline-heavy professions, etc. With their unmedicated ADD brain, such ADDers will almost always be better in "emergencies" of all types than someone with a non-ADD brain. However, when the ADDer's EB brain and working memory return to low-baseline levels during less emergent situations, like around the family dinner table or studying for school, there are huge downsides to their then "untreated" ADD brain.

16.3 The Difference Between an Illness and a "Condition"

Although it may *not* be something you may have thought about, the terms "illness" and "disorder" clearly convey the meaning that there is *no* upside to such a condition — (1) *illness*: a disease or indisposition; sickness; a state of ill health[687]; or, an unhealthy condition of body or mind[688]; and (2) *disorder*: an abnormal physical or mental condition.[689]

Note that the meaning of the words "normal" and "abnormal" are highly debatable. "Normal" can mean "average" or "ideal." If normal stands for ideal when it comes to brain function, that "ideal" is far from being understood yet. If normal stands for average when it comes to brain function, that "average" is far from being understood. In this book, I claim that a more dopamine-deficient brain is the majority brain found in the Western Hemisphere of planet Earth. Thus, I am asserting that the "average" or "normal" brain in the Western Hemisphere has one kind of dopamine deficiency or another.

The untreated ADD brain is one of the most well-understood conditions related to dopamine deficiency, second only to Parkinson's Disease. In that regard, ADD is the poster child for the many significantly-documented dopamine-deficiency conditions which will be discussed in my forthcoming book *The Culture Genes* (to be published in early 2012) — "nicotinism," alcoholism, obesity, other eating disorders, insomnia, fibromyalgia, and the over-use of marijuana, cocaine, illicit methamphetamine, and opioids, not to mention rampant gambling, over-spending, and impulse-control problems of all kinds.

16.4   Two Brains can be Better than One

For those who fit the criteria for ADD, guess what? You can have two brains. Since all the medications that are utilized for ADD treatment are short-acting except for atomoxetine (Strattera), you can have your ADD brain when it is the better one to have in certain situations, *and* you can have a more non-ADD brain (better working memory, more "responsive" EB) when you want to have that brain.

Those people with brains that are already dopamine-optimized, well, they only get to have "one" brain. There is no approved method for consistently or reliably reducing dopamine in the already dopamine-optimized brain so that people with such non-ADD brains can jump out of planes (a metaphor) as well as those who fit the criteria for ADD. You can change the peripheral effects of "too much adrenaline" by using beta blocker medications, but that does not change the longer-lasting central effects of an over-stimulated EB.

SSRIs can reduce central dopamine but it is inconsistent and can reduce cognitive performance.

It is unfortunate that Russell Barkley does not recognize the upside of the ADD brain, at all, at least up to the publication of his 2008 book *ADHD in Adults — What the Science Says.*

> "Some clinicians and advocates for the adult ADHD community have claimed that ADHD has a good side, and that it brings with it positive traits or special gifts individuals would not otherwise possess. 'People with ADD have special gifts, even if they are hidden. The most common include originality, creativity, charisma, energy, liveliness, and unusual sense of humor, areas of intellectual brilliance, and spunk' (Hallowell & Ratey, 2005, p. 6). Others have claimed likewise (Hartmann, 1993; Sarkis, 2005).
>
> We wish we could say there is evidence in these two large projects supporting such a romantic view of this disorder. But none was found above. Nor is any found in the remaining chapters of this book, at least not at the group level of analysis. In not a single instance on hundreds of measures did we find that ADHD conferred some advantage over our various control groups.
>
> Admittedly, we did not examine any specific and positive affinity ADHD may have with hunting or military combat ability, but neither did those who have asserted such special adaptive capacities as being associated with ADHD. Certainly there is nothing here that would suggest such special talents as likely to exist within those domains of life activities. Yet if this ideal were true, we should see it at the group level, not just in a few individual and

exceptional cases cited by advocates. The exceptions are just that - exceptions.

They likely represent unique individual positive traits in those cases, which have no relationship to ADHD and would have been present anyway, whether the disorder had been present or not.

Clinicians should, by all means, help patients identify and celebrate their individual strengths and use them where feasible to compensate for their disorder. But let us not portray those individual talents as somehow resulting directly from the presence of this disorder. It is not only false to claim so but - given the prevailing scientific evidence mustered here - *also misleading.*" (emphasis mine) Russell A. Barkley, Kevin R. Murphy, Mariellen Fischer. *ADHD in Adults: What the Science Says* (pp. 148-149). Kindle Edition.

I guess Dr. Barkley would say that *I am misleading you* by claiming that all the studies that have clearly documented the "risk-tolerance" of a vast majority of those who fit the criteria for ADD supports the conclusion that there is a significant upside to the ADD brain. Really? I am misleading you and there is no significant scientific evidence of an upside to the ADD brain? Could have fooled me.

I guess for Barkley, the ability to calmly face down the saber-toothed cat at your cave entrance with faster reaction times, increased focus and better judgment, among other things, instead of the opposite, has no significant upside. If I was given a choice as to who should guard the entrance to my cave, I would choose the person who fits the criteria for ADD. As far as I can tell from most, if not all, the scientific findings, most ADDers make the best defenders.

In that regard, I am very thankful for the high percentage of ADDers in our midst. They, quite likely, are why we non-ADDers are still here. I can tell you this, if that had been my job in those old days, and my clan had depended on me for defending them, I am sure there would *not* have been a good outcome.

17 Creativity, Novelty-Seeking, Sensation-Seeking, Criminality, "Deviance," and "Aversion"

"Creativity," "novelty-seeking," "sensation-seeking," and "harm avoidance" have been the subjects of many studies as they relate to various dopamine and norepinephrine functions and genes. "Criminality" and "deviance," not so much.

17.1 "Creativity"

When last checked in November 2011, "creativity" took up about 22 pages of text at Wikipedia.com,[690] which notes that "creativity" has been defined more than 100 different ways in the scientific literature according to M.D. Mumford in a 2003 article.[691]

The difficulty with studying "creativity" is in clearly defining what constitutes "creativity." Are people who fit the criteria for ADD more creative? That question is very important, since it is a common belief that carries a lot of emotional weight. That belief affects perceptions about the upside of untreated ADD and about the medications that are helpful with the downside of ADD.

Clearly, if people who have the dopamine deficiencies of ADD and other dopamine-deficiency conditions are more creative because of that, then, the downside of a medication strategy for the symptoms of such a condition could possibly be the loss of creativity. However, it is my professional and scientific opinion, based on my experience and on the literature, that there are so many variables involved in the "creative" process, that it is far from clear whether dopamine deficiencies or excesses significantly contribute or interfere with the creative process.

What can be said with certainty, however, is that dopamine excesses produced by too much of the right medication or by the wrong medication in a person with ADD will clearly cause cognitive problems, including decreased performance in many cognitive areas and increased perseveration (possibly the opposite of divergent thinking) as noted in several sections of this book. One study published in 2009 showed that mixed salts of amphetamine (Adderall) given to healthy individuals did not have an overall negative effect on creativity as measured by divergent and convergent tasks.[692] It has not been replicated to date (November 2011).

Creativity in many of the scientific studies has been repeatedly measured by divergent thinking tests which claim to measure something that is outside of both fluid intelligence and crystallized intelligence — something called "long-term storage and retrieval" which is characterized as "fluent retrieval of information through association." [693] How this significant variable is affected by lower than optimal dopamine levels in the PFC is still not fully understood, but it appears to be related to the DRD2 gene (dopamine receptor 2 gene). Since we do not know which typical ADD medications might affect such D2 receptors the most, we cannot predict, on this data, whether or not a given medication may interfere with creative processes for an ADDer. It is a trial-and-error process, and if a medication for ADD is found to be interfering with the creative processes of an ADDer, then it can be considered a significant side-effect and other medications should be explored.

It is my contention that creativity is more than "wandering" or "thinking outside of the box." Creativity is a process that starts with a novel idea or a novel connection of data not previously connected, but which cannot be called creative until it is made observable — that is, until it is more than a novel thought or image or connection of data points. Creativity implies an action. To create means to "bring into existence." [694] Creativity clearly implies follow-through and action, not just creative thoughts. Thus, one could argue that those who fit the criteria for ADD, although they might be very good at wandering, thinking outside of the box, and the discovery of things off the beaten path, they are not so good at the "bring-into-existence" part of the creative process (follow-through).

Higher-than-average IQ with its very important higher-than-average fluid intelligence is likely a much more powerful factor with respect to creativity than the distractibility-quotient of the ADD brain with normal IQ or not.

17.2 "Novelty Need," "Novelty Addiction," "Novelty Seeking" or "Novelty Tolerance"?

"Novelty seeking" is a common term used in the scientific literature — "The personality trait of novelty seeking measures the extent to which a person responds to novel stimuli or situations with exploratory activity and positive excitement." The term is often used interchangeably with "sensation-seeking," which creates significant confusion in understanding the research findings.[695] In my opinion, however, they are quite different constructs.

"Sensation-seeking" does not necessarily imply seeking a novel situation or experience. In fact, it often involves doing the same "sensation-intense" experience again and again. "Novelty seeking" is more aligned with the concept of curiosity than with sensation-intense, EB-stimulating activities. In addition, novelty awareness — the ability to identify and react to novelty within an environment is fundamental to survival.[696]

Novelty "seeking" is often assessed using the Tridimensional Personality Questionnaire (Cloninger),[697] which measures novelty "seeking," harm avoidance and reward dependence. Cloninger suggested that those three dimensions, novelty seeking, harm avoidance and reward dependence, are correlated with low basal dopaminergic activity.

Sensation-seeking has been traditionally measured using the Sensation Seeking Scale developed by Marvin

Zuckerman, Ph.D. He defined the trait of sensation-seeking as the seeking of novel and intense stimuli, and outlined four subtypes representing the various ways sensation-seeking is expressed behaviorally:

(1) Thrill and Adventure Seeking: the pursuit of physical activities that are exciting, unusual and potentially dangerous (e.g., sky-diving).

(2) Experience Seeking: stimulation through the mind and senses; the pursuit of unfamiliar and complex environmental stimuli, as through travel or meeting new people.

(3) Disinhibition: sensation-seeking through engagement with other people; searching for opportunities to lose inhibitions by engaging in variety in sex, alcohol, drugs, etc.

(4) Boredom Susceptibility: the tendency to be easily bored by familiar or repetitive situations or people, or by routine work.[698]

"Homo sapiens were the only group of early hominids to emigrate over the entire world, which entailed great risk, so I think humans as a species are characterized by novelty- and intensity-seeking," says Zuckerman, arguing that this "must have been an adaptive trait." Early humans also needed to hunt to survive, and those who were more willing to take risks were likely to be more successful hunters, so a certain degree of risk-taking behavior — fueled by the promise of reward — maybe programmed into human DNA." [699]

17.3 Look Mom, No Speed Bumps!

In my opinion, Zukerman and many others who utilize words like "willing," "seeking," and "taking" are erroneously attributing motive to the indulgences in such behaviors. A tolerance is clearly not a motive. It is an ability — an innate one in the ADD scenario.

When there is no speed bump (overstimulating side effects) in the way of EB stimulating behaviors, the behaviors proceed "naturally" and *without* a second thought (also not very possible with the low working memory of dopamine deficiency).

After a few non-aversive and "healing" forays into such behaviors, the brain-sets connected to such behaviors clearly take on characteristics of addiction — need, seeking, and withdrawal. The addiction process moves ahead easily if there are relatively no initial aversive speed bumps in the way of such behaviors.

I am hoping that you are getting this: the untreated *ADD brain* **can**, and the *non-ADD brain* **cannot**, tolerate the early significantly increased levels of sensation-induced dopamine and norepinephrine. That speed bump in the non-ADD brain is the aversive side-effects of above-optimal levels of dopamine and norepinephrine.

This speed-bump phenomena is one of the major reasons why those who do *not* fit the criteria for ADD have a much more difficult time with smoking cigarettes. Their first several cigarettes may make them feel quite ill. Not so with a vast majority of ADDers. They feel smarter, faster, and better with the very first puff and there is no aversive, sick-feeling, above-optimal-dopamine-side-effects speed bump to slow them down.

17.4   Novelty and Sensation Tolerance

Along with the Guo 2010 Study (the "straight-arrow" gene) that clearly revealed the power of the aversive qualities of above-optimal levels of dopamine in the PFC and EB, there are other studies that show that so-called "novelty seekers" are not necessarily motivated by actual reward-predicting stimulus properties.[700] [701] In other words, the key to the vulnerability to, and the continuation of, sensation- or novelty-intense behaviors is the lack of a "speed bump" (initial and sometimes persistent aversive symptoms caused by above-optimal levels of dopamine and norepinephrine in relatively "straight-arrow" brains).

In my opinion, much better terms for describing the tolerance and increased vulnerability of the ADD brain to sensation- and novelty-related behaviors is "sensation or novelty tolerance." (As far as I can tell, I have invented this term.) However, the idea and the documentation of such "tolerance" is not new. A key 2009 study entitled *Cognitive and emotional processing in high novelty seeking associated with the L-DRD4 genotype* (the "Roussos Study")[702] clearly establishes such "tolerance" but does not use the term "tolerance." Instead, the Roussos Study uses the term "under-reactivity to unconditioned aversive stimuli." "Under-reactivity" by another name is "higher tolerance."

The fact is, if you can tolerate adventuring into the relative unknown or thinking certain thoughts or doing certain behaviors that are known to produce EB stimulation, you *will* likely do them. One more time, "there are relatively no early physiological disincentives (physiological speed bumps)."

17.5 Curiosity and Meaning-Seeking are Human Constants

Curiosity is a clearly-established, ever-present constant in human beings. Such novelty awareness — the ability to identify and react to novelty within an environment — is fundamental to survival.[703]

According to Kurt Goldstein,[704] Carl Rogers,[705] Abraham Maslow,[706] Erich Fromm,[707] and others, once an environment allows for time to focus on less threat- and physical survival-related novelty challenges, humans automatically turn their attention to less threat-related self-actualization.

In my opinion, self-actualization, is a very misunderstood word. A very significant part of the "self" is the "universal" or the "community of selves." Thus "self-actualization" automatically includes "species actualization" (in my book). As Erich Fromm put it —"I believe that the man choosing progress can find a new unity through the development of all his human forces, which are produced in three orientations.

These can be presented separately or together: biophilia, love for humanity and nature, and independence and freedom."

If there is one axiomatic, all encompassing truth about animals it is that, at some level, whether unconscious or conscious, they know what they may be able to do and they know what they need.

However, the most influential variables that affect what you will do with your equal helping of curiosity and highly-developed human novelty *awareness* is your dopamine and norepinephrine levels.

The drive to actualize is automatic. *Actualizing has no direction of its own.* Murder, *for instance, can be an actualization of your humanity* (humans are *capable* of murder). However, it may be an actualization that is based on erroneous, limited, or chaotic neurological processes. The actualization process is automatic throughout the whole animal kingdom. What gets actualized clearly depends on your stimulation tolerance and your ability to do working-memory dependent long-term thinking (mindfulness).

So, sensation-tolerance is not about sensation-seeking until you are hooked. It is about *not having an aversive reaction* to the idea of or the actual early participation in such "stimulating" activities *and* feeling more "alive" when you first engage in those activities. If you are a more dopamine-optimized "straight arrow," you will have to be highly motivated to get "hooked" because you will have to submit to some significant "torture" before you develop enough tolerance to actually "enjoy" what used to be the over-stimulation side-effects of such thoughts and behavior (it is a process sometimes called desensitization). At that point, however, you are actually not "enjoying" the thoughts and behavior so much as you are preventing withdrawal symptoms. Although necessary to feel "good," preventing withdrawal symptoms is clearly a "secondary enjoyment."

17.6 Startle Response, Cortisol Response, "Callousness," Empathy, Criminality, and More About "Speed Bumps"

As noted earlier, there are many things that can increase dopamine in the CNS, and many of those things are problematic. So fixing your dopamine-deficiencies with things that have the least side-effects is very important.

Some of the unfortunate directions that dopamine-deficient lives can take include significant "anti-social" (not pro-social), "callous," criminal, sociopathic and psychopathic behavior. This is *not* to say that a majority of ADDers go down these roads. It is to say, the speed bumps to those roads are absent or very small compared to the speed bumps present for non-ADDers with optimal dopamine. See earlier discussion of the *Straight-Arrow Gene* in Section 15.10.2. Other studies have replicated the findings in the 2010 Guo Study.[708] [709]

ADDers clearly share many of the same downsides of dopamine-deficiencies as those found in "delinquents," "sociopaths," and "psychopaths" in terms of impulsivity, impatience, distractibility, short-term reward vulnerabilities, and high tolerances for fear, pain, and threat.[710]

The same high-risk ADD genes are also present to a similar degree in populations displaying serious and violent delinquency.[711] [712] [713] As noted in Section 14.3, large numbers of prisoners fit the criteria for ADD.[714] [715] [716]

The scientific investigation of such dopamine-deficient behaviors has included studies of "callousness," fear tolerance, decreased startle-reflex, blunted cortisol response, low insula and amygdala dopamine-dependent activity, the contribution of inattention (distractibility) to psychopathy, and the neural bases of empathy, emotion and moral cognition.

One of my favorite review articles, which does an excellent job of comprehensively detailing almost all such "non-speed bump" research up to early 2009, is *Neurobiology of empathy and callousness: implications for the development of antisocial behavior* ("2009 Shirtcliff Review").[717] Although it utilizes 206 studies to inform us, only two of them directly relate to the overlapping dopamine-deficient characteristics and mechanisms of the ADD brain. I could not begin to cover all the excellent data presented in the 2009 Shirtcliff Review, so I recommend reading it.

It appears to me, and I may have this wrong (don't forget to tell me, if I am), but the studies and discussions of sociopathy and psychopathy seem clearly tainted by the words themselves, making it difficult to use them without being accused of inappropriately dramatizing the downside of the ADD brain.

Let me be clear. Just because someone has a vulnerability to certain types of mindsets and behaviors and a significant *lack of speed bumps* in the way of going down hurtful, impulsive, or inattentive roads, which behaviors may, at some point in history be classified as sociopathic or psychopathic, does *not* mean that such people *are* sociopathic or psychopathic. The terms are pejorative, not unlike "self-mutilation" was pejorative and inaccurate for describing "self-injury." "Callousness" and "unemotional" are also value-laden terms. By far, "non-empathic" and "other-hurtful" are better terms. There is clearly a spectrum of such behaviors from zero to ten. We know a heck of a lot about the neural bases of such spectrums of behavior.

Clearly and convincingly, the literature shows that the variation of "empathic" mindsets and behaviors is influenced by one's own sensitivity to threat. More threat tolerance (less active dopamine-dependent insula, anterior cingulate cortex, and amygdala), makes it difficult to notice or understand other people's fears or threat sensitivities. We are each very limited in our awareness of the nuances of the experiences of others by *our own* brain and mind-sets, and tolerance to threat, disgust, and fear.

In that regard, it is interesting to note that many of the least value-laden studies of the overlap of ADD characteristics and criminality have come out of Australia, United Kingdom, Germany. and Sweden. One very excellent late-2010 review, *The heterogeneity of disruptive behavior disorders — implications for neurobiological research and treatment* ("2010 Stadler Review"),[718] extensively describes many of the structural, chemical, cognitive, and behavioral overlaps between "criminality" and "ADD-ality." The term "ADHD" appears in that report 13 times.

In any earlier German study *Developmental psychopathology: Attention Deficit Hyperactivity Disorder (ADHD)*,[719] the authors do not shy away from the use of the terms ADHD along with psychopathology. Similarly, the 2010 Swedish Study, *Attention Deficit Hyperactivity Disorder (ADHD) among longer-term prison inmates is a prevalent, persistent and disabling disorder*,[720] does not shy away from using criminality terms in conjunction with "ADHD."

The Youth Psychopathic Traits Inventory accurately predicts various forms of increased interpersonal aggression, theft, and drug selling. Scores on this and other measures of non-empathic mindsets and behaviors also correlate with measures of attention deficit hyperactivity disorder (ADHD).[721]

The most significant areas of the brain clearly implicated in the empathic response include the dopamine-dependent insula, anterior cingulate cortex ("ACC") and amydala. In both non-empathic ADD types ("psychopaths") and empathic ADD types ("non-psychopaths"), there is clear malfunctioning of both the insula and ACC. They have that in common.

The important question is "Does this mean that empathic and non-empathic ADDers are neurophysiologically quite similar or quite different?" The answer is, they appear to differ in amygdala function *only*. Imaging studies show more evidence of amygdala dysfunction in the non-empathic ADDer as opposed to the empathic ADDer. One gets tagged a "psychopath" or "sociopath" and the other *does not.* In certain ways, that makes sense, since there is at least one clear difference in both neurophysiology and behavior but, in another way, it does *not* make sense.

We should probably not be so reassured by the less "dangerous" downsides of the ADD-brain. Aggressive screening for ADD and assistance on many levels with its downside is important whether we actually know if any particular ADDer has the additional "burden" of a low-functioning amygdala (the "psychopath"), or not.

17.7 "Deviance"

It could be claimed that a very large percentage of ADDers can tolerate "deviance" better than the non-ADDer who already possesses the dopamine-optimized brain. In that sense, "deviance," not unlike other perceived "risky," "rude," "disgusting," "fringe," or unconventional thoughts and behaviors, can lead the ADD brain to a different state of brain — more dopamine optimized and, therefore, calmer, faster, and better working memory ("normalized").

A detailed discussion of how "deviancy" and the waves of seemingly endless fads (phasic "newness" or "temporary deviancy") that take place in the United States clearly arise from the dopamine-deficiency status of the Western Hemisphere is beyond the scope of this book. It will be discussed in detail in the forthcoming book *The Culture Genes.*

17.8 Who Decided What Constitutes "Threat" Stimuli?

Another discussion which is beyond the scope of this book is the neurobiological basis of "moral" and "altruistic" behavior.

What activates the EB circuits, which then gets the attention of the PFC and, in the dopamine-optimized brain, frequently creates aversive physiological responses that discourage continuation of certain thoughts and behaviors related to perceived threat — disgust, anticipation of pain, fairness, guilt, empathy, mismatch (for instance, lying versus truthfulness) — is being documented on a daily basis in the scientific community. Since about 2005, there has been an explosion of research looking at the neural correlates (neural activity, dopamine responsiveness, etc.) related to social cognition, moral judgment, guilt, empathy, and positive emotionality.[722][723][724][725][726]

Clearly, there is a very close relationship between optimal dopamine levels and the connectivity and activity in the prefrontal cortex and many parts of the EB and so-called "moral" behavior. I say "so-called" moral behavior, because the definition of moral is highly arguable. Recent discussions and research regarding the neurobiology of moral behavior use the terms "implicit" and "explicit" processes. Implicit "moral" processes are defined as those which are intimately connected to EB circuit influences. Explicit "moral" processes are defined as primarily related to PFC oversight processes — cognitive control processes.[727]

EB influences on moral decisions and behavior would be variable dependent upon the "sensitivity" of a particular person's EB. In a sense, all moral decisions, including ones in which a person delays or terminates possible personal gain for the purpose of "fairness" can be analyzed against the template of "threat assessment and response." Someone attempting to cheat you may be a threat to you which may involve additional assessment against the competing data of the other threats that might be part of the same scenario (a person who would try to cheat you might be assessed as more dangerous than the threat of the actual cheating behavior).

More "traditional" theories of moral development have highlighted the role of "controlled cognition in the moral judgment process." More recent theories emphasize the role of "automatic" emotional process (various threat assessment circuitry) on moral imagination, decisions, and behavior.

Morality, for the most part, is highly threat-assessment related and, thus, those who are more threat-tolerant or slower to "feel" the aversive effects of threat-related dopamine flooding, are much more likely to have a "different" morality.

How certain sensory data became the triggering mechanisms that would lead to EB dopamine flooding in humans seems to be clearly related to threat to life and limb and, thus, have been likely naturally selected, since those species and subtypes with significantly less discriminative and responsive EB's would have been selected out by less effective threat responses and activities.

However, in the human domain, the correlates of such threats to "life and limb" in the social context are much harder to dissect out. The variability in reactivity is very dependent on EB responsiveness which is highly modified by PFC cognitive processes related to assessment of both critical and ancillary data, such as long-term consequences, trade-offs, and the good of the survival of the group.

The prefrontal cortex is very important to fairness-related decisions. The PFC oversight and influence on the EB votes (dopamine signaling) is necessary to prevent personal moral violations in moral dilemma scenarios.[728] [729] [730] [731]

The term "reappraisal" has gained popularity for describing the PFC processes involved in the manipulation of the initial EB threat data resulting in modifications to initial thoughts and behaviors and then leading to "final" threat response(s). Such reappraisal of initial EB data involves intense working memory operations, since the reappraisal process is relatively immediate and short-lived.

During reappraisal and the maintenance of such reappraisal processes, neural activity shifts from left-posterior to right-anterior lateral frontal cortical areas.[732] Similarly, distinctions have been drawn between "low-level" and "high-level" appraisal, with low-level defined as more automatic (EB controlled) and high-level defined as less automatic (PFC modification of EB signaling). High-level (a term that is value-laden) appraisal is the same as "reappraisal," and involves intense attentional and working memory resources.[733] In other words, since such operations which allow for sustained reappraisal processes are highly dependent on working memory, the unmedicated ADDer is at a decided disadvantage for such operations.

One of my favorite thought-provoking studies with respect to the EB's dopamine-dependent sensitivity variations from highly sensitive (dopamine optimal) to more insensitive (low baseline dopamine) is the 2010 *Psychopaths know right from wrong but don't care.*[734] It clearly supports my hypothesis that it isn't the knowledge of what hurts (threats, wrongs) and what does not hurt (non-threat, right) to self and others that is all that different from person to person as it is the level of "caring." Almost instantaneous, aversive dopamine-flooding in the dopamine-optimized brain not only initiates "caring" but makes it significantly unavoidable. Guilt, which is a feeling of above-optimal dopamine "sickness" may be much higher in the dopamine-optimized EB due to its low tolerance for conflicts in data, disgust, and the imagination of hurt.

18   The Truth about "Wandering," "Discovery," and "Migration"

Clearly, a dopamine-deficient brain (ADD being a prime example) is distractible for all the reasons noted earlier. It wanders.

The upside of wandering is "being off of the beaten path" (out of the box). Wandering is not creativity; it is wandering. It can make a large contribution to the creative process, but it is not the whole process. Wandering clearly leads to discoveries off the beaten path. What you do with those discoveries constitutes the main process of creativity.

So, if you have a high IQ and an ADD brain, you are not only going to be good at wandering but you will also be good at connecting heretofore unconnected dots — that does not mean you will necessarily "create" something from those realizations.

The role of fluid intelligence in the creative process, in connecting dots that have not been connected before, can contribute to significant new discoveries within the "beaten path." Creating new connections within the "beaten path" is just as creative, as long as there is follow through.

18.1   Human Migration

Migrations of humans have been occurring for tens of thousands of years. As noted by Zukerman, "early hominids emigrated over the entire world, which entailed great risk, so I think humans as a species are characterized by novelty- and intensity-seeking."

In my scientific world, Zukerman's conclusion that sensation-tolerance is present throughout the human species is called a "very broad generalization," now known to not reflect the facts. Yes, a large number of migrants were "gifted" with the ability to *not* get sick just thinking about such adventures and the risks inherent therein. But, just because there was and is a large number of such humans who can tolerate increased dopamine and norepinephrine without getting "sick" *decidedly does not mean* that *all* humans possess such abilities.

As I will discuss in detail in the chapter "The New World" in my forthcoming book *The Culture Genes* — the vast majority of those who migrated to the entire Western Hemisphere in at least two of the well-known migrations, were sensation-tolerant, ADD-brain types. In that regard, I wish to thank Thaddeus Russell for his clear and wonderful description of the huge numbers of ADD-types who inhabited U.S. pre-revolution communities in his book *A Renegade History of the United States* (2010).[735]

You don't think the "straight arrows" were hopping on boats to adventure across large oceans to relatively unknown lands, now do you? Just the thought of such exploits is enough to produce aversive feedback (above-optimal dopamine over-stimulation) in the non-ADD brain.

The majority of the people who migrated to the Western Hemisphere were people who *could* — *not the people who couldn't*, you know, the people who got "sick" just thinking about it. (Yes, of course, they brought along a large number of reluctant types — non-ADDer spouses, children, servants and slaves. More about that later.)

18.2   ADD-Related Dopamine Genes

Polymorphisms of the DAT1 and DRD4 genes are *widely accepted* as the most significant contributors to risk tolerance in ADDers.[736 737 738 739 740 741 742 743 744 745 746 747 748] Other genes that have been implicated in the manifestation of ADD characteristics include the D5 receptor gene[749 750] and the D1 receptor gene.[751] The same or very similar genes are also very influential for academic achievement, verbal skills, reading comprehension, sexual promiscuity, and reaction time performance.[752 753 754 755 756]

The DAT1 gene and its variations (alleles) produces the dopamine transporter that plays a very important role in regulating the amount of dopamine bridges available for information processing. The DAT1 gene comes in two alleles — DAT1 10 and DAT1 9. People who inherit two 10 alleles (10/10) are said to be at greater risk for developing ADHD than people who inherit 10/9 alleles. Rarely does someone inherit two 9R alleles (see "Straight Arrow Gene" in Section 15.10.2).

DAT1-created dopamine transporters are responsible for sucking bridges back into the nerve cell. We don't know the exact purpose of that mechanism — whether it is to recycle and thus economize on brain cell pressures to manufacture dopamine, or whether it is just a regulatory process with no particular special meaning.

The DAT1 10/10 gene type creates too many dopamine transporters in nerve cells producing a situation where tonic (longer-lasting) dopamine bridges between nerve cells are sucked back into the nerve cell too soon or too completely which results in fewer bridges being available for working memory operations (cache and data buffer functions).[757] [758]

Major genetic influences on dopamine synthesis, presence, and function originate in genes that are responsible for all the dopamine receptors (D1 through D5), the dopamine transporter mechanism (DAT1), and enzymes responsible for breaking down ("trashing") extracellular active-dopamine to inactive metabolic by-products.

Again, the majority of the current ADD diagnostic criteria are clearly related to deficient dopamine processes, even when studied as stand-alone characteristics (endophenotypes). Since the current criteria for the diagnosis of ADD is outdated and quite arbitrary (DSM IV, 1994), it is a result of excellent observational skills and some luck that many of those identified individual ADD characteristics have been found to be associated with certain genes in ways that were never envisioned 17 years ago.

18.3   What Did it Take to Emigrate to the Western Hemisphere?

We don't even have to speculate about the so-called "migrant brainset" too much. The question "what does it take to emigrate?" has been researched. Significantly more studies than not have arrived at the conclusion that emigration takes "risk-taking" or, in my world, *risk tolerance*. In other words, it takes something like the DAT1 *any**R/10R gene *and/or* the DRD4 7R/7R gene. [759] [760] [761] [762] [763] [764] [765]

In other words, it takes someone who can jump out of planes better than I can.

On that note, I need to say this. I am *so* tired of hearing the same-old, same-old from Dr. Hallowell. Today, October 12, 2011, Hallowell states in a New York Times Room for Debate[766] article:

Consider also the positives that so often accompany A.D.H.D.: being a dreamer and a pioneer, being creative, entrepreneurial, having an ability to think outside the box (with some difficulty thinking inside of it!), a tendency to be independent of mind and able to pursue a vision that goes against convention. Well, who colonized this country? People who have those traits!

Back in the 1600s and 1700s, you had to have special qualities — some would say special craziness — to get on one of those boats and come over to this uncharted, dangerous land. And the waves of immigration in subsequent centuries also drew people who possessed the same special qualities. In many ways, the qualities associated with A.D.H.D. are central to the American temperament, for better or worse. I often tell people that having A.D.H.D. is like having a Ferrari engine for a brain, but with bicycle brakes. If you can strengthen your brakes, you can win races and be a champion, as so many highly accomplished people with A.D.H.D. are. But if you don't strengthen your brakes you can crash and burn as, sadly, many people who have A.D.H.D. but don't know how to manage it ultimately do."

Okay. This just makes my dopamine over-amp and I start to get nauseous. *I will say this one more time, for everyone, including Dr. Hallowell.*

Romanticizing the alleged upside of the ADD brain with words like "dreamer and a pioneer, being creative, entrepreneurial, having an ability to think outside the box" and "able to pursue a vision that goes against convention" is almost unforgivably and unspeakably unscientific. Pursue? Has Hallowell *not* heard of poor follow-through?

The upside of the ADD brain is NOT a motivation, it is a capability. It is NOT risk taking. It is risk tolerance. NO

SPEED BUMP! That's not a trait. That is a physiological reality. A huge percentage of ADDers do not experience physiological speed bumps related to contemplating or doing "threatening" activities. *Curiosity is a given in all humans.* When there is practically no speed bump in the way of pursuing curiosity, guess what? You pursue it, automatically. Curiosity is all the motivation you need. Threat tolerance is all the capability you need.

As for "brakes"? It is *not* about brakes. It's about having an adequate data buffer. It is about working memory, which allows for mindfulness, retention, and slowing and organizing streaming data, among other things.

18.4 "Self-Selection" and the Humans of the Western Hemisphere

This is how the conversation would have gone between me and a self-selected new worlder anytime between the late 1600s and the mid-1800s. "You're going where? On what? Are you out of your mind? It makes me sick just to think about it. Honestly, it makes me queasy." Self-selected new worlder reply: "Sick? What do you mean sick? I feel better just thinking about it. Can't wait to get started."

Until proven otherwise, my hypothesis about the self-selected new worlder up to around 1850 (when steamships became the favored mode of transportation across the Atlantic) is *there was a huge percentage of ADDers whose dopamine-deficient risk tolerance clearly greased the wheels to such risky travel — they felt better, faster, more grounded and engaged, and calmer in the face of such threats. They were "up for it."*

Immigration up to 1790 in the United States totaled 950,000. At that time, however, the total population was around 3,900,000. That means that around 3 million US residents were born (and alive and countable in 1790) during the years of about 1607 to 1790. In New England, alone, 700,000 people were added through high birth rates. It doesn't take a rocket scientist to figure out that whoever showed up early did their best to procreate. The slave trade contributed about 360,000 newcomers who increased their population to about 750,000 by 1790.[767] [768]

Since no one was screening for ADD back then, there is no way to directly prove or disprove the high prevalence of ADD in those "self-selected" emigrant populations. However, a huge majority of available data about the characteristics of emigrants during those 200 years leads clearly to that conclusion.

In that regard, as I said before, I am so glad that Thaddeus Russell documents the huge numbers of ADD-types who inhabited our pre-revolution communities in his book *A Renegade History of the United States* (2010).[769] In the first chapter entitled *Laggards, Prostitutes, Pirates, and Other Heroes of The American Revolution,* Russell quotes from many reliable sources, clearly describing the characteristics of the majority of inhabitants of the cities of New York, Philadelphia, Boston and Charleston during the late 1700s. The following are a small percentage of the possible relevant quotations from Russell's book.

> *Indeed, there is one enemy, who is more formidable than famine, pestilence, and the sword," John Adams wrote to a friend from Philadelphia in April [1777]. "I mean the corruption which is prevalent in so many American hearts, a depravity that is more inconsistent with our republican governments than light is with darkness."*
>
> *Adams was right. Many, and probably most, inhabitants of early American cities were corrupt and depraved, and the Founding Fathers knew it. Alexander Hamilton called the behaviors of Americans "vicious" and "vile." Samuel Adams saw a "torrent of vice" running through the new country. John Jay wrote of his fear that "our conduct should*

confirm the tory maxim 'that men are incapable of governing themselves.'"

James Warren, the president of the Provincial Congress of Massachusetts and a Paymaster General of the Continental army, declared during the Revolution that Americans lived "degenerate days."

As the war with the British thundered on, John Adams grew so disgusted at what he saw on the streets that at times he believed Americans deserved death more than freedom . . .

Nonmarital sex, including adultery and relations between whites and blacks, was rampant and unpunished. Divorces were frequent and easily obtained. Prostitutes plied their trade free of legal or moral proscriptions. Black slaves, Irish indentured servants, Native Americans, and free whites of all classes danced together in the streets. Pirates who frequented the port cities brought with them a way of life that embraced wild dances, nightlong parties, racial integration, and homosexuality. European visitors frequently commented on the "astonishing libertinism" of early American cities. Renegades held the upper hand in Philadelphia, Boston, New York, and Charleston, and made them into the first centers of the American pleasure culture . . .

To get the whole picture that Russell documents, please review his book. Russell's hypothesis, to which I ascribe, is essentially:

To solve the lack of order they saw all around them, the fathers seized on one of the great — and often missed — ironies in world history: the only thing that could make men forsake their own freedom and still believe they were free was self-rule.

A government of the people, John Adams argued, would make the people disciplined, stern, hard working, and joyless—the qualities he most admired. It would "produce Strength, Hardiness Activity, Courage, Fortitude, and Enterprise; the manly noble and Sublime Qualities in human Nature, in Abundance."

A monarchy, on the other hand, would let them have too much fun and, paradoxically, allow them too much liberty.

In my forthcoming book, *The Culture Genes*, I will discuss Russell's hypothesis in much more detail.

There were a lot of people who were not "self-selected" who "traveled" to the new world during those almost 200 years. I will write more about them soon.

It is beyond the scope of this book to write extensively about my hypothesis that there was at least one, long, huge dopamine-deficiency emigration (the "Great Migration"), to the Western Hemisphere starting in the 1400s, and at least one earlier, not-so-huge emigration, but dopamine-deficient, nonetheless (the "First Migration"). However, it would be inconsiderate of me to not highlight the major variables related to my claim that the average brain in the Western Hemisphere *is* the dopamine-deficient brain, of which the ADD brain is a prime, currently well-documented, example.

There are three major variables to keep in mind about the Great Migration: (1) the immigration from what is generally the Eastern Hemisphere to the Western Hemisphere was the *only* huge human migration in human history that occurred across thousands of miles of ocean; (2) the 1600 A.D to 1790 A.D. self-selected migrant procreators traveled on slow-moving, relatively small, "rickety," generally square-rigged, triple-masted, wooden, sailing ships that were usually less than 100 feet long and around 200-400 tons, which took anywhere from six weeks to 26 weeks to reach Western Hemisphere lands; and, (3) those who were not self-selected, but forced to bear the torture of such travel, included wives, children, servants and slaves.

Although, the First Migration was much smaller and much earlier (15,000 to 13,000 B.C.), the progeny of that migration had thousands of years to procreate and produce the "native" populations of the Western Hemisphere. Estimates of pre-Columbian Western Hemisphere native populations have, unfortunately, ranged from 1.2 million to over 100 million.[770] In a sense, for this discussion, it does not matter how many pre-Columbian people there were in the Americas. What matters more is what were the characteristics of their dopamine functions?

The native American dopamine gene characteristics have been documented several times as noted in the first-paragraph endnotes in Section 18.3 — *What Did it Take to Emigrate to the Western Hemisphere?* I will briefly summarize the findings. Two different dopamine genes that control D4 receptor functions and dopamine transporter function have been researched in descendants of pre-Columbian native populations. Scientists in Chile and Brazil,[771] in particular, have done a significant amount of research related to ADD and DRD4 gene-types in their populations.

One study is not only particularly clear about the high prevalence of the "risk-tolerance" DRD4 7R/7R in the Western Hemisphere, but also about the "*linear increase* of long alleles of DRD4 *with distance* of migration across several different migration routes certainly points to the possibility of natural selection" (emphasis mine).[772] This 1999 study has been supported by further analysis in 2011.[773]

Five other studies are important to note. Three of them address the question "Did the DRD4 7R/7R risk-tolerance polymorphism arise before or after major human migrations?"[774 775 776] Two studies address the question "What is the global distribution of the DRD4 7R/7R allele?"[777 778]

The DRD4 7R/7R polymorphism *arose long before* the major human migrations took place, somewhere around 50,000 to 40,000 B.C. The worldwide distribution of the DRD4 alleles (DRD4 7R/7R, 4R/4R, 2R/2R, etc.) is significantly documented by the above two studies. DRD4 4R/4R is most prevalent in all continents. Second is the DRD4 7R/7R (risk-tolerance gene), but it is *uncommon* in Asia. South America is notable for the DRD4 7R/7R gene being the *most prevalent*. In the studies endnoted as 736 and 737, *Population Migration and the Variation of Dopamine D4 Receptor (DRD4) Allele Frequencies Around the Globe* and *Novelty-seeking DRD4 polymorphisms are associated with human migration distance out-of-Africa after controlling for neutral population gene structure*, the largest prevalence of the DRD4 7R/7R polymorphism is found in the far south of South America and it gradually decreases in frequency as you move north up the Western Hemisphere western coastline until it all but disappears completely in Asia.

There are also clear global variations in the dopamine transporter gene (DAT1 or SLC6A3 gene), with some populations showing a very high prevalence of the "protective" DAT1 9R/9R such as Italians, Druze and Yeminite Jews, and some showing very low frequencies such as Chinese. There were wide prevalence variations in DAT1 polymorphisms among European populations.[779]

However, the DAT1 gene and its resultant effects on the dopamine transporter mechanism have not been shown to be significant contributors to "risk-tolerance." DAT1 genes affect working memory operations and striatal dopamine function. In addition, since dopamine transporter operations are important for all dopamine receptor and bridge dynamics, one would expect it to have a wide influence on both PFC and EB functions, compared to the D4 receptor, which is likely specialized in certain parts of the EB.

fMRI imaging of the D4 receptor has not yet been perfected enough [780 781] to accurately identify many of its distributions in the EB or PFC, but the D4 gene variations (alleles), have been shown to have clear influences on certain mental operations and areas of brain functioning by fMRI and SPECT scans, including the cingulate cortex, cerebellum, insula, and ventral striatum.[782] [783] [784]

18.5 "Natural Selection" and the Humans of the Western Hemisphere

A precise definition of "natural selection" is "a nonrandom process by which biologic traits become more or less common in a population as a function of differential reproduction of their bearers. What matters is the total lifetime reproduction of the variant."

However, there is more to the natural selection process than reproductive rates. You have to exist to reproduce, and, thus, characteristics of a particular variant that encourage greater numbers of survivors (faster, smarter, stronger, harder to kill, etc.) will make for a larger population of that variant, as long as it reproduces well. The environment in which the variant thrives will likely become its "home."

In population genetics, "directional selection" is a mode of natural selection in which a single phenotype is favored, causing the allele frequency to shift in a particular direction. Under directional selection, the advantageous allele increases in frequency independently of its dominance relative to other alleles; that is, even if the advantageous allele is recessive, it will eventually become fixed. Directional selection occurs most often under environmental changes and when populations migrate through or to new areas with different environmental pressures.

Until proven otherwise, my hypothesis about new worlders up to around 1870, when larger, faster, and more stable steamships became the favored mode of transportation across the Atlantic, is: *There was a huge percentage of ADDers whose dopamine deficiencies clearly facilitated their survival during the tortured travel circumstances of those trips across 3,400 or more miles of ocean which both selected low-dopaminers and deselected optimal-dopaminers through the mechanisms of seasickness, vomiting, dehydration, and subsequent vulnerability to illness and death.*

18.6 Resistance to Seasickness — Motion/Mismatch Tolerance

You may not know this, but the most effective treatments for seasickness in the last 50 years have always been medications that decrease CNS dopamine — cyclizine (Merazine), prochlorperazine (Compazine), and promethazine (Phenergan).[785] More recently, anticholinergics and antihistaminics have been utilized for mitigating the symptoms of motion sickness. However, their actions are not considered to be centrally-acting (CNS) but more peripheral by inhibiting vestibular input to the EB.

I hope you find that interesting.

Other than ginger,[786] there were no effective medications for mitigating seasickness until about 1940, when research clearly ramped up due to military planning and the grave concerns about motion sickness related to operations on sea and in the air.[787]

There are many other medications that can be helpful for minimizing the symptoms of seasickness and motion sickness, however, they work on other variables in the motion-sickness process than the suppression of extracellular dopamine in parts of the EB.[788]

There are several variables involved in producing seasickness and the resultant nausea and vomiting: (1) hypersensitive or mis-calibrated vestibular system (semicircular canals, otoliths); (2) over-stimulation of cingulate cortex and other EB parts due to mismatch processing of conflicting sensory signals from vestibular system, eyes, and proprioceptors; and (3) CNS adrenergic receptor mutations (chromosome 10 α2-AR 6.3-kb allele).[789] [790] [791]

All the ADD medications that have significant effects on dopamine and norepinephrine levels can cause nausea and vomiting when they are the wrong medication for you or you are taking too much of the right medication. They "over-stimulate" EB circuits involved in processing disgust, sensory conflict, noxious stimuli, and nausea and vomiting centers.

Again, if you fit the criteria for ADD, and you are going to do some skydiving or similar "threat-triggering" activity, do it unmedicated, unless, well, you want some nausea and vomiting. I have adjusted more than a few medications for high-level ADDer athletes (baseball, basketball, track, etc.) due to how sick they got during performances while utilizing long-acting ADD medications. One high-level athlete I evaluated had been prescribed long-acting methylphenidate and was wondering why he vomited on the pitcher's mound during games.

I hope you find it significant that too much CNS dopamine and/or norepinephrine can cause nausea and vomiting. The reason I hope you find it significant is that I am hoping it brings to your mind my earlier discussion of the higher "threat tolerance" of the ADD EB due to low baseline dopamine. The same dopamine tolerance exists in the ADD EB for the threshold stimulation needed for the nausea and vomiting related to above-optimal-dopamine triggered seasickness symptoms.

My hypothesis, until proven otherwise, is the ADD brain (and body) is seasick resistant (motion and mismatch tolerant).

It seems so obvious to me that I had a difficult time justifying the citation of all the forthcoming facts to make this hypothesis as bullet-proof as possible. All you have to do is survey ADDers and you will find out (1) they have gotten jobs on fishing boats in Alaska by beating out other applicants who got seasick too easily; (2) 80% never get seasick; (3) they love to ride extreme roller-coasters and other upside-down, circling, or twisting carnival thrill rides, like the Zipper.[792]

However, you will *not* find any studies noting this ADD phenomenon. I have no explanation for why this hypothesis has *not* been investigated in the past.

Here are the supportive data points, which, for the most part have been substantiated through significant replication.

(1) *Dopamine suppressors prochlorperazine and metoclopramide are antiemetic drugs.* Prochlorperazine inhibits apomorphine induced vomiting by blocking dopamine D2 receptors in the chemoreceptor trigger zone (CTZ) (area of medulla oblongata that measures blood-borne toxins).

Metoclopramide directly affects the CTZ in the area postrema by blocking DRD2, increasing CTZ threshold and decreasing sensitivity of visceral nerves that transmit triggering impulses from the gastrointestinal tract to "vomiting" processors in the lateral reticular formation.[793]

(2) *Risk of post-operative nausea and vomiting is reduced in the cigarette smoker* by mechanisms that have not been completely identified, but are more-likely-than-not related to either the smoker's pre-smoking low baseline dopamine (which exists again when smoking is withdrawn) or a non-ADD smoker's large tolerance for increased dopamine that they developed by enduring their "sickness" associated with smoking long-enough to develop a significant tolerance (addiction).[794]

As noted in Section 9.1, cigarette smoking clearly increases CNS dopamine.

Motion sickness tolerance was aided by short-term smoking deprivation in mild to heavy smokers. In other words, their tobacco-induced dopamine levels were gone, and they did not experience above-optimal-dopamine induced motion sickness due to the zone of dopamine tolerance as noted in the graphic on page 107.

Motion sickness vulnerability was dramatically increased by nicotine in non-smokers (generally non-ADDers) and even in smokers who were *not* deprived.

In other words optimal dopamine levels in the presence of motion-induced mismatch increased dopamine to *above-optimal* and created "stimulation" side effects —nausea, vomiting, cognitive impairment, longer reaction times.

(3) *Motion sickness tolerance is clearly highly heritable.*[795]

(4) *Ethnic differences in motion sickness tolerance are dramatic and well-established.* Asian and Chinese subjects are very vulnerable to motion sickness as compared to Caucasians and Africans.[796] [797]

As noted in several places in this book, the distribution of the higher risk DRD4 7R/7R allele in Chinese populations is all but entirely absent (they are relatively dopamine optimized). In addition, such populations are also cortisol optimized.

Clearly such dopamine optimized individuals are more vulnerable to dopamine over-stimulation related to the processing of mismatch signaling related to the etiology of motion sickness, resulting in increased nausea and vomiting.

Need I say more? Well, yes. Okay. So, the crucial question is "Can you die from seasickness?"

Yes, you can.

On one hand, I feel like I have spent way too many hours reading and researching first-person accounts of traveling on ships across the Atlantic Ocean during the period 1600 to 1850. On the other hand, I had no choice. I needed to know just what it was like and what the challenges and hazards were like. I can say this without any reservations: "It was brutal."

Almost without exception, every detailed personal account of such "self-selected" or "forced" travel across the Atlantic revealed high percentages of morbidity and mortality. Seasickness was high on the list of causes. The detailed accounts of two particularly popular writers are readily available at Google Books:

(1)   Gottlieb Mittelberger: Organ master and schoolmaster who left a small German state in May 1750 to make his way to America. He returned to his homeland in 1754. Among many other things, he had this to say about "self-selected" new worlders:[798]

But during the voyage there is on board these ships terrible misery, stench, fumes, horror, vomiting, many kinds of sea-sickness, fever, dysentery, headache, heat, constipation, boils, scurvy, cancer, mouth-rot, and the like...

No one can have an idea of the sufferings which women in confinement have to bear with their innocent children on board these ships. Few of this class escape with their lives; many a mother is cast into the water with her child as soon as she is dead. One day, just as we had a heavy gale, a woman in our ship, who was to give birth and could not give birth under the circumstances, was pushed through a loop-hole [port-hole] in the ship and dropped into the sea, because she was far in the rear of the ship and could not be brought forward.

Children from 1 to 7 years rarely survive the voyage. I witnessed misery in no less than 32 children in our ship, all of whom were thrown into the sea. The parents grieve all the more since their children find no resting-place in the earth, but are devoured by the monsters of the sea.

(2) Alexander Falconbridge: British surgeon employed on four voyages of slave ships between 1780 and 1787. Among many other things, he had this to say about the "coerced new worlders" (slaves).[799]

The hardships and inconveniences suffered by the Negroes during the passage are scarcely to be enumerated or conceived. They are far more violently affected by seasickness than Europeans. It frequently terminates in death, especially among the women.

But the exclusion of fresh air is among the most intolerable . . . whenever the sea is rough and the rain heavy it becomes necessary to shut these and every other conveyance by which the air is admitted. The fresh air being thus excluded, the Negroes' rooms soon grow intolerable hot. The confined air, rendered noxious by the effluvia exhaled from their bodies and being repeatedly breathed, soon produces fevers and fluxes which generally carries off great numbers of them.

Chapter 13 in the book *The Atlantic Slave Trade: Effects on Economies, Societies, and Peoples in Africa, the Americas, and Europe*[800], is very informative and well-sourced on the huge slave mortality rates resulting from dehydration due to seasickness (vomiting), profuse sweating, and diarrhea. In my opinion, although the authors, Thomas W. Wilson and Clarence Grim, were off the mark about their hypothesis that the natural-selection process of the Atlantic slave trade selected out slaves who would be "salt-loss" resistant and, thus, create African American descendants with a much higher prevalence of high blood pressure, they were clearly on to something. What they were on to, they have not followed-up on. I am not sure why, and I don't have time to ask them directly. Maybe they will explain some day. Many scientific discoveries have taken place since Wilson's and Grim's 1991 Hypertensive African-American Hypothesis.[801]

Are you ready for this? Hypertension is less prevalent in ADD populations than it is in non-ADD populations.[802] Hypertension in the United States and Canada is much less prevalent than in many parts of Europe — 60% higher in six European countries (Germany, Finland, Italy, England, Sweden and Spain).[803] This certainly does *not* support Wilson and Grim's Hypothesis.

In fact, the difference between "Western" and "Eastern" Hemisphere blood pressures is twice as high as the difference between European-ancestry Americans and African-Americans. In other words, even African-American descendants of slave emigrants have less hypertension going on as the Europeans who stayed in Europe.

This 2003 study reporting the Western/Eastern differences, however, comes to the conclusion that "genetics is *not* a plausible explanation of the finding reported herein." (emphasis mine) This is somewhat understandable, given the limited information available in the 1990s about the genetics of hypertension and the extensive role of dopamine in the regulation of sodium, water retention, and vascular tone, among other things. However, it is quite incorrect. We know a lot more, now.

So, why do I even bring this up, these statistics about lower blood pressure in ADDers, and blood pressure differences between Western and Eastern Caucasian populations? Mostly, because the hypothesis that I propose about the powerful self-selection and natural-selection processes that significantly influenced the dopamine characteristics of emigrants who made it to the Western Hemisphere during the Great Migration does not have the same "weaknesses" that Wilson and Grim's 1991 Hypertensive African-American Hypothesis had.[804]

With one exception, worldwide ADD statistics and hypertension statistics are inversely related — the lower the

ADD prevalence in a geographic area, the higher the hypertension prevalence. The one exception is Central and South America with 11.8% ADD prevalence but with areas of hypertension (Mexico, Peru, Venezuela) of around 36%. Asia and Middle East ADD prevalence is very small, but hypertension prevalence is much higher than in the United States.[805] [806] [807]

With respect, however, to Wilson and Grim's discussion of the dynamics of dehydration and the related death rates of self-selected (less) and naturally-selected (more) dopamine-deficient emigrants, they are spot on.

It is beyond the scope of this book to discuss even a few of the large number of variables involved in the control of blood pressure, sodium retention, and vascular tone. However, a majority of those variables are clearly influenced by the same genetic and structural mechanisms that influence ADD prefrontal and EB functional variations — dopamine and norepinephrine receptors, synthesis, and function in the CNS and in kidneys and arteries,[808] [809] [810] and dopamine/norepinephrine-dependent processes in the hypothalamus, pituitary[811] and adrenal glands.

18.7 Prevalence of Dopamine Deficiencies in the Western Hemisphere

As noted in the early sections of this book, many other "disorders" are diagnosed instead of ADD and such misdiagnosed ADDers are treated incorrectly for their alleged "standalone" anxiety, clinical depression, insomnia, panic attacks, anger, moodiness (bipolar and other), narcissism, borderline personality disorder, various addictions, impulsiveness, eating disorders, passive-aggressiveness, dissociation, compulsions, pain and chronic fatigue syndromes, fibromyalgia, asthma, atopy, auto-immune diseases, social phobia, self-injury, gambling disorders, over-attachments, and problematic impulsive, intrusive, obsessive and "sociopathic" behaviors, among others.

As noted, one study (only one so far) showed that about 33% of people referred to an anxiety disorder clinic for anxiety (not for ADD), when screened for ADD, were found to clearly fit the criteria for ADD. That would be, again, 33% of those with apparent standalone anxiety disorders fit the criteria for ADD.

Honestly, that is just the tip of the iceberg of misdiagnosed "standalone" anxiety disorders which are actually part of the undiagnosed ADDer's clinical presentation. With respect to all the other diagnoses I have just listed in the above paragraph, no significant effort has taken place to validly establish the percentages of incorrect standalone diagnoses made on the basis of the various serious ADD symptoms and behavior.

Co-morbid studies have established many ADD "co-morbidities," but such co-existing disorders have not been studied further with respect to whether they exist *because* of untreated ADD or they exist *in spite of* treated ADD.

The same can be said for all of the dopamine/norepinephrine-fixing behaviors of frequent over-users of tobacco, alcohol, marijuana, cocaine, street methamphetamine, heroin, street opioids, diverted pharmaceutical amphetamines and methylphenidate and food — no significant effort has taken place to screen for ADD among such populations, even though it is clear that the primary mission of such behaviors is to fix dopamine and norepinephrine dysfunction (feel calmer, better cognition, less moody).

If you screened those who experience chronic sleep-onset insomnia, a majority of them would fit the criteria for ADD. The percentage of prison inmates who fit the criteria for ADD is about 60%.

To repeat: ADD co-morbidity is only *true* co-morbidity if the co-morbidity continues to exist after proper treatment of ADD. Although there is a large overlap of populations, it is possible to do the approximate math for the United States.

"Diagnosis"	% of US	% Coexisting ADD
ADD	5 to 10	5 to 10
Alcohol overuse	9.7	18 to 22
Anxiety disorders	11.9	15-33
Asthma	14	24 to 30
Bipolar I and II	7	5.4 to 27
Cocaine overuse	1 to 3	20 to 21
Dysthymia	1	12 to 22.6
Eating disorders	3	7 to 21
Gambling disorders	.42	10 to 15
High school dropouts	25 to 30	25 to 40
Hoarding disorder	5.8	80
Insomnia	28 to 40	70 to 80
Learning/reading disorder	5	46
Major depression	6.7 to 13.3	10 to 17.6
Marijuana overuse	2 to 7	14 to 20
Methamphetamine (street)	2 to 3	?
Obesity	28 to 60	26 to 61
"Obsessive" disorders	2	8-51
Panic attacks and disorders	11	12 to 20
Personality disorders	10	25 to 35
Prison inmates/parolees	3	50 to 60
Seasonal affective disorder	1 to 10	≈ 20
Drug use disorders	8 to 10	28 to 44
Tobacco overuse	13.5 to 30	23 to 46

The sources for all the statistics in the above table are far too many to list completely, but here are a few.[812 813 814 815 816 817 818 819 820 821 822 823 824 825 826 827 828 829 830 831 832 833 834 835 836 837 838 839 840 841 842]

One study analyzed age of onset of ADD and the subsequent or previous co-morbidities and found that 68% to 99% of any such co-morbidities (mood, anxiety, phobia and substance abuse) emerged much later in the untreated ADD person's life.[843] Other studies have followed girls and boys for 10 to 11 years (starting ages at 6-18 years old) and found high risk ratios for the development of several disorders, including anxiety, antisocial personality, developmental, and mood disorders.[844 845]

One of my favorite reports is a 2011 study entitled *Prevalence of the addictions: a problem of the majority or the minority?* They completed a systematic literature review of 11 addictions — cigarette (nicotine) dependence, alcohol abuse/dependence, illicit/other drug abuse/dependence, food disorders/addiction (with a focus on binge-eating disorder but not excluding examination of anorexia nervosa and bulimia if examined concurrently with binge-eating disorder), gambling addiction (i.e., pathological gambling), Internet addiction, love addiction, sex addiction, exercise addiction, workaholism, and shopping (spending) addiction. Those addictions were selected due to the existence of extensive published relevant research.

Not unlike what I am proposing in this book that the majority of brains in the Western Hemisphere are dopamine-deficient, the authors of the study state

> "Depending on which assumptions are made, overall 12-month prevalence of an addiction among U.S. adults varies from 15% to 61%. The authors assert that it is most plausible that 47% of the U.S. adult population suffers from maladaptive signs of an addictive disorder over a 12-month period and that it may be useful to think of addictions as due to problems of lifestyle as well as to person-level factors."[846]

As you already know, and as the authors of this 2011 study note, dopaminergic CNS systems are clearly involved in such addictions.

If you add up all the people who would fit the criteria for ADD in the populations noted in the above-table, the conclusion would clearly be that the majority brain, the so-called "average" or "normal" brain of the Western Hemisphere, *is* the ADD brain.

You don't think American culture fits the criteria for the diagnosis of ADD by chance, do you? People create culture. It doesn't just fall out of the sky. If you think it is just an American dilemma, you would be wrong. We got lucky. Our "founding fathers" knew what we needed.[847] You can't say the same for Central and South American populations.

What we do about the high prevalence of dopamine-deficiencies in the Western Hemisphere is up for grabs. Hopefully, it will not require medicating huge numbers of dopamine-deficient adults. Hopefully, it will involve understanding and accepting the significance of the widespread dopamine-deficiencies found in the Western Hemisphere and utilizing structural and mindful strategies for dealing with the downside and the upside of those deficiencies.

18.8   America's "Amphetamine Epidemics"

That's what Nicolas Rasmussen calls the periods of time between about 1929 and 1970 and between about 1995 and the present — "America's Amphetamine Epidemics":

> *By the late 1970s, America's speed epidemic seemed almost a concern of the past. This one-time miracle drug still refused to retire gracefully, however. Speed remains with us today, despite relentless narcotics enforcement. Indeed, we are now suffering another epidemic of amphetamine abuse and addiction, driven by a recent surge in the popularity of crystalline methamphetamine or "ice," as well as the amphetamine derivatives known as "ecstasy."*

> *And, once again, amphetamine and its close relatives have become enormously popular pharmaceuticals, this time for Attention Deficit Disorder.* [848]

In addition to Rasmussen's 2008 book, in 2008 the American Journal of Public Health published his article *America's First Amphetamine Epidemic 1929-1971: A quantitative and qualitative retrospective with implications for the present.* [849]

The abstract from that article reads:

Using historical research that draws on new primary sources, I review the causes and course of the first, mainly iatrogenic amphetamine epidemic in the United States from the 1940s through the 1960s. Retrospective epidemiology indicates that the absolute prevalence of both nonmedical stimulant use and stimulant dependence or abuse have reached nearly the same levels today as at the epidemic's peak around 1969. Further parallels between epidemics past and present, including evidence that consumption of prescribed amphetamines has also reached the same absolute levels today as at the original epidemic's peak, suggest that stricter limits on pharmaceutical stimulants must be considered in any efforts to reduce amphetamine abuse today.

I almost don't know where to begin in my discussion of Rasmussen's (and a few others) rather "dramatic" writings, which use a lot of value-laden language and creative quoting of statistics about frequency of use, "addiction," and availability of both non-medical and medical "speed" formulations in ways that are clearly meant to impress us with how out-of-control are the uses of illicit, diverted, *and* prescribed amphetamine-like chemicals. Neither Rasmussen's 2008 book or article take any serious look at what might be the causes of the high prevalence of the use of dopamine/norepinephrine enhancers in the United States. Instead, he attributes such high illicit and medical use to "the medicalization of social problems."

Rasmussen follows that accusation with this statement:

Soon millions seeking help for failing to meet society's standards around good cheer, ambition, accomplishment, and physique received absolution with a diagnosis and, with the wave of a prescription pen, an amphetamine benediction. What might have been a moral issue of substandard conduct, or instead might have brought standards of conduct into question, became commonplace mental health problems, managed medically with amphetamines. (2008 Book)

Rasmussen then goes on to promote his explanation of the current "epidemic" with

Then, in the 1990s, the idea was abandoned that Attention Deficit was something that could only affect children. The broader the definition, the more people it has applied to, even if the prevalence and experience of the symptoms have remained unchanged over time. (2008 Book)

He then offers these thoughts before moving on to propose his theories about the roots of the current "epidemic."

Perhaps video games or junk food or modern advertising methods are causing neural damage. It is also possible that a large fraction of the population have always had this same condition, only doctors now understand and recognize it much better. There are, however, a number of factors to consider that make both these answers too simple, if not altogether wrong. (2008 Book)

Rasmussen proposes that the main causes of such high usage of both legal and illegal "stimulants" is (1) today patients more aggressively demand a medical diagnosis for a given level of discomfort; (2) today a given level of mental distraction is more likely than before to count as a medical problem; (3) the definition of the condition we now call Attention Deficit/Hyperactivity Disorder has expanded; (4) it relieves them [parents] of blame for their child's behavior and may give access to special school programs; (5) "The diagnosis can also confer benefits for adults, especially in contexts where disability is compensated by competitive advantages, such as special consideration for a student at a university or extra protection from dismissal for the working adult. One commentator has even gone so far as to call Attention Deficit Disorder 'affirmative action for white people,' referring to the middle-class, predominantly white majority who receive the diagnosis. This third explanation fits with much lower diagnosis and medication rates outside the United States"; (6) the presence of highly active support and lobby groups for Attention Deficit sufferers that spread the word about how common and terrible the condition is, push for special benefits for sufferers, and try to make the drugs more widely available; (7) incentives from within the medical system for doctors to make the Attention Deficit diagnosis for complaints of distraction, bad behavior, and poor performance; (8) high levels of diversion due to the "over-prescribing" of restricted medications; and (9) American needs for "success" and the competitive edge.

I apologize for quoting so extensively from Rasmussen's 2008 Book, but his superficial analysis of the "epidemic" use of amphetamine-like chemicals leaves me no choice.

More from Rasmussen's 2008 Book:

Sociologically rather than pharmacologically speaking, what is the demand for speed today? Or to put the question another way, how many Americans now use drugs for the same reasons that they once took amphetamine, when it was an ordinary pharmaceutical? To answer this question, we must count not just those who today are taking amphetamine-like drugs recreationally, for weight loss, and for Attention Deficit. We must also count the drugs that took amphetamine's place in its original, major market: minor depression and emotional distress in general practice. [the SSRIs]

Kramer [Rasmussen quoting *Listening to Prozac*] *goes on perceptively to equate the use of Prozac, particularly by people with mild or no depression, to the use of amphetamines on the street: in both cases, the drugs are taken "for overcoming inhibitions and inspiring zest," for boosting confidence, and for accelerating thought and speech. The main difference is that Prozac is taken by the well-to-do with prescriptions, whereas amphetamines are now taken mainly by poorer people, outside the law, or else by prescription for Attention Deficit.*

When Americans cannot live up to society's values and norms, they may seek help in medicine. Medicine, aided and urged by the pharmaceutical industry, welcomes the opportunity to manage such mismatches between individuals and social norms as treatable medical problems.

In case Rasmussen wants to know the truth about why there have been and will continue to be "speed epidemics" in the whole Western Hemisphere (he ignores Canada, and Central and South America) and why the rates of ADD in the Western Hemisphere are so high, he should read this book.

In addition, Kramer got it wrong when it comes to the "casual use of Prozac,"[850] but I don't have time to go there right now. Maybe someday. And, maybe someday, I will discuss the book *Running on Ritalin* by Lawrence Diller, M.D.[851]

Clearly, people, not just in the United States, but worldwide, will try to fix whatever they feel needs to be fixed, whether it is sanctioned by law, or science, or the medical establishment. It is the thing that uniquely characterizes humans — the search for solutions. If you connect the dots, it is very clear what plagues the Western Hemisphere — the downside of very prevalent dopamine-deficiencies.

On the upside, Rasmussen at least hits the nail on the head as to possible solutions when he says:

> *Judging by today's expanded drug consumption for the conditions that drove amphetamine use in the 1960s, we are now considerably sicker with the ailments that amphetamines remedy—twice as sick, if we combine medical and nonmedical speed use as equivalent "technologies of the self." But if amphetamines and their substitutes are medicines for a social disease, it might now be time to question whether the ailment may lie not chiefly in the physiology of the one out of every eight Americans now taking drugs with amphetamine-like effects. Perhaps we should consider that the problem lies instead in a sick social system fundamentally at odds with natural human capacities and fulfillments.*
> (2008 Book)

I could not agree more with the idea that in the United States "a sick social system" exploits and cannibalizes its own for the purposes of making profits, but the existence of the high prevalence of ADD-like dopamine deficiencies in the entire Western Hemisphere, is *not* a problem that is created by our culture.

If you wish to reduce the amount of dopamine/norepinephrine enhancers of all kinds that are currently ravaging our Western societies, including nicotine, over-eating, over-spending, impulse control problems, gambling, criminality, alcohol, marijuana, cocaine, illicit methamphetamine, and the diversion of pharmaceuticals, you are going to have to make radical changes in the cultural, capitalist and corporate priorities and processes that clearly exploit those with non-optimal CNS dopamine and norepinephrine (the majority of Western Hemisphere populations). I will be writing much more about that radical change in my forthcoming book *The Culture Genes.*

19   Free Will, Destiny, and "Taking Credit"

Here's a couple of crucial questions.

If a "straight-arrow" *cannot* do something that other people with a different brain *can* do, does that mean they are a more "responsible," "disciplined," or a "better" more "moral" person?

If such things as gambling, binge eating, binge spending, doing drugs, being promiscuous, smoking cigarettes, speeding, shooting a gun, bullying, fighting, and enjoying conflict are *not* your thing, is it because the most important variable to *not* doing such things is a decision you made? Well, only partially.

Clearly, in my opinion, if you recognize the dots and you are willing to connect them, the most influential variable found in the non-ADD brain for staying out of "trouble" is the *aversive effect* of above-optimal dopamine and norepinephrine levels that just thinking about such behaviors produces (the non-ADD brain speed bump).

Most, if not all, people *with dopamine-optimized* brains *cannot* think about or participate in "risky" behaviors without feeling "sick" (at least in the beginning). However, people *with dopamine-deficient* brains *can.*

"Look mom, no speed bump!"

The significance of that, I hope, is not lost on you.

19.1   Individual Differences in Executive Functioning are Almost Entirely Genetic in Origin

A very credible twin study published in 2008 [852](the "Friedman 2008 Study") came to the following conclusion:

"The present multivariate twin study of three executive functions (inhibiting dominant responses, updating working memory representations, and shifting between task sets), measured as latent variables, examined why people vary in these executive control abilities and why these abilities are correlated but separable from a behavioral genetic perspective.

Results indicated that executive functions are correlated because they are influenced by a highly heritable (99%) common factor that goes beyond general intelligence or perceptual speed, and they are separable because of additional genetic influences unique to particular executive functions. This combination of general and specific genetic influences places *executive functions among the most heritable psychological traits. . . possibly even more heritable than IQ.*" (emphasis mine)

19.2   The Plasticity Quotient and "Culture"

From the results of the Friedman 2008 Study, it is tempting to conclude that executive functions are possibly all "nature" and no "nurture." However, high heritability does not necessarily mean "unalterable by environment or training." There are a number of studies that show it is possible to improve performance in certain areas of executive functioning by training, mostly with respect to working memory.

Michael Posner and Mary Rothbart (University of Oregon) published a 2009 study entitled *Toward A Physical Basis of Attention and Self Regulation* (the "2009 Posner Self-Regulation Study").[853] I consider it one of the most important studies that clearly demonstrated the high vulnerability to environmental influences (plasticity [854]or ability to be "molded") of four-to-seven year-old children with high risk ADD genes. It showed that such plasticity cuts both ways.

When I use the word "plasticity" for the children with the high-risk ADD genes in the 2009 Posner Self-Regulation

Study, I am referring to how vulnerable they were shown to be with respect to their family culture (parenting style). Children with the high-risk ADD gene DRD4 7R/7R were significantly more susceptible to the influences of their family culture than children *without* the DRD4 7R/7R.

19.3 Learning Self-Regulation is Possible Even With a High-Risk Set of Plasticity Genes

If the child's family culture taught "self-regulation" and "effortful control" (families defined in the study as "high quality"), the DRD4 7R/7R children could learn it. In other words, they may not be doomed, so to speak, to a life characterized by poor self-regulation and risky behavior. However, if the DRD4 7R/7R children were part of a more "laid-back" family culture, they were molded by that environment to be less capable of self-regulation. The family cultures were rated on characteristics developed by the National Institute of Child Health and Human Development: support, autonomy, stimulation, lack of hostility and confidence in the child.

What about the non-DRD4 7R/7R children in the study? Essentially, their behaviors were *significantly independent* of family culture and family culture had less impact on their scores on impulsivity and risk taking. In other words, their "self-regulation" was a given, no unlike winning the dopamine-optimized, self-regulation lottery. In other words, their environment had less ability to "program" them.

The study showed that during middle childhood, along with increased projection cells involved in remote connections of dorsal anterior cingulate and prefrontal and parietal cortex, executive network connectivity increases and shifts from predominantly short to longer range connections. During *that* period of childhood, specific experiences (even, possibly, exercises) can influence network development and improve self-regulation. The next big question is "Will they follow those kids into adulthood to see if that 'positive plasticity' sticks?"

The high-risk ADD DRD4 7R/7R genotype high plasticity quotient (suggestibility, compliance, vulnerability, easy mark, etc.) has been substantially established by several other studies:

(1) "Maternal insensitivity was associated with externalizing (oppositional, aggressive) behaviors, but only in the presence of the DRD4 7-repeat polymorphism" [855];

(2) "We found support for the differential susceptibility hypothesis predicting not only more negative outcomes for susceptible children [those with DRD4 7R/7R] in unfavorable environments, but also positive outcomes for susceptible children in favorable environments" [856];

(3) Our findings indicate that children are differentially susceptible to intervention effects dependent on the presence of the 7-repeat DRD4 allele" [857];

(4) Increased vulnerability for ADHD only in the presence of inconsistent parenting and increased susceptibility to self-blame for parental conflict [858]; and,

(5) The DRD4 7R/7R genotype in adults increases the risk for heavy alcohol use or abuse in the company of heavy-drinking peers. [859]

Have I mentioned the word "sheep"? [860]

Thus, study (5) above, about vulnerability to "peer pressure" shows that such susceptibility to "molding" does not disappear after childhood. More studies are clearly needed, but the anecdotal data is huge. Ask any ADDer about how easily they are victimized, influenced, lead astray, or otherwise thrown off course. [861 862 863]

The high distractibility quotient of the ADD brain (and other dopamine-deficiency conditions) clearly creates difficulties with staying on track, sticking to a plan, and/or following-through.

Similar to a sailboat with a weak steering mechanism, ADDers can get blown in one direction or another at the whim of the wind.

19.4 A Few Words About Advertising, Marketing, and Peer Pressure in America

Given the proven high influence-ability quotient of those with the high-risk ADD DRD4 7R/7R genotype, you would think there would be concern about how that vulnerability could be taken advantage of by various forms of persuasion (advertising, marketing, propaganda, brainwashing, peer pressure, etc.). However, I have not been able to find a single study that examines the relationship between such dopamine-deficiency vulnerabilities to environmental influences ("brainwashing processes") like advertising, propaganda, and peer pressure.

The closest I got was finding two articles *Impulsive and Self-Conscious: Adolescents' Vulnerability to Advertising and Promotion* (Pechmann 2005 Study) [864] and *Why Didn't I Think of That? Self-Regulation Through Selective Information Processing* (Trudel 2011 Study).[865]

I found it particularly loathsome that the Pechmann and Trudel studies were published in marketing association journals, not *anti*-marketing association journals. I found it even more galling that such vulnerability studies are not present in the "scientific" literature database of pubmed.com.

However, I did find one significant 2010 Harvard publication — *Defining neuromarketing: practices and professional challenges*[866] — which is a good review and discussion of the state of the art, practices and ethics of "applied consumer neuroscience." Scary.

The 2005 Pechmann Study was interesting in that it was very detailed and heavily sourced. It also contained a table entitled "Reasons *Adolescents* Might Show Heightened

Vulnerability to Marketing Efforts and Possible Remedies" (emphasis mine).

Their table could have just as easily been titled "Reasons *Adult ADDers* Might Show Heightened Vulnerability to Market Efforts and Possible Remedies" (emphasis mine).

I guess it is *not okay to exploit adolescent characteristics in adolescents* for marketing purposes, but *it is just fine to exploit adolescent characteristics in adult ADDers* for marketing purposes. The 2005 Pechmann Study did not mention the term ADD or ADHD.

One other relevant marketing article that I discovered is *Why I am less persuaded than you: People's intuitive understanding of the psychology of persuasion.* [867] It refers to a fairly new term —"need for cognition" [868] — the need of people who have a greater inclination for thinking things through and tend to be less swayed by advertising that uses superficial tricks like beautiful models and slick graphics. They are more persuaded by advertising that makes an intelligent argument.

The term "need for cognition" in the world of, let's say, The Journal of Consumer Psychology (yes, it exists), is not much different than "the ability to be a straight arrow" in a more impulsive, superficial, aversive-to-delay, capable-of-not-being-overstimulated dopamine-deficiency population.

I am hoping that the concept of the well-documented high programmability (plasticity) of the thoughts, ideas, beliefs, and behaviors of those with various dopamine-deficiency conditions is not lost on you.

I will be writing much more about the high prevalence of dopamine-deficiency conditions in the Western Hemisphere and how, unfortunately, many of the Western Hemisphere societies are not only ignorant of the widespread "plasticity problem" of their populations, but are actually facilitating the exploitation of those vulnerabilities to the maximum allowable by law, and then some.

Believe me when I say, "it's a downward spiral, similar to cannibalism."

19.5 Free Will is a Minor Variable; Taking Total Credit can be Just Plain Ill-Informed

Free will is clearly a variable, but it is a variable that is substantially influenced by brain structure and function. Taking credit for "mindful," "civil," "organized," "peace-filled" and "disciplined" thinking and behavior should be possible, but, scientifically, only *realistically* in the context of knowing just how easy the dopamine-optimized brain makes it for those who have it.

I suppose if you are someone who chose your biological parents wisely, you could argue with me.

In a very real sense, these genetically-loaded, neurotransmitter disparities which lead to clear vulnerabilities to certain kinds of thinking and behaviors have unwittingly become another battleground between the haves and the have-nots. The haves (the straight-arrows) claim willpower, hard work and discipline is what is needed, when, in fact, what controls them is as unconscious as what controls the "have-nots." One wonders, or, at least I do, if humans have really evolved beyond certain animals when it comes to rationally overriding their urges for territorialism.

Please note, I said "urges" for territorialism. The struggle between any groups of people over any particular "territory," may be triggered by several different variables including population density, resource competition (air, water, food, space, climate, energy, and money — which relies on controlling factors such as force, connections, inheritance, and reputation). In my view, both Robert Ardrey and Ashley Montague got it wrong. [869] The urge to territorialism is different from the manifestation of territorialism.

In humans, there are clear triggering mechanisms which a majority of humans have not chosen to "evolve" beyond.

(Maybe it's their dopamine-deficiencies leading to short-term, illogical thinking, as Spock[870] would say.)

You would think that given the high capacity of humans for reason, logic, and comprehension, that the urge to territorialism would be under better control. Clearly, it is not. We look for any excuse to get a "leg up."[871] Sometimes, that "leg-up" effort has dual meanings — picture the classic male dog urination stance.

19.6   A Serious Man

When I discuss issues like free will and taking credit, I am often challenged with questions about "responsibility," "discipline," and "punishment." Believe it or not, for wisdom and answers to such questions since 2009, I turn to the movie *A Serious Man*.[872] At the beginning of the movie, for a few seconds, the following paraphrased quote appears, by itself, on the screen.

"Receive with simplicity everything that happens to you." — Rashi

Rashi is an acronym for RAbbi SHlomo Itzhaki who lived from 1040–1105 A.D. He was a Jewish exegete, grammarian, and legal authority in Troyes, France. His Bible and Talmud commentaries and interpretations are beloved for their great clarity. His writings are among the most inclusive and authoritative in Jewish exegesis and are still important in Jewish life. He examined the literal meaning of those texts and used allegory, parable, and symbolism to analyze their non-literal meaning. His landmark commentary on the Talmud is known as a classic introduction to biblical and post-biblical Judaism.[873]   The original text according to Steven Menashi[874] is "Conduct yourself with Him with simplicity and depend on Him, and do not inquire of the future; rather, accept whatever happens to you with simplicity and then, you will be with Him and to His portion."

In the film, Rabbi Marshak paraphrases Darby Slick's *Somebody to Love* lyrics made popular by Jefferson Airplane, which the Rabbi had been listening to, and offers this advice to the recently bar mitzvahed Danny (as he returns Danny's radio to him) — *When the truth is found to be lies and all the hope within you dies, then what? ... Be a good boy.*

As humans, most of us have the capacity to rise above our bodies and our genes and honor the mystery of our existence, if we can learn, through such honoring, the humbleness to accept that our destinies are substantially shaped by forces beyond our control, which includes our genes. Should we complain and whine? Not really. Should such forces (genes and such) allow us to evade personal responsibility or constitute valid excuses for hurting others? Not in the least. It is not a fair world, as Larry, the mathematician, learns in *A Serious Man*. Such an unfair world is no honorable excuse for engaging in further unfairness or hurt.

Before I had that movie to refer to, I turned to Viktor Frankl. (Actually, I still do.) Frankl's English book *Man's Search for Meaning* was originally titled *trotzdem ja zum Leben sagen (Ein Psychologe erlebt das Konzentrationslager)* — "...*saying yes to life* in spite of everything; A Psychologist Experiences the Concentration Camp."[875] *Saying yes to life* in spite of everything — to be the good person (honorable person) within the means available to you without damaging others or yourself too much.

Frankl often said that the Statue of Liberty on the East Coast of the United States should be complemented by a Statue of Responsibility on the West Coast.[876]

Such attention to "responsibility" by those of us who have won the dopamine-gene lottery means understanding and appreciating our own brain-set and its upside and downside and understanding the upside and downside of the less optimal dopamine brain-set. It means understanding and appreciating what the Western Hemisphere needs and responding to those needs.

And, if you want my opinion about what the Western Hemisphere needs and, specifically, what the United States needs with respect to the high level of dopamine deficiencies in their populations, please read my forthcoming book *The Culture Genes.* I'll give you a hint — it's not a bunch of medications.

20 If the Shoe Fits, Wear It

If the shoe fits, wear it.

It is a phrase that most of us learned when we were exposed to the Cinderella Story. But, it actually originated much earlier as the phrase, "if the hat fits, wear it." It means, literally: "If it has all of the characteristics of a thing, it probably *is* that thing." When the shoe fits, it is generally a very significant and memorable emotional moment.

As I noted in the Introduction, one of the significant obstacles to a widespread understanding of ADD has been that most of the traditional explanations of the processes that produce ADD characteristics have *not* been accurate enough to "stick." What that means is that those who experience the ADD brain could not completely identify with the "traditional" explanations of their distractibility, reading problems, forgetfulness, anxiety, dread, insomnia, restlessness, and procrastination, among other things. When I say "traditional" explanations, I am referring to any explanations that did *not* highlight the readily recognizable downside of the ADD brain, working memory, or the readily recognizable upside of the ADD brain, emergency capability.

Without explaining either of those very significant and highly influential characteristics of the ADD brain, most ADDers and non-ADDers did not get it. That is, they could not identify fully with such traditional explanations that were heavy on "lack of inhibition," "hyperactivity," "troublemaking," and "impulsivity." Clearly, they have sensed and experienced the upside of their brains but none of the "traditional" explanations of that upside (if any) came close enough for them to say "yep, the shoe fits."

When checking the most recent writings of some of the "giants" of ADD understanding, such as Russell Barkley, Ph.D., Edward Hallowell, M.D., Stephen Faraone, Ph.D., and John Ratey, M.D., it appears that only Dr. Barkley has systematically updated his writings and thinking since 2006 with respect to the widely-reported processes involved in the production of the typical characteristics of ADD. However, as noted earlier, Dr. Barkley apparently does not believe there is an upside to the ADD brain. As you may already know from reading Section 16.4, I respectfully disagree.

In addition, Dr. Barkley's most recent updating of his online continuing education course last revised 1/10/2011 (accessed on the Internet on 11/10/11) entitled *ADHD: Nature, Course, Outcomes and Comorbidity,*[877] does *not* cite any significant scientific literature since 2008, and the literature he does cite with a later date is mostly his own. There is almost no discussion of dopamine and norepinephrine processes, although hundreds of studies were published before 1/10/2011 confirming the contribution of such neurotransmitter functional variations to the characteristics of ADD processing and behavior.

I cannot understand why such omissions have taken place and I do not have the time to ask these leaders in the field what those omissions are all about. If there is a reason to ignore all the findings cited in this book regarding such processes and all the ancillary data pointing to such ADD-related processes, then, at least, Dr. Barkley should have said something like "Although hundreds of studies have been done implicating deficient dopamine and norepinephrine processes in the prefrontal cortex and emotional brain circuits that contribute to low working memory, impulse control difficulties, and 'risk-taking' behavior, none of it seems to me to be substantial." At least, then, we would know he did his homework.

"If the shoe fits, wear it," can be a little more complicated in the scientific arena, and maybe I should discuss that, at least briefly. There are certain guiding principles that scientists generally try to keep in mind when they offer up and test hypotheses.

One of the most significant ones is called Occam's Razor.[878] A full discussion of the principles and meanings related to Occam's Razor ("OR") is beyond the scope of this book. However, it would be inconsiderate of me not to discuss its ramifications at least enough for you to get a sense of the calibrations I have brought to the hypotheses I have offered in this book.

OR is named after William of Ockham (1285-1349) who was a not-so-well-known logician. However, although he promoted the principle of economy, he never actually offered up the phrase that fits the OR maxim the best "simpler explanations are, other things being equal, generally better than more complex ones." This has also been called the principle of "parsimony."

There have been many heated discussions of the principle and some criteria offered for when it should be abandoned, however, it has stood the test of time and trials. Karl Popper introduced the concept of falsifiability — a hypothesis or explanation of a phenomena should be testable.

I bring this up because, in my opinion, many of the earlier theories of ADD rely on too many somewhat independent constructs to explain what is producing all the various characteristics that have been identified as the criteria for the diagnosis of ADD.

One of my favorite articles is the 2009 *What would Karl Popper say? Are current psychological theories of ADHD falsifiable?*[879] It discusses the four major psychological theories of ADD: (1) Executive Dysfunction, (2) State Regulation, (3) Delay Aversion, and (4) Dynamic Developmental. The authors analyzed each of those theories on (a) their ability to explain symptoms, (b) their testability, and (c) their openness to falsification.

Their recommendation is that "theoreticians should focus, to a greater extent than currently practiced, on developing refutable theories of ADHD." They also concluded that the Dynamic Developmental Theory ("DDT") of ADD comes the closest to the principles of OR and Karl Popper's falsifiability test. Developed and fine-tuned by Sagvolden and colleagues in Norway since the late 1980s, DDT is a comprehensive theory which attempts to explain the behavioral manifestations of ADD from a neurotransmitter through to a societal level and aims to explain all the traditional characteristics of ADD.

Reinforcement and extinction processes are hypothesized to be the core problems in ADD due to abnormally low levels of dopamine, affecting the functioning of the anterior cingulate, dorsolateral prefrontal and motor circuits and consequently, producing the variety of traditional ADD behaviors and characteristics. The Sagvolden group clearly demonstrated the interaction between phasic and tonic dopamine and how that significantly affects reinforcement and extinction (learning).[880]

With respect to parsimonious hypotheses, I cannot think of a more parsimonious hypothesis than the main one I offer in this book with respect to ADD. It is similar to the Dynamic Developmental Theory, but even simpler. It similarly relies on the substantial findings with respect to dopamine (and likely norepinephrine) deficiencies in the prefrontal cortex (in general) and the emotional brain. My hypothesis, one more time, is:

(1) Dopamine and norepinephrine deficiencies ("malfunctions" in synthesis, receptors, transporters and enzymes) produce the *low working memory* (low RAM and relatively no data buffer or cache) of the ADD brain, which then so negatively affects information processing speed, depth, and maintenance (appraisal and reappraisal) that it produces 90% of the downside experiences of

the ADDer — distractibility, inaccurate targeting, "dyslexia," over-attention to certain "spiky" sensory input (poor screening) and inner-talk (poor screening) and insomnia (poor screening), over-whelmed easily (poor handling of baseline data loads and panic with new data challenges), irritable ("Leave me alone!"), short-tempered ("Didn't I say I was overwhelmed?"), forgetful (including, have a difficult time remembering the beginning of a sentence when reaching the end of a sentence or short paragraph), impatient, impulsive, delay aversive, restless (behavior created by streaming, non-buffered data), fidgety (behavior to increase working memory), moody (created by streaming, non-buffered thoughts and data), disorganized, indecisive, can't prioritize well, lose track of time (not enough RAM to have a task program open at the same time as a clock program not to mention that to notice the passing of time you have to hold in a cache at least for a few seconds, a beginning time marker and an ending time marker to notice the "length of time"); short-term thinking (consequences?), and, I could go on.

(2) The other significant downside of the ADD experience created by "malfunctions" in synthesis, receptors, transporters and enzymes, is the *ability to engage in "risky" thinking and behavior without much aversive EB feedback*. This sets up the ADDer for some serious problems, unless they have above-average IQ, and then, there is no guarantee.

(3) The same malfunctioning neurotrans-mitter processes in the EB that produce the higher risk tolerance of the ADD brain are also almost entirely responsible for *the upside of the ADD brain — better in emergencies*.

Emergencies actually treat ADD, and the ADDer gets faster, sharper (better working memory) and calmer (grounded, focused).

I consider this to be as parsimonious and as accurate as you can get, based on the available data at this time. (I am sure you will let me know your thoughts.) Is it a further iteration of the DDT? Sort of, but not really.

The DDT still relies on too many variables to explain ADD characteristics, and, in my view, the reliance on constructs such as reinforcement and extinction makes it relatively non-testable, since reinforcement and extinction are very complicated in humans as compared to rats. The top-down influences (feedback and priming) and voting done by the human cortex and prefrontal cortex cannot begin to be understood by utilizing the less "cortical" brains of animals.

In my practice, in the last year alone, I have repeatedly experienced how much the descriptions found in this book have resonated and fit with clients who have been 99% self-referred by way of reading what I have posted at www.AdultADDFacts.com (out-dated as of 11/10/11, compared to this book). (I will update the website soon to reflect a leaner version of this book. Promise.)

In other words, the shoe fit for them.

Once the shoe fits, the lights turn on and there is a clear recognition of one's inner workings and *then* there is the opportunity to meaningfully engage in changing certain processes by correctly targeting underlying causes and setting measurable goals, not just shooting in the dark.

Sure, given the many possible different combinations of the gene polymorphisms known to negatively impact dopamine and norepinephrine function (synthesis, receptors, transporters, and de-activating enzymes), and, thus, all the different possible neurobiological subtypes of ADD, we *are* "shooting in the semi-dark." However, frankly, I would choose the semi-dark over the full dark, any day.

I have been astounded by the number of highly intelligent 20-50 year olds I have evaluated in the last year with IQs in the range of 130-160 who have had significant struggles with reading processes — distractibility leading to substantial slowness (rereading a lot) with poor retention and then subsequent aversion to reading, picking classes where reading and writing were minimal, and all the time not knowing what was wrong, or, if anything was really wrong, since they were so smart ("If *I* have this problem, so must everyone else"). Almost 100% of them were self-referred to me after discovering how well they fit the criteria for ADD as it is "untraditionally" described at AdultADDFacts.com.

In other words, the shoe fit.

With respect to shoes fitting, I wish to continue to be a good cobbler and actively keep my shoes updated and wearable.

21   Controversies and Civil Rights

So, I wish I could finish this book, right here, right now. But, I can't. I still need to say something about certain controversies and about civil rights.

I have already addressed the controversies and misunderstanding related to traditional, restricted ADD medications.

I have not fully addressed the controversies related to the diagnosis, itself, in terms of how it is made and by whom.

I have not fully addressed the controversy, now rather smothered by governmental powers and propaganda, regarding the significant negative healthcare impacts of restricting the most useful ADD medications and declaring them dangerous, as if, as I said, alcohol and tobacco are less dangerous, among other things.

I have not addressed the controversy over the huge and ongoing shortages of ADD medications that have lasted almost this entire year (2011). (As if our government really wants our populations to be that competitive world-wide.) Given the American ruling class behavior over the last several years, it seems that the real goal of that wealth-governmental complex is to economically hammer the majority of Americans into full submission, in the hope that they will accept living in huts and eating gruel.

I have not addressed the controversies spawned by articles such as *ADHD is best understood as a cultural construct* [881] or the countless articles that attempt to discredit the diagnosis.

Sure, the official diagnosis has huge problems. I bet so does your 17 year-old car that has been driven 200,000 miles without an oil change. But, the fact is, with only a few omissions, the downside characteristics of ADD (not the developmental timelines) noted in the official ADD criteria clearly relate to a significantly well-understood common denominator. *That common denominator is less than optimal dopamine and norepinephrine functions in the ADD brain and body.*

It is unfortunate that the proposed criteria for the diagnosis of ADD in the forthcoming revision of the DSM IV (to be called DSM-5),[882] to be published in the next two years, does not adequately address working memory, insomnia, distractibility, and reading challenges.[883] Dr. Barkley and several others made presentations to the DSM-5 ADHD and Disruptive Behavior Disorders Work Group ("ADD Group")[884] during a conference that took place February 14-17, 2007.[885] He and others proposed creating a new ADD symptom pool based on criteria related to executive functioning — inhibition, working memory, organization to time and future events, emotional self-control, self-motivation and planning. So far, none of them have been incorporated. Additionally, it is noteworthy that the word "insomnia" is not present in the report of the February 2007 conference. The word "reading" only appears once. And, finally, the ADD Group is sticking with the current three subtype classifications. You may have winced as you noted that the conference was early 2007. If you have read this book to this point, you know how many new and significant research findings have taken place since then.

This book stands on its own. Most of the controversies you might run across, you should be able to analyze in the light of what has been written in this book. If you are interested, Wikipedia has a short, but fairly comprehensive discussion of several ADD controversies.[886]

As for civil rights, it looks like it is going to take more than a few Million ADDer Marches on Washington to make sure the government understands and positively responds to the needs of its citizens.

* * * * * * * * *

Your move

22 Endnotes

To make it easier for you to view these citations quickly, I chose to not use traditional citation styles. For most of these citations, you can just enter the last 7 or 8 digits in the search box at pubmed.com, and quickly access the cited article.

[1] http://www.ncbi.nlm.nih.gov/pubmed/19380515
[2] http://www.ncbi.nlm.nih.gov/pubmed/19037178
[3] http://www.ncbi.nlm.nih.gov/pubmed/16585449
[4] http://www.ncbi.nlm.nih.gov/pubmed/19193347
[5] http://www.ncbi.nlm.nih.gov/pubmed/21654176
[6] http://www.medscape.org/viewarticle/713528
[7] http://www.ncbi.nlm.nih.gov/pubmed/18590022
[8] Mayes, R., Rafalovich, A. *Suffer the Restless Children: The Evolution of ADHD and Pediatric Stimulant Use*, 1900-1980. November, 2006. https://facultystaff.richmond.edu/~bmayes/ADHD_Mayes_Rafalovich_HistoryofPsychiatry.pdf
[9] http://www.ncbi.nlm.nih.gov/pubmed/17484934
[10] http://www.ncbi.nlm.nih.gov/pubmed/17463342
[11] http://www.ncbi.nlm.nih.gov/pubmed/18216729
[12] Mental Health America, June 2006. *Public Understanding and Comfort with Mental Illnesses Still Lag Behind Other Major Diseases* http://www.mentalhealthamerica.net/index.cfm?objectid=FD502854-1372-4D20-C89C30F0DEE68035
[13] Englund, W. *Windows Of Opportunity -- We're still a bootstrap nation. Few Americans see government as the best hope for improving their lives.* National Journal, January 2011. http://www.nationaljournal.com/njmagazine/nj_20090725_6544.php
[14] http://www.ncbi.nlm.nih.gov/pubmed/19105857
[15] http://www.ncbi.nlm.nih.gov/pubmed/17593149
[16] http://www.ncbi.nlm.nih.gov/pubmed/20576645
[17] http://www.mass.gov/?pageID=cagopressrelease&L=1&L0=Home&sid=Cago&b=pressrelease&f=2011_08_01_risperdal&csid=Cago
[18] http://voiceofdetroit.net/2011/08/07/u-s-johnson-johnson-wrongly-marketed-risperdal-to-kids/
[19] http://blogs.nature.com/news/2011/07/harvard_scientists_disciplined.html

[20] New York Times. *Joseph Biederman*, March 2009. http://topics.nytimes.com/topics/reference/timestopics/people/b/joseph_biederman/index.html

[21] http://en.wikipedia.org/wiki/Chuck_Grassley

[22] Carey, B., Harris G. *Psychiatric Group Faces Scrutiny Over Drug Industry Ties*. NY Times, July 12, 2008. http://www.nytimes.com/2008/07/12/washington/12psych.html?hp

[23] http://www.russellbarkley.org/about-dr-barkley.htm

[24] http://www.ronsterling.com/disclosure.htm

[25] Hallowell E., Ratey J. *Driven to Distraction*, New York, Pantheon Books, 1994.

[26] Hallowell E., Ratey J. *Delivered from Distraction*, 2004 Random House, Inc.

[27] http://www.medscape.com/viewarticle/571537

[28] http://www.ncbi.nlm.nih.gov/pubmed/21432575

[29] http://www.ncbi.nlm.nih.gov/pubmed/21158602

[30] http://www.ncbi.nlm.nih.gov/pubmed/19835674

[31] http://www.ncbi.nlm.nih.gov/pubmed/20732624

[32] http://www.ncbi.nlm.nih.gov/pubmed/20452044

[33] *Diagnostic and Statistical Manual of Mental Disorders, 4th Ed.*, 1994, American Psychiatric Association

[34] http://www.ncbi.nlm.nih.gov/pubmed/20815868

[35] http://www.ncbi.nlm.nih.gov/pubmed/17709814

[36] http://www.ncbi.nlm.nih.gov/pubmed/20815868

[37] Edwards, H., Behave net ® Clinical Capsule ™ web page. http://www.behavenet.com/capsules/disorders/adhd.htm

[38] *Diagnostic and Statistical Manual of Mental Disorders, 4th Ed.*, 1994, American Psychiatric Association

[39] http://www.ncbi.nlm.nih.gov/pubmed/21041618

[40] http://www.ncbi.nlm.nih.gov/pubmed/20060129

[41] http://www.ncbi.nlm.nih.gov/pubmed/21041618

[42] http://www.ncbi.nlm.nih.gov/pubmed/21575934

[43] http://www.ncbi.nlm.nih.gov/pubmed/19193347

[44] http://www.ncbi.nlm.nih.gov/pubmed/16982202

[45] http://www.ncbi.nlm.nih.gov/pubmed/16982202

[46] http://www.ncbi.nlm.nih.gov/pubmed/19759528

[47] http://www.ncbi.nlm.nih.gov/pubmed/21434915

[48] http://www.ncbi.nlm.nih.gov/pubmed/21664605

[49] http://en.wikipedia.org/wiki/Neurotransmitter

[50] http://www.ncbi.nlm.nih.gov/pubmed/16741205

[51] http://www.ncbi.nlm.nih.gov/pubmed/20123910

[52] http://www.ncbi.nlm.nih.gov/pubmed/20595414

[53] http://www.ncbi.nlm.nih.gov/pubmed/16110052

[54] http://www.amenclinics.com/cybcyb/online-tests-calculators/add-test/

[55] http://www.npjulie.com/Acrobat_forms/amen_complete.pdf

[56] http://www.addcoach4u.com/documents/adultadhdscreenertest1.pdf

[57] http://www.ncbi.nlm.nih.gov/pubmed/18803914

[58] http://www.ncbi.nlm.nih.gov/pubmed/19738093

[59] Volkow, N. et al. *Depressed Dopamine Activity in Caudate and Preliminary Evidence of Limbic Involvement in Adults With Attention-Deficit/Hyperactivity Disorder. Arch Gen Psychiatry.* 2007;64(8):932-940. http://www.ncbi.nlm.nih.gov/pubmed/17679638

[60] http://www.ncbi.nlm.nih.gov/pubmed/17126039

[61] http://www.ncbi.nlm.nih.gov/pubmed/15691523

[62] http://www.ncbi.nlm.nih.gov/pubmed/19183781

[63] http://www.ncbi.nlm.nih.gov/pubmed/17318414

[64] Lund beck Institute. *CNS Forum, CNS Image Bank Brain Physiology.* (Undated) http://www.cnsforum.com/imagebank/section/Bp_Normal_brain/default.aspx

[65] http://www.ncbi.nlm.nih.gov/pubmed/20596295

[66] http://www.ncbi.nlm.nih.gov/pubmed/20641880

[67] http://www.ncbi.nlm.nih.gov/pubmed/17909794

[68] http://www.ncbi.nlm.nih.gov/pubmed/17979789

[69] http://www.ncbi.nlm.nih.gov/pubmed/18000665

[70] http://www.ncbi.nlm.nih.gov/pubmed/21489408

[71] http://www.ncbi.nlm.nih.gov/pubmed/15858063

[72] http://www.ncbi.nlm.nih.gov/pubmed/10782925

[73] http://www.medscape.org/viewarticle/523887

[74] http://en.wikipedia.org/wiki/Norepinephrine

[75] http://www.ncbi.nlm.nih.gov/pubmed/17725997

[76] http://www.ncbi.nlm.nih.gov/pubmed/21207241

[77] http://www.hippocampus.us

[78] http://www.ncbi.nlm.nih.gov/pubmed/18403120

[79] http://docrotz.com/present_fidget.htm

[80] http://www.ncbi.nlm.nih.gov/pubmed/20813245

[81] http://www.ncbi.nlm.nih.gov/pubmed/21244440

[82] http://www.ncbi.nlm.nih.gov/pubmed/20146828

[83] http://www.ncbi.nlm.nih.gov/pubmed/18358675

[84] http://www.ncbi.nlm.nih.gov/pubmed/20958329

[85] http://www.ncbi.nlm.nih.gov/pubmed/16953002

[86] http://www.ncbi.nlm.nih.gov/pubmed/20682457
[87] http://www.ncbi.nlm.nih.gov/pubmed/19339599
[88] http://www.ncbi.nlm.nih.gov/pubmed/18563061
[89] http://www.ncbi.nlm.nih.gov/pubmed/20456288
[90] http://www.ncbi.nlm.nih.gov/pubmed/19184649
[91] http://www.ncbi.nlm.nih.gov/pubmed/21187978
[92] http://www.ncbi.nlm.nih.gov/pubmed/19631753
[93] http://www.ncbi.nlm.nih.gov/pubmed/20849328
[94] http://www.ncbi.nlm.nih.gov/pubmed/10403500
[95] http://www.ncbi.nlm.nih.gov/pubmed/18559805
[96] http://www.ncbi.nlm.nih.gov/pubmed/19154629
[97] http://www.ncbi.nlm.nih.gov/pubmed/20622144
[98] http://www.ncbi.nlm.nih.gov/pubmed/11210998
[99] http://www.ncbi.nlm.nih.gov/pubmed/21603099
[100] http://www.ncbi.nlm.nih.gov/pubmed/20881128
[101] http://www.ncbi.nlm.nih.gov/pubmed/21603099
[102] http://www.ncbi.nlm.nih.gov/pubmed/21430137
[103] http://www.ncbi.nlm.nih.gov/pubmed/20116437
[104] http://www.ncbi.nlm.nih.gov/pubmed/20875835
[105] http://www.ncbi.nlm.nih.gov/pubmed/20875835
[106] http://www.ncbi.nlm.nih.gov/pubmed/20875435
[107] http://www.ncbi.nlm.nih.gov/pubmed/10426490
[108] http://www.ncbi.nlm.nih.gov/pubmed/16111831
[109] http://www.ncbi.nlm.nih.gov/pubmed/21605572
[110] http://www.ncbi.nlm.nih.gov/pubmed/20881401
[111] http://www.ncbi.nlm.nih.gov/pubmed/21714067
[112] http://www.ncbi.nlm.nih.gov/pubmed/18617195
[113] http://www.ncbi.nlm.nih.gov/pubmed/18690117
[114] http://www.ncbi.nlm.nih.gov/pubmed/15530728
[115] http://www.ncbi.nlm.nih.gov/pubmed/7752065
[116] http://www.ncbi.nlm.nih.gov/pubmed/12093592
[117] http://www.ncbi.nlm.nih.gov/pubmed/20182035
[118] http://www.ncbi.nlm.nih.gov/pubmed/20182030
[119] http://www.ncbi.nlm.nih.gov/pubmed/18554731
[120] http://www.ncbi.nlm.nih.gov/pubmed/21698275
[121] http://www.ncbi.nlm.nih.gov/pubmed/12858935
[122] http://www.ronsterling.com/disclosure.htm
[123] http://www.ncbi.nlm.nih.gov/pubmed/20739076
[124] http://www.ncbi.nlm.nih.gov/pubmed/21053468
[125] http://www.ncbi.nlm.nih.gov/pubmed/21391409
[126] http://www.ncbi.nlm.nih.gov/pubmed/19372494

[127] http://www.ncbi.nlm.nih.gov/pubmed/16775518

[128] http://www.ncbi.nlm.nih.gov/pubmed/21318193

[129] http://www.ncbi.nlm.nih.gov/pubmed/20739076

[130] http://www.ncbi.nlm.nih.gov/pubmed/20638739

[131] http://www.ncbi.nlm.nih.gov/pubmed/11556624

[132] National Institute of Mental Health. *Teenage Brain: A work in progress (Fact Sheet)*, (Undated, circa 2000). http://www.nimh.nih.gov/health/publications/teenage-brain-a-work-in-progress-fact-sheet/index.shtml

[133] Mitchell, D. *Parents Say Drugs, Changing Schools Best for ADHD Kids*. Emaxhealth.com, July 2010. http://www.emaxhealth.com/1275/parents-say-drugs-changing-schools-best-adhd-kids

[134] http://www.adders.org/info16.htm

[135] http://www.ncbi.nlm.nih.gov/pubmed/16961424

[136] http://www.ncbi.nlm.nih.gov/pubmed/18480677

[137] http://www.ncbi.nlm.nih.gov/pubmed/20416377

[138] http://www.ncbi.nlm.nih.gov/pubmed/19293415

[139] http://www.ncbi.nlm.nih.gov/pubmed/20352415

[140] http://www.ncbi.nlm.nih.gov/pubmed/20592211

[141] http://www.ncbi.nlm.nih.gov/pubmed/19037178

[142] http://www.ncbi.nlm.nih.gov/pubmed/16585449

[143] http://www.askdrjones.com/adhd/ssri-type-antidepressants-for-adhd/ (Accessed 6/30/2011; unavailable 8/1/2011)

[144] http://www.ncbi.nlm.nih.gov/pubmed/15323590

[145] http://www.ncbi.nlm.nih.gov/pubmed/15671124

[146] http://www.ncbi.nlm.nih.gov/pubmed/1938791

[147] http://www.ncbi.nlm.nih.gov/pubmed/17103304

[148] http://www.ncbi.nlm.nih.gov/pubmed/21179515

[149] http://www.ncbi.nlm.nih.gov/pubmed/15361919

[150] http://www.ncbi.nlm.nih.gov/pubmed/20051220

[151] http://www.ncbi.nlm.nih.gov/pubmed/18720661

[152] http://www.ncbi.nlm.nih.gov/pubmed/18720662

[153] http://www.ncbi.nlm.nih.gov/pubmed/20863843

[154] http://www.ncbi.nlm.nih.gov/pubmed/20399622

[155] http://blog.lib.umn.edu/psy/psychair/Grice-Patil.pdf

[156] http://www.ncbi.nlm.nih.gov/pubmed/19457373

[157] http://www.ncbi.nlm.nih.gov/pubmed/17974940

[158] http://www.ncbi.nlm.nih.gov/pubmed/18720662

[159] Amen Clinics (author unknown). *How Brain SPECT Imaging Can Help with ADHD/AD*. Undated web page. http://www.amenclinics.com/clinics/information/ways-we-can-help/adhd-add/

[160] http://www.jneurosci.org/content/30/29/9910.long
[161] http://www.ncbi.nlm.nih.gov/pubmed/18476765
[162] http://www.ncbi.nlm.nih.gov/pubmed/19818382
[163] http://www.ncbi.nlm.nih.gov/pubmed/19005068
[164] http://www.ncbi.nlm.nih.gov/pubmed/18066057
[165] http://www.ncbi.nlm.nih.gov/pubmed/11682348
[166] http://www.ncbi.nlm.nih.gov/pubmed/12088697
[167] http://www.ncbi.nlm.nih.gov/pubmed/12559240
[168] http://www.ncbi.nlm.nih.gov/pubmed/21247797
[169] http://www.ncbi.nlm.nih.gov/pubmed/21089242
[170] National Institute of Mental Health (author unknown).
Medications for ADHD. Web page last updated
September 23, 2010.
http://www.nimh.nih.gov/health/publications/attention-deficit-hyperactivity-disorder/medications.shtml
[171] http://www.ncbi.nlm.nih.gov/pubmed/21295057
[172] http://www.ncbi.nlm.nih.gov/pubmed/19445548
[173] http://www.ncbi.nlm.nih.gov/pubmed/19293415
[174] http://www.ncbi.nlm.nih.gov/pubmed/16961428
[175] http://www.ncbi.nlm.nih.gov/pubmed/17712350
[176] http://www.ncbi.nlm.nih.gov/pubmed/18698321
[177] http://www.ncbi.nlm.nih.gov/pubmed/12685517
[178] http://www.ncbi.nlm.nih.gov/pubmed/15950015
[179] http://www.ncbi.nlm.nih.gov/pubmed/19587853
[180] http://www.ncbi.nlm.nih.gov/pubmed/18591484
[181] http://www.ncbi.nlm.nih.gov/pubmed/19969097
[182] http://www.ncbi.nlm.nih.gov/pubmed/18708076
[183] http://www.ncbi.nlm.nih.gov/pubmed/18720661
[184] Amen Clinics (author unknown). *SPECT Image Gallery*. (Web
page undated)
http://www.amenclinics.com/amenclinics/brain-science/spect-image-gallery/
[185] http://www.ncbi.nlm.nih.gov/pubmed/11177522
[186] http://www.ncbi.nlm.nih.gov/pubmed/19434551
[187] http://www.ncbi.nlm.nih.gov/pubmed/19014677
[188] http://www.ncbi.nlm.nih.gov/pubmed/20602089
[189] http://www.ncbi.nlm.nih.gov/pubmed/18585681
[190] http://www.ncbi.nlm.nih.gov/pubmed/20352415
[191] http://www.ncbi.nlm.nih.gov/pubmed/21146447
[192] http://www.ncbi.nlm.nih.gov/pubmed/20484709
[193] http://www.ncbi.nlm.nih.gov/pubmed/20416377
[194] http://www.ncbi.nlm.nih.gov/pubmed/20381522

[195] http://www.ncbi.nlm.nih.gov/pubmed/21339852
[196] http://www.ncbi.nlm.nih.gov/pubmed/21335017
[197] http://www.ncbi.nlm.nih.gov/pubmed/20808821
[198] http://www.ncbi.nlm.nih.gov/pubmed/17694051
[199] http://www.ncbi.nlm.nih.gov/pubmed/19961035
[200] Welsh, C. *Seizure Induced by Insufflations of Bupropion.* N Engle J Med 2002; 347:951, September 19, 2002. http://www.nejm.org/doi/full/10.1056/NEJM200209193471222
[201] http://www.ncbi.nlm.nih.gov/pubmed/20219165
[202] http://www.ncbi.nlm.nih.gov/pubmed/16723965
[203] http://www.ncbi.nlm.nih.gov/pubmed/8746293
[204] http://www.ncbi.nlm.nih.gov/pubmed/17132052
[205] http://www.ncbi.nlm.nih.gov/pubmed/17525776
[206] http://www.ncbi.nlm.nih.gov/pubmed/19428492
[207] http://www.ncbi.nlm.nih.gov/pubmed/12008858
[208] http://www.ncbi.nlm.nih.gov/pubmed/10863885
[209] http://www.ncbi.nlm.nih.gov/pubmed/10863885
[210] http://www.ncbi.nlm.nih.gov/pubmed/16797080
[211] http://www.ncbi.nlm.nih.gov/pubmed/10763190
[212] http://www.ncbi.nlm.nih.gov/pubmed/19779354
[213] http://www.ncbi.nlm.nih.gov/pubmed/20075642
[214] http://www.ncbi.nlm.nih.gov/pubmed/16390910
[215] http://www.ncbi.nlm.nih.gov/pubmed/21286371
[216] http://ajp.psychiatryonline.org/cgi/content/full/165/7/918
[217] http://www.ncbi.nlm.nih.gov/pubmed/15898970
[218] http://www.ncbi.nlm.nih.gov/pubmed/6133446
[219] http://www.ncbi.nlm.nih.gov/pubmed/21286371
[220] http://ajp.psychiatryonline.org/cgi/content/full/165/7/918
[221] http://www.ncbi.nlm.nih.gov/pubmed/8889907
[222] http://www.ncbi.nlm.nih.gov/pubmed/21448114
[223] http://www.nlm.nih.gov/medlineplus/ency/article/000949.htm
[224] http://www.ncbi.nlm.nih.gov/pubmed/18032401
[225] http://www.globaldrugpolicy.org/2/2/1.php
[226] http://www.ncbi.nlm.nih.gov/pubmed/19281939
[227] http://www.ncbi.nlm.nih.gov/pubmed/8268747
[228] http://www.ncbi.nlm.nih.gov/pubmed/19116378
[229] http://www.ncbi.nlm.nih.gov/pubmed/20104069
[230] http://www.ncbi.nlm.nih.gov/pubmed/16473984
[231] http://www.ncbi.nlm.nih.gov/pubmed/21508938
[232] http://www.globaldrugpolicy.org/2/2/1.php

[233] http://www.ncbi.nlm.nih.gov/pubmed/21494335
[234] http://www.ncbi.nlm.nih.gov/pubmed/20675840
[235] http://www.ncbi.nlm.nih.gov/pubmed/14613439
[236] http://www.medscape.org/viewarticle/708287
[237] http://www.ncbi.nlm.nih.gov/pubmed/16721314
[238] http://www.additudemag.com/adhd/article/757.html
[239] http://www.additudemag.com/web/article/677.html
[240] http://www.ncbi.nlm.nih.gov/pubmed/20605120
[241] http://www.ncbi.nlm.nih.gov/pubmed/17520787
[242] http://www.ncbi.nlm.nih.gov/pubmed/18363314
[243] http://www.ncbi.nlm.nih.gov/pubmed/19646365
[244] http://www.ncbi.nlm.nih.gov/pubmed/20920224
[245] http://www.ncbi.nlm.nih.gov/pubmed/19721722
[246] http://www.ncbi.nlm.nih.gov/pubmed/18026719
[247] http://www.ncbi.nlm.nih.gov/pubmed/20051220
[248] http://www.ncbi.nlm.nih.gov/pubmed/21089242
[249] http://www.ncbi.nlm.nih.gov/pubmed/11177522
[250] http://www.ncbi.nlm.nih.gov/pubmed/20806841
[251] http://www.ncbi.nlm.nih.gov/pubmed/20849328
[252] http://www.ncbi.nlm.nih.gov/pubmed/15229250
[253] http://www.ncbi.nlm.nih.gov/pubmed/20409426
[254] http://www.ncbi.nlm.nih.gov/pubmed/20508803
[255] http://www.ncbi.nlm.nih.gov/pubmed/20484709
[256] http://www.ncbi.nlm.nih.gov/pubmed/19630724
[257] http://www.ncbi.nlm.nih.gov/pubmed/19278795
[258] http://www.ncbi.nlm.nih.gov/pubmed/20129754
[259] http://www.ncbi.nlm.nih.gov/pubmed/20958854
[260] http://www.ncbi.nlm.nih.gov/pubmed/18316421
[261] http://www.ncbi.nlm.nih.gov/pubmed/12509574
[262] http://www.ncbi.nlm.nih.gov/pubmed/18838643
[263] http://www.ncbi.nlm.nih.gov/pubmed/16262596
[264] http://www.ncbi.nlm.nih.gov/pubmed/18381904
[265] http://www.ncbi.nlm.nih.gov/pubmed/18617195
[266] http://www.ncbi.nlm.nih.gov/pubmed/12509561
[267] http://www.ncbi.nlm.nih.gov/pubmed/20441004
[268] http://www.ncbi.nlm.nih.gov/pubmed/20632134
[269] http://www.ncbi.nlm.nih.gov/pubmed/20881401
[270] http://www.ncbi.nlm.nih.gov/pubmed/18326548
[271] http://www.ncbi.nlm.nih.gov/pubmed/17766314
[272] http://www.ncbi.nlm.nih.gov/pubmed/20584517
[273] http://www.ncbi.nlm.nih.gov/pubmed/20812768

[274] http://www.ncbi.nlm.nih.gov/pubmed/15705013
[275] http://www.ncbi.nlm.nih.gov/pubmed/16841618
[276] http://www.ncbi.nlm.nih.gov/pubmed/21977356
[277] http://www.ncbi.nlm.nih.gov/pubmed/21184783
[278] http://www.ncbi.nlm.nih.gov/pubmed/19410652
[279] http://www.ncbi.nlm.nih.gov/pubmed/19120127
[280] http://www.ncbi.nlm.nih.gov/pubmed/14570949
[281] http://www.ncbi.nlm.nih.gov/pubmed/16204425
[282] Armstrong, T. *Why I Believe that Attention Deficit Disorder is a Myth*. First published in Sydney's Child [Australia], September, 1996.
http://www.thomasarmstrong.com/articles/add_myth.php
[283] http://www.ncbi.nlm.nih.gov/pubmed/21391409
[284] http://www.ncbi.nlm.nih.gov/pubmed/20739076
[285] http://www.ncbi.nlm.nih.gov/pubmed/20638739
[286] http://www.ncbi.nlm.nih.gov/pubmed/19372494
[287] http://www.ncbi.nlm.nih.gov/pubmed/18083961
[288] http://www.nytimes.com/2010/12/14/health/14klass.html
[289] http://www.psychologytoday.com/blog/attention-please/201006/adhd-brains-the-quintessential-supercomputer (A further note about Dr. Goodman's writings. Although I consider him to be way off base as to his understanding of RAM and how the function of RAM can be used to think about human brain processes, he deserves a lot of credit. He may have been one of the loudest voices in the 1990s about SSRI addiction syndromes and several other important matters related to norepinephrine and dopamine and what he calls the Neurosomatic Syndrome. See his blog at http://www.jorygoodmanmd.com.)
[290] http://www.ncbi.nlm.nih.gov/pubmed/20522277
[291] http://www.ncbi.nlm.nih.gov/pubmed/20576645
[292] http://www.ncbi.nlm.nih.gov/pubmed/19936275
[293] http://www.ncbi.nlm.nih.gov/pubmed/21108990
[294] http://www.ncbi.nlm.nih.gov/pubmed/18434203
[295] http://www.ncbi.nlm.nih.gov/pubmed/19936275
[296] http://www.ncbi.nlm.nih.gov/pubmed/21390261
[297] http://www.ncbi.nlm.nih.gov/pubmed/18443283
[298] http://www.ncbi.nlm.nih.gov/pubmed/18095280
[299] http://www.ncbi.nlm.nih.gov/pubmed/18760263
[300] http://www.ncbi.nlm.nih.gov/pubmed/18095280
[301] http://www.ncbi.nlm.nih.gov/pubmed/18760263
[302] http://www.ncbi.nlm.nih.gov/pubmed/18095280
[303] http://www.ncbi.nlm.nih.gov/pubmed/18760263

[304] http://www.ncbi.nlm.nih.gov/pubmed/19420282
[305] http://www.ncbi.nlm.nih.gov/pubmed/18815437
[306] http://www.ncbi.nlm.nih.gov/pubmed/21200330
[307] http://precedings.nature.com/documents/2343/version/1
[308] http://www.ncbi.nlm.nih.gov/pubmed/21115182
[309] http://www.ncbi.nlm.nih.gov/pubmed/18815437
[310] http://www.ncbi.nlm.nih.gov/pubmed/2600242
[311] http://www.ncbi.nlm.nih.gov/pubmed/20692779
[312] http://www.ncbi.nlm.nih.gov/pubmed/21415916
[313] http://www.ncbi.nlm.nih.gov/pubmed/20571323
[314] http://www.ncbi.nlm.nih.gov/pubmed/8946568
[315] http://www.ncbi.nlm.nih.gov/pubmed/14754823
[316] http://www.ncbi.nlm.nih.gov/pubmed/18004732
[317] http://www.ncbi.nlm.nih.gov/pubmed/19207280
[318] http://www.ncbi.nlm.nih.gov/pubmed/19270267
[319] http://www.ncbi.nlm.nih.gov/pubmed/18004732
[320] Unknown author, blog reference to research. *Single neurons have RAM-like activity*. Jan. 2009. References Don Cooper's work at UT Southwestern Medical Center (http://www3.utsouthwestern.edu/psychlab/cooper/) http://scienceblogs.com/neurophilosophy/2009/01/single_neurons_have_ram-like_activity.php
[321] http://www.ncbi.nlm.nih.gov/pubmed/19169252
[322] Unknown author, *People With Lots Of Working Memory Are Not Easily Distracted*. ScienceDaily.com, August 2009. http://www.sciencedaily.com/releases/2009/08/090806141712.htm
[323] http://www.ncbi.nlm.nih.gov/pubmed/18066057
[324] http://www.ncbi.nlm.nih.gov/pubmed/20660273
[325] http://www.ncbi.nlm.nih.gov/pubmed/19281801
[326] http://www.ncbi.nlm.nih.gov/pubmed/20576647
[327] http://www.ncbi.nlm.nih.gov/pubmed/20726037
[328] http://www.ncbi.nlm.nih.gov/pubmed/21286223
[329] http://www.ncbi.nlm.nih.gov/pubmed/12371514
[330] http://en.wikipedia.org/wiki/Dynamic_random-access_memory
[331] http://www.ncbi.nlm.nih.gov/pubmed/15381316
[332] http://www.ncbi.nlm.nih.gov/pubmed/19654866
[333] http://www.ncbi.nlm.nih.gov/pubmed/19642882
[334] http://www.ncbi.nlm.nih.gov/pubmed/18213617
[335] http://www.ncbi.nlm.nih.gov/pubmed/16741204
[336] http://www.ncbi.nlm.nih.gov/pubmed/21546000

[337] http://www.ncbi.nlm.nih.gov/pubmed/21596533
[338] http://www.ncbi.nlm.nih.gov/pubmed/21489409
[339] http://www.ncbi.nlm.nih.gov/pubmed/18400958
[340] http://www.ncbi.nlm.nih.gov/pubmed/21059342
[341] http://www.ncbi.nlm.nih.gov/pubmed/20634975
[342] http://www.ncbi.nlm.nih.gov/pubmed/21029780
[343] http://www.ncbi.nlm.nih.gov/pubmed/21073458
[344] Previc, Fred. H. *The Dopaminergic Mind in Human Evolution and History*. 2009, Cambridge University Press.
[345] http://www.ncbi.nlm.nih.gov/pubmed/21839810
[346] http://www.ncbi.nlm.nih.gov/pubmed/21072167
[347] http://www.ncbi.nlm.nih.gov/pubmed/17679637
[348] http://www.ncbi.nlm.nih.gov/pubmed/18951431
[349] http://www.ncbi.nlm.nih.gov/pubmed/15737658
[350] http://www.ncbi.nlm.nih.gov/pubmed/19107752
[351] http://www.ncbi.nlm.nih.gov/pubmed/16876137
[352] http://www.ncbi.nlm.nih.gov/pubmed/16876137
[353] http://www.ncbi.nlm.nih.gov/pubmed/21575934
[354] http://www.ncbi.nlm.nih.gov/pubmed/20374289
[355] http://www.ncbi.nlm.nih.gov/pubmed/21546000
[356] http://www.ncbi.nlm.nih.gov/pubmed/19759528
[357] http://www.ncbi.nlm.nih.gov/pubmed/19565262
[358] http://en.wikipedia.org/wiki/Alzheimer's_disease
[359] http://en.wikipedia.org/wiki/Parkinson's_disease
[360] http://en.wikipedia.org/wiki/Stem_cell
[361] Unknown author. *Inconsistent Performance Speed Among Children With ADHD May Underlie How Well They Use Memory*. ScienceDaily.com, March 2009. http://www.sciencedaily.com/releases/2009/03/090324141047.htm
[362] http://www.ncbi.nlm.nih.gov/pubmed/18234898
[363] http://www.ncbi.nlm.nih.gov/pubmed/21503140
[364] http://www.ncbi.nlm.nih.gov/pubmed/21432617
[365] http://www.ncbi.nlm.nih.gov/pubmed/19787447
[366] http://www.ncbi.nlm.nih.gov/pubmed/17173676
[367] Cloud, J. *Kids with ADHD May Learn Better by Fidgeting*. Time Magazine, Mar. 25, 2009. http://www.time.com/time/health/article/0,8599,1887486,00.html
[368] http://www.ncbi.nlm.nih.gov/pubmed/19083090
[369] http://www.ncbi.nlm.nih.gov/pubmed/19088741
[370] http://www.ncbi.nlm.nih.gov/pubmed/21182852

[371] Klinberg, Torkel. *The Overflowing Brain*, 2009. Oxford University Press.

[372] http://www.ncbi.nlm.nih.gov/pubmed/18066057

[373] http://www.ncbi.nlm.nih.gov/pubmed/20349365

[374] http://www.ncbi.nlm.nih.gov/pubmed/21477197

[375] http://www.ncbi.nlm.nih.gov/pubmed/21477196

[376] http://www.ncbi.nlm.nih.gov/pubmed/18443283

[377] http://www.ncbi.nlm.nih.gov/pubmed/21670271

[378] Shipstead, Zach, et al., *Does Working Memory Training Generalize?* Psychologica Belgica, 2010: 50-3&4, 245-276. (http://www.ingentaconnect.com/content/acad/psyb/2010/000 00050/F0020003/art00007)

[379] http://www.ncbi.nlm.nih.gov/pubmed/20407435

[380] http://www.ncbi.nlm.nih.gov/pubmed/19197069

[381] http://www.ncbi.nlm.nih.gov/pubmed/20179754

[382] http://www.ncbi.nlm.nih.gov/pubmed/19176830

[383] http://www.ncbi.nlm.nih.gov/pubmed/18815437

[384] http://www.ncbi.nlm.nih.gov/pubmed/21488750

[385] http://www.ncbi.nlm.nih.gov/pubmed/21436147

[386] http://www.ncbi.nlm.nih.gov/pubmed/21432614

[387] http://www.ncbi.nlm.nih.gov/pubmed/18264813

[388] http://www.ncbi.nlm.nih.gov/pubmed/18465700

[389] http://www.ncbi.nlm.nih.gov/pubmed/21383110

[390] http://www.ncbi.nlm.nih.gov/pubmed/11513378

[391] http://www.ncbi.nlm.nih.gov/pubmed/15950015

[392] Hsu, S. *Neuroenhancement*. Information Processing Blog, Apr. 25,2009. http://www.technologyreview.com/blog/post.aspx?bid=354& bpid=23443

[393] Talbot, M. *Brain Gain: The underground world of "neuroenhancing" drugs*. The New Yorker, Apr. 27, 2009. http://www.newyorker.com/reporting/2009/04/27/090427fa_f act_talbot?printable=true

[394] http://www.ncbi.nlm.nih.gov/pubmed/19776378

[395] http://www.ncbi.nlm.nih.gov/pubmed/19293415

[396] http://www.ncbi.nlm.nih.gov/pubmed/21146447

[397] http://www.ncbi.nlm.nih.gov/pubmed/20605137

[398] http://www.ncbi.nlm.nih.gov/pubmed/20381522

[399] http://www.ncbi.nlm.nih.gov/pubmed/20700786

[400] http://www.ncbi.nlm.nih.gov/pubmed/20416377

[401] http://www.ncbi.nlm.nih.gov/pubmed/20484709

[402] http://www.ncbi.nlm.nih.gov/pubmed/20416377

[403] http://www.ncbi.nlm.nih.gov/pubmed/20381522

[404] http://www.ncbi.nlm.nih.gov/pubmed/19654866
[405] http://www.ncbi.nlm.nih.gov/pubmed/18478205
[406] http://www.ncbi.nlm.nih.gov/pubmed/20969573
[407] http://www.ncbi.nlm.nih.gov/pubmed/16310964
[408] http://www.ncbi.nlm.nih.gov/pubmed/19621976
[409] http://www.ncbi.nlm.nih.gov/pubmed/20855046
[410] http://www.ncbi.nlm.nih.gov/pubmed/19005068
[411] Lundbeck Institute. *CNS Forum, CNS Image Bank Brain Physiology.* (Undated)
http://www.cnsforum.com/imagebank/section/
Bp_Normal_brain/default.aspx
[412] http://www.ncbi.nlm.nih.gov/pubmed/21281093
[413] http://www.ncbi.nlm.nih.gov/pubmed/20080053
[414] http://www.ncbi.nlm.nih.gov/pubmed/20876182
[415] http://www.ncbi.nlm.nih.gov/pubmed/20828676
[416] http://www.ncbi.nlm.nih.gov/pubmed/18838044
[417] http://www.ncbi.nlm.nih.gov/pubmed/20920224
[418] http://www.ncbi.nlm.nih.gov/pubmed/19646365
[419] http://www.ncbi.nlm.nih.gov/pubmed/19480234
[420] http://www.ncbi.nlm.nih.gov/pubmed/20605120
[421] http://www.ncbi.nlm.nih.gov/pubmed/18363314
[422] http://www.ncbi.nlm.nih.gov/pubmed/17520787
[423] http://www.additudemag.com/adhd/article/757.html
[424] http://www.ncbi.nlm.nih.gov/pubmed/20679155
[425] http://www.ncbi.nlm.nih.gov/pubmed/20936546
[426] http://www.ncbi.nlm.nih.gov/pubmed/19754502
[427] http://www.ncbi.nlm.nih.gov/pubmed/12959497
[428] http://www.ncbi.nlm.nih.gov/pubmed/21470583
[429] http://www.ncbi.nlm.nih.gov/pubmed/21483434
[430] http://www.ncbi.nlm.nih.gov/pubmed/19694631
[431] http://www.medscape.com/viewarticle/571537
[432] http://www.ncbi.nlm.nih.gov/pubmed/17546345
[433] http://www.ncbi.nlm.nih.gov/pubmed/20556242
[434] http://www.ncbi.nlm.nih.gov/pubmed/20944770
[435] http://www.ncbi.nlm.nih.gov/pubmed/20140491
[436] http://www.ncbi.nlm.nih.gov/pubmed/20140491
[437] http://www.ncbi.nlm.nih.gov/pubmed/18573510
[438] http://www.ncbi.nlm.nih.gov/pubmed/19135135
[439] http://www.ncbi.nlm.nih.gov/pubmed/19118170
[440] http://www.ncbi.nlm.nih.gov/pubmed/19940168
[441] http://www.ncbi.nlm.nih.gov/pubmed/19778504

[442] http://www.ncbi.nlm.nih.gov/pubmed/20034014
[443] http://www.ncbi.nlm.nih.gov/pubmed/19803628
[444] http://www.ncbi.nlm.nih.gov/pubmed/19564796
[445] http://www.ncbi.nlm.nih.gov/pubmed/19564796
[446] http://www.ncbi.nlm.nih.gov/pubmed/17433881
[447] http://www.ncbi.nlm.nih.gov/pubmed/19368898
[448] http://www.ncbi.nlm.nih.gov/pubmed/19583473
[449] http://www.ncbi.nlm.nih.gov/pubmed/21765593
[450] http://www.ncbi.nlm.nih.gov/pubmed/21765593
[451] http://en.wikipedia.org/wiki/Impulsivity
[452] http://www.ncbi.nlm.nih.gov/pubmed/21765593
[453] http://www.ncbi.nlm.nih.gov/pubmed/20399590
[454] http://www.ncbi.nlm.nih.gov/pubmed/21833346
[455] http://www.ncbi.nlm.nih.gov/pubmed/20921120
[456] http://www.ncbi.nlm.nih.gov/pubmed/19699060
[457] http://www.ncbi.nlm.nih.gov/pubmed/18778384
[458] http://www.ncbi.nlm.nih.gov/pubmed/19349309
[459] http://www.ncbi.nlm.nih.gov/pubmed/20731961
[460] http://www.ncbi.nlm.nih.gov/pubmed/21158602
[461] Cloud, J. *Kids with ADHD May Learn Better by Fidgeting.* Time Magazine, Mar. 25, 2009. http://www.time.com/time/health/article/0,8599,1887486,00.html
[462] http://www.ncbi.nlm.nih.gov/pubmed/19083090
[463] http://www.ncbi.nlm.nih.gov/pubmed/20199487
[464] http://www.ncbi.nlm.nih.gov/pubmed/20977559
[465] http://www.ncbi.nlm.nih.gov/pubmed/19199417
[466] http://www.ncbi.nlm.nih.gov/pubmed/17214562
[467] http://www.ncbi.nlm.nih.gov/pubmed/19568995
[468] http://www.ncbi.nlm.nih.gov/pubmed/17401608
[469] http://www.ncbi.nlm.nih.gov/pubmed/17188897
[470] http://www.ncbi.nlm.nih.gov/pubmed/20558302
[471] http://www.ncbi.nlm.nih.gov/pubmed/17214308
[472] http://www.ncbi.nlm.nih.gov/pubmed/18392181
[473] http://www.ncbi.nlm.nih.gov/pubmed/19739058
[474] http://www.ncbi.nlm.nih.gov/pubmed/16919226
[475] http://www.ncbi.nlm.nih.gov/pubmed/17007602
[476] http://www.ncbi.nlm.nih.gov/pubmed/21483267
[477] http://www.ncbi.nlm.nih.gov/pubmed/21156266
[478] http://www.ncbi.nlm.nih.gov/pubmed/12108804
[479] http://www.ncbi.nlm.nih.gov/pubmed/20183697

[480] http://www.ncbi.nlm.nih.gov/pubmed/18695621

[481] http://www.ncbi.nlm.nih.gov/pubmed/20658352

[482] Angier, N. *Searching for the Source of a Fountain of Courage.* The New York Times, Jan. 3, 2011. http://www.nytimes.com/2011/01/04/science/04angier.html

[483] http://www.ncbi.nlm.nih.gov/pubmed/17433881

[484] http://www.ncbi.nlm.nih.gov/pubmed/20687105

[485] http://www.ncbi.nlm.nih.gov/pubmed/20001112

[486] http://www.ncbi.nlm.nih.gov/pubmed/21664605

[487] http://www.ncbi.nlm.nih.gov/pubmed/16741206

[488] http://www.ncbi.nlm.nih.gov/pubmed/20856811

[489] http://www.ncbi.nlm.nih.gov/pubmed/20955808

[490] http://www.ncbi.nlm.nih.gov/pubmed/19741115

[491] http://www.ncbi.nlm.nih.gov/pubmed/20179766

[492] http://www.ncbi.nlm.nih.gov/pubmed/20235795

[493] http://www.ncbi.nlm.nih.gov/pubmed/17126039

[494] http://www.ncbi.nlm.nih.gov/pubmed/20179766

[495] http://www.ncbi.nlm.nih.gov/pubmed/19519258

[496] http://www.ncbi.nlm.nih.gov/pubmed/17063150

[497] http://www.ncbi.nlm.nih.gov/pubmed/18295157

[498] http://www.ncbi.nlm.nih.gov/pubmed/15827573

[499] http://www.ncbi.nlm.nih.gov/pubmed/15602501

[500] http://www.ncbi.nlm.nih.gov/pubmed/19295165

[501] http://www.ncbi.nlm.nih.gov/pubmed/21314209

[502] http://www.ncbi.nlm.nih.gov/pubmed/20418943

[503] http://www.ncbi.nlm.nih.gov/pubmed/20393190

[504] http://www.ncbi.nlm.nih.gov/pubmed/20732901

[505] http://www.ncbi.nlm.nih.gov/pubmed/21229616

[506] http://www.ncbi.nlm.nih.gov/pubmed/21681856

[507] http://www.ncbi.nlm.nih.gov/pubmed/20393190

[508] http://www.vetmed.wsu.edu/research_vcapp/Panksepp/

[509] http://www.ncbi.nlm.nih.gov/pubmed/21319497

[510] http://en.wikipedia.org/wiki/Joseph_E._LeDoux

[511] http://www.dartmouth.edu/~dons/figures/ chapt_8/Fig_8_1.htm

[512] http://en.wikipedia.org/wiki/Reflex_arc

[513] http://en.wikipedia.org/wiki/Primitive_reflexes

[514] http://www.ncbi.nlm.nih.gov/pubmed/20959860

[515] http://www.thebrainwiki.com/ pmwiki.php?n=Forebrain.Thalamus

[516] http://www.ncbi.nlm.nih.gov/pubmed/16469510

[517] http://www.ncbi.nlm.nih.gov/pubmed/17101911

[518] http://www.ncbi.nlm.nih.gov/pubmed/19251247
[519] http://www.ncbi.nlm.nih.gov/pubmed/21939738
[520] LeDoux, J. *The Emotional Brain - The Mysterious Underpinnings of Emotional Life*. 1996, New York, Simon and Schuster Inc.
[521] http://www.ncbi.nlm.nih.gov/pubmed/12965291
[522] http://www.ncbi.nlm.nih.gov/pubmed/18805486
[523] http://www.ncbi.nlm.nih.gov/pubmed/20589100
[524] http://www.ncbi.nlm.nih.gov/pubmed/19966840
[525] http://www.ncbi.nlm.nih.gov/pubmed/21664605
[526] http://www.ncbi.nlm.nih.gov/pubmed/20498850
[527] http://www.ncbi.nlm.nih.gov/pubmed/19883142
[528] http://en.wikipedia.org/wiki/Insular_cortex
[529] http://en.wikipedia.org/wiki/Cingulate_cortex
[530] http://en.wikipedia.org/wiki/Amygdala
[531] http://en.wikipedia.org/wiki/Nucleus_accumbens
[532] http://en.wikipedia.org/wiki/Caudate_nucleus
[533] http://en.wikipedia.org/wiki/Ventral_tegmental_area
[534] http://www.ncbi.nlm.nih.gov/pubmed/21389234
[535] http://www.ncbi.nlm.nih.gov/pubmed/20959860
[536] http://www.ncbi.nlm.nih.gov/pubmed/21888979
[537] http://www.ncbi.nlm.nih.gov/pubmed/20331363
[538] http://www.ncbi.nlm.nih.gov/pubmed/21818311
[539] http://www.ncbi.nlm.nih.gov/pubmed/19940188
[540] http://www.ncbi.nlm.nih.gov/pubmed/21921543
[541] http://www.ncbi.nlm.nih.gov/pubmed/21534994
[542] http://www.ncbi.nlm.nih.gov/pubmed/20207692
[543] http://www.ncbi.nlm.nih.gov/pubmed/14976305
[544] http://www.ncbi.nlm.nih.gov/pubmed/21444827
[545] http://www.ncbi.nlm.nih.gov/pubmed/21939738
[546] http://www.ncbi.nlm.nih.gov/pubmed/12526986
[547] http://www.ncbi.nlm.nih.gov/pubmed/20420924
[548] http://www.ncbi.nlm.nih.gov/pubmed/21515927
[549] http://www.scholarpedia.org/article/Amygdala
[550] http://www.ncbi.nlm.nih.gov/pubmed/15850729
[551] http://www.ncbi.nlm.nih.gov/pubmed/20181600
[552] http://www.ncbi.nlm.nih.gov/pubmed/20181600
[553] http://www.ncbi.nlm.nih.gov/pubmed/21940454
[554] http://www.ncbi.nlm.nih.gov/pubmed/20980303
[555] http://en.wikipedia.org/wiki/Thalamus
[556] http://www.ncbi.nlm.nih.gov/pubmed/20364374

[557] http://www.ncbi.nlm.nih.gov/pubmed/21939738
[558] http://www.ncbi.nlm.nih.gov/pubmed/20731637
[559] http://www.ncbi.nlm.nih.gov/pubmed/20550755
[560] http://www.ncbi.nlm.nih.gov/pubmed/21264642
[561] http://www.ncbi.nlm.nih.gov/pubmed/21088699
[562] http://www.scholarpedia.org/article/Hypothalamus
[563] http://en.wikipedia.org/wiki/Pituitary_gland
[564] http://en.wikipedia.org/wiki/Glucocorticoid
[565] http://www.ncbi.nlm.nih.gov/pubmed/21945794
[566] http://www.ncbi.nlm.nih.gov/pubmed/19124688
[567] http://www.ncbi.nlm.nih.gov/pubmed/20808870
[568] http://www.ncbi.nlm.nih.gov/pubmed/20681231
[569] http://www.cbc.ca/news/background/friendlyfire/verdict.html
[570] http://en.wikipedia.org/wiki/Tarnak_Farm_incident
[571] http://leda.law.harvard.edu/leda/data/534/Hoffman.html
[572] http://www.airpower.au.af.mil/airchronicles/apj/
apj08/fal08/caldwell.html
[573] http://www.ncbi.nlm.nih.gov/pubmed/20681231
[574] http://www.ncbi.nlm.nih.gov/pubmed/16120100
[575] http://www.ncbi.nlm.nih.gov/pubmed/19836143
[576] http://www.ncbi.nlm.nih.gov/pubmed/20970071
[577] http://www.ncbi.nlm.nih.gov/pubmed/17574217
[578] http://www.ncbi.nlm.nih.gov/pubmed/20620172
[579] http://www.ncbi.nlm.nih.gov/pubmed/14754765
[580] http://www.ncbi.nlm.nih.gov/pubmed/15028776
[581] http://www.ncbi.nlm.nih.gov/pubmed/20001112
[582] http://www.ncbi.nlm.nih.gov/pubmed/19294447
[583] http://www.ncbi.nlm.nih.gov/pubmed/17564829
[584] http://www.ncbi.nlm.nih.gov/pubmed/19899671
[585] http://archpsyc.ama-assn.org/cgi/content/full/64/8/932
[586] http://www.ncbi.nlm.nih.gov/pubmed/19738093
[587] http://www.ncbi.nlm.nih.gov/pubmed/18978778
[588] http://www.ncbi.nlm.nih.gov/pubmed/21147996
[589] http://www.ncbi.nlm.nih.gov/pubmed/19853006
[590] http://www.ncbi.nlm.nih.gov/pubmed/20181600
[591] http://www.ncbi.nlm.nih.gov/pubmed/19679543
[592] http://www.ncbi.nlm.nih.gov/pubmed/9621734
[593] http://www.ncbi.nlm.nih.gov/pubmed/19447132
[594] http://www.ncbi.nlm.nih.gov/pubmed/20418943
[595] http://www.ncbi.nlm.nih.gov/pubmed/21906725
[596] http://www.ncbi.nlm.nih.gov/pubmed/17896226

[597] http://www.ncbi.nlm.nih.gov/pubmed/18534149
[598] http://www.ncbi.nlm.nih.gov/pubmed/19941180
[599] http://www.ncbi.nlm.nih.gov/pubmed/19462309
[600] http://www.ncbi.nlm.nih.gov/pubmed/21807433
[601] http://www.womenandpolicing.org/violenceFS.asp
[602] Unknown author. *Military Domestic Violence - Learn about Domestic Violence and Abuse in the Military.* Web page undated, but circa 2008.
http://www.allpsychologycareers.com/topics/military-domestic-violence.html
[603] http://www.ncbi.nlm.nih.gov/pubmed/19368898
[604] http://www.ncbi.nlm.nih.gov/pubmed/21445667
[605] http://www.ncbi.nlm.nih.gov/pubmed/21765900
[606] http://www.ncbi.nlm.nih.gov/pubmed/1343357
[607] http://www.ncbi.nlm.nih.gov/pubmed/20192787
[608] http://www.ncbi.nlm.nih.gov/pubmed/20192787
[609] http://www.ncbi.nlm.nih.gov/pubmed/14691363
[610] http://www.ncbi.nlm.nih.gov/pubmed/19784715
[611] http://www.ncbi.nlm.nih.gov/pubmed/16105680
[612] http://www.ncbi.nlm.nih.gov/pubmed/17091447
[613] http://www.ncbi.nlm.nih.gov/pubmed/21833346
[614] http://www.ncbi.nlm.nih.gov/pubmed/12900314
[615] Pendower, J. *Why Do Some Teenagers With ADHD Self Harm?* Web page updated Sept. 18, 2010.
http://www.addandadhd.co.uk/why-do-teenagers-with-adhd-self-harm.html
[616] http://thechart.blogs.cnn.com/2011/08/23/self-injury-a-silent-epidemic/
[617] Adler, Patricia; Adler, Peter. *The Tender Cut: Inside the Hidden World of Self-Injury.* 2011, New York University Press
[618] http://www.ncbi.nlm.nih.gov/pubmed/20192787
[619] Kuhn, C., Swartzwelder, S., Wilson W. 2003. *Buzzed: The Straight Facts about the Most Used and Abused Drugs from Alcohol to Ecstasy.* New York: Norton.
[620] http://www.ncbi.nlm.nih.gov/pubmed/12900314
[621] http://www.ncbi.nlm.nih.gov/pubmed/19486726
[622] http://www.ncbi.nlm.nih.gov/pubmed/21034383
[623] http://www.ncbi.nlm.nih.gov/pubmed/10974364
[624] http://www.ncbi.nlm.nih.gov/pubmed/17126914
[625] http://www.ncbi.nlm.nih.gov/pubmed/20218798
[626] http://www.ncbi.nlm.nih.gov/pubmed/17050717
[627] http://www.ncbi.nlm.nih.gov/pubmed/15721212

[628] http://www.ncbi.nlm.nih.gov/pubmed/20465845

[629] http://www.ncbi.nlm.nih.gov/pubmed/20465845

[630] http://www.ncbi.nlm.nih.gov/pubmed/20620028

[631] http://www.ncbi.nlm.nih.gov/pubmed/17610577

[632] http://www.ncbi.nlm.nih.gov/pubmed/18216200

[633] http://www.ncbi.nlm.nih.gov/pubmed/19577398

[634] http://www.ncbi.nlm.nih.gov/pubmed/20620028

[635] http://www.ncbi.nlm.nih.gov/pubmed/17285103

[636] http://www.ncbi.nlm.nih.gov/pubmed/19208556

[637] http://www.ncbi.nlm.nih.gov/pubmed/18537459

[638] http://www.ncbi.nlm.nih.gov/pubmed/20108102

[639] http://www.ncbi.nlm.nih.gov/pubmed/21678632

[640] http://www.ncbi.nlm.nih.gov/pubmed/17048717

[641] http://www.ncbi.nlm.nih.gov/pubmed/21127082

[642] http://www.ncbi.nlm.nih.gov/pubmed/21576306

[643] http://www.ncbi.nlm.nih.gov/pubmed/19692717

[644] http://www.ncbi.nlm.nih.gov/pubmed/21206547

[645] http://www.ncbi.nlm.nih.gov/pubmed/10086401

[646] http://www.ncbi.nlm.nih.gov/pubmed/19732962

[647] http://www.ncbi.nlm.nih.gov/pubmed/19896530

[648] http://www.ncbi.nlm.nih.gov/pubmed/20236043

[649] http://www.ncbi.nlm.nih.gov/pubmed/20670813

[650] http://www.ncbi.nlm.nih.gov/pubmed/21560489

[651] http://www.ncbi.nlm.nih.gov/pubmed/20574059

[652] http://en.wikipedia.org/wiki/Cortisol

[653] http://www.ncbi.nlm.nih.gov/pubmed/18155557

[654] http://www.ncbi.nlm.nih.gov/pubmed/20633637

[655] http://www.ncbi.nlm.nih.gov/pubmed/21872917

[656] http://www.ncbi.nlm.nih.gov/pubmed/14624291

[657] http://www.ncbi.nlm.nih.gov/pubmed/10543319

[658] http://www.ncbi.nlm.nih.gov/pubmed/11343812

[659] http://www.ncbi.nlm.nih.gov/pubmed/20496460

[660] http://en.wikipedia.org/wiki/Benzedrine

[661] http://www.ncbi.nlm.nih.gov/pubmed/20164771

[662] http://en.wikipedia.org/wiki/Cortisol

[663] http://www.ncbi.nlm.nih.gov/pubmed/19466988

[664] Douglas, G., Elward, K. *Asthma - Clinician's Desk Reference.* 2010, Manson Publishing Ltd.

[665] http://www.ncbi.nlm.nih.gov/pubmed/20492543

[666] http://www.ncbi.nlm.nih.gov/pubmed/20019071

[667] http://www.ncbi.nlm.nih.gov/pubmed/17541055

[668] http://www.ncbi.nlm.nih.gov/pubmed/11835982

[669] http://www.ncbi.nlm.nih.gov/pubmed/12776394

[670] http://www.ncbi.nlm.nih.gov/pubmed/15889301

[671] http://www.ncbi.nlm.nih.gov/pubmed/11074867

[672] http://www.ncbi.nlm.nih.gov/pubmed/21152404

[673] http://www.ncbi.nlm.nih.gov/pubmed/16619053

[674] http://www.ncbi.nlm.nih.gov/pubmed/16619053

[675] http://www.ncbi.nlm.nih.gov/pubmed/20130091

[676] http://www.ncbi.nlm.nih.gov/pubmed/17484426

[677] http://www.ncbi.nlm.nih.gov/pubmed/15686575

[678] http://www.ncbi.nlm.nih.gov/pubmed/14754765

[679] http://www.ncbi.nlm.nih.gov/pubmed/15028776

[680] http://www.ncbi.nlm.nih.gov/pubmed/20001112

[681] http://www.ncbi.nlm.nih.gov/pubmed/19294447

[682] http://www.ncbi.nlm.nih.gov/pubmed/17564829

[683] http://www.ncbi.nlm.nih.gov/pubmed/19899671

[684] http://archpsyc.ama-assn.org/cgi/content/full/64/8/932

[685] http://www.ncbi.nlm.nih.gov/pubmed/19738093

[686] http://www.ncbi.nlm.nih.gov/pubmed/20980303

[687] Collins English Dictionary - Complete & Unabridged 10th Ed. 2009, William Collins Sons & Co. Ltd.

[688] Merriam-Webster's Medical Dictionary, © 2007 Merriam-Webster, Inc.

[689] Merriam-Webster's Medical Dictionary, © 2007 Merriam-Webster, Inc.

[690] http://en.wikipedia.org/wiki/Creativity

[691] Mumford, M. D. (2003). *Where have we been, where are we going? Taking stock in creativity research.* Creativity Research Journal, 15, 107–120

[692] http://www.ncbi.nlm.nih.gov/pubmed/19011838

[693] http://www.ncbi.nlm.nih.gov/pubmed/20498850

[694] http://www.thefreedictionary.com/create

[695] http://www.ncbi.nlm.nih.gov/pubmed/8501447

[696] http://www.ncbi.nlm.nih.gov/pubmed/17132050

[697] http://www.ncbi.nlm.nih.gov/pubmed/1784653

[698] Zuckerman, M. (2007), *Sensation Seeking and Risky Behavior.* Washington, DC: American Psychological Association.

[699] http://www.apa.org/monitor/julaug06/frisky.aspx

[700] http://www.ncbi.nlm.nih.gov/pubmed/18835480

[701] http://www.ncbi.nlm.nih.gov/pubmed/21596760

[702] http://www.ncbi.nlm.nih.gov/pubmed/20875435

[703] http://www.ncbi.nlm.nih.gov/pubmed/17132050

[704] Goldstein, Kurt. *The Organism: A Holistic Approach to Biology Derived from Pathological Data in Man.* 1934. New York: Zone Books, 1995

[705] Carl Rogers, *On Becoming a Person* (1961) p. 350-1

[706] Maslow, Abraham H. *A Theory of Human Motivation.* Psychological Review 50 (1943): 370-396. 17 October 2006

[707] Fromm, Erich *On Being Human* London: The Continuum International Publishing Group Ltd, 1997

[708] http://www.ncbi.nlm.nih.gov/pubmed/17245411

[709] http://www.ncbi.nlm.nih.gov/pubmed/19350760

[710] http://www.ncbi.nlm.nih.gov/pubmed/18473259

[711] http://www.ncbi.nlm.nih.gov/pubmed/19829167

[712] http://www.ncbi.nlm.nih.gov/pubmed/17120049

[713] http://www.ncbi.nlm.nih.gov/pubmed/18366104

[714] http://www.ncbi.nlm.nih.gov/pubmed/19270267

[715] http://www.ncbi.nlm.nih.gov/pubmed/21176203

[716] http://www.ncbi.nlm.nih.gov/pubmed/15538605

[717] http://www.ncbi.nlm.nih.gov/pubmed/19319834

[718] http://www.ncbi.nlm.nih.gov/pubmed/21423432

[719] http://www.ncbi.nlm.nih.gov/pubmed/19761584

[720] http://www.ncbi.nlm.nih.gov/pubmed/21176203

[721] http://www.ncbi.nlm.nih.gov/pubmed/18514316

[722] http://www.ncbi.nlm.nih.gov/pubmed/20350167

[723] http://www.ncbi.nlm.nih.gov/pubmed/20173686

[724] http://www.ncbi.nlm.nih.gov/pubmed/20493953

[725] http://www.ncbi.nlm.nih.gov/pubmed/21847383

[726] http://www.ncbi.nlm.nih.gov/pubmed/20842749

[727] http://www.ncbi.nlm.nih.gov/pubmed/18158145

[728] http://www.ncbi.nlm.nih.gov/pubmed/19925181

[729] http://www.ncbi.nlm.nih.gov/pubmed/20946057

[730] http://www.ncbi.nlm.nih.gov/pubmed/21167765

[731] http://www.ncbi.nlm.nih.gov/pubmed/21964488

[732] http://www.ncbi.nlm.nih.gov/pubmed/21922013

[733] http://www.ncbi.nlm.nih.gov/pubmed/16388969

[734] http://www.ncbi.nlm.nih.gov/pubmed/20053752

[735] Russell, Thaddeus. *A Renegade History of the United States,* 2010 Free Press, a Division of Simon and Schuster, Inc.

[736] http://www.ncbi.nlm.nih.gov/pubmed/20421851

[737] http://www.ncbi.nlm.nih.gov/pubmed/20206707

[738] http://www.ncbi.nlm.nih.gov/pubmed/19713452

[739] http://www.ncbi.nlm.nih.gov/pubmed/20172533

[740] http://www.ncbi.nlm.nih.gov/pubmed/19906444

[741] http://www.ncbi.nlm.nih.gov/pubmed/18769827

[742] http://www.ncbi.nlm.nih.gov/pubmed/20145962

[743] http://www.ncbi.nlm.nih.gov/pubmed/18729135

[744] http://www.ncbi.nlm.nih.gov/pubmed/19890261

[745] http://www.ncbi.nlm.nih.gov/pubmed/20888040

[746] http://www.ncbi.nlm.nih.gov/pubmed/21527290

[747] http://www.ncbi.nlm.nih.gov/pubmed/12808433

[748] http://www.ncbi.nlm.nih.gov/pubmed/21207241

[749] http://www.ncbi.nlm.nih.gov/pubmed/20856918

[750] http://www.ncbi.nlm.nih.gov/pubmed/15108184

[751] http://www.ncbi.nlm.nih.gov/pubmed/14569274

[752] Author unknown. *Low Grades in Adolescence Linked to Dopamine Genes, Says Biosocial Criminologist.* ScienceDigest.com, posted Sept. 3, 2010. http://www.sciencedaily.com/releases/2010/09/100902131740.htm

[753] http://www.ncbi.nlm.nih.gov/pubmed/20532925

[754] http://www.ncbi.nlm.nih.gov/pubmed/21318082

[755] http://www.ncbi.nlm.nih.gov/pubmed/21152404

[756] http://www.ncbi.nlm.nih.gov/pubmed/20807239

[757] Unknown author. *Gene Linked to ADHD Allows Memory Task to Be Interrupted by Brain Regions Tied to Daydreaming.* ScienceDigest.com, posted Nov. 24, 2010. http://www.sciencedaily.com/releases/2010/11/101116122850.htm

[758] http://www.ncbi.nlm.nih.gov/pubmed/16123773

[759] http://www.ncbi.nlm.nih.gov/pubmed/8682515

[760] http://www.ncbi.nlm.nih.gov/pubmed/10418689

[761] http://www.ncbi.nlm.nih.gov/pubmed/11756666

[762] Chen, et al. *Population Migration and the Variation of Dopamine D4 Receptor (DRD4) Allele Frequencies Around the Globe.* Evolution and Human Behavior, 20:309-324 (1999)

[763] http://www.ncbi.nlm.nih.gov/pubmed/15077199

[764] http://www.ncbi.nlm.nih.gov/pubmed/20019071

[765] http://www.ncbi.nlm.nih.gov/pubmed/19713452

[766] http://www.nytimes.com/roomfordebate/2011/10/12/are-americans-more-prone-to-adhd

[767] http://en.wikipedia.org/wiki/History_of_immigration_to_the_United_States

[768] http://www.digitalhistory.uh.edu/historyonline/us3.cfm - Digital History -- The Peopling of America

[769] Russell, Thaddeus. *A Renegade History of the United States,* 2010 Free Press, a Division of Simon and Schuster, Inc.
[770] http://cogweb.ucla.edu/Chumash/Population.html
[771] http://www.ncbi.nlm.nih.gov/pubmed/20623607
[772] http://www.ehbonline.org/article/S1090-5138(99)00015-X/abstract
[773] http://www.ncbi.nlm.nih.gov/pubmed/21469077
[774] http://www.ncbi.nlm.nih.gov/pubmed/11756666
[775] http://www.ncbi.nlm.nih.gov/pubmed/15077199
[776] http://www.ncbi.nlm.nih.gov/pubmed/21909391
[777] http://www.ncbi.nlm.nih.gov/pubmed/20019071
[778] http://www.ncbi.nlm.nih.gov/pubmed/8682515
[779] http://www.ncbi.nlm.nih.gov/pubmed/10418689
[780] http://www.ncbi.nlm.nih.gov/pubmed/21232805
[781] http://www.ncbi.nlm.nih.gov/pubmed/20873719
[782] http://www.ncbi.nlm.nih.gov/pubmed/12773616
[783] http://www.ncbi.nlm.nih.gov/pubmed/17893706
[784] http://www.ncbi.nlm.nih.gov/pubmed/20646063
[785] http://www.ncbi.nlm.nih.gov/pubmed/19081819
[786] http://www.umm.edu/altmed/articles/ginger-000246.htm
[787] Noble, RI, Sellers, EA, Best, CH. *The treatment of motion sickness.* Canada M.A.J., April 1947.
[788] http://www.ncbi.nlm.nih.gov/pubmed/21365391
[789] http://www.ncbi.nlm.nih.gov/pubmed/17183916
[790] http://www.ncbi.nlm.nih.gov/pubmed/14742450
[791] http://www.ncbi.nlm.nih.gov/pubmed/11286016
[792] http://en.wikipedia.org/wiki/Zipper_(ride)
[793] http://www.ncbi.nlm.nih.gov/pubmed/21365391
[794] http://www.ncbi.nlm.nih.gov/pubmed/21036110
[795] http://www.ncbi.nlm.nih.gov/pubmed/17086768
[796] http://www.ncbi.nlm.nih.gov/pubmed/16313141
[797] http://www.ncbi.nlm.nih.gov/pubmed/17081956
[798] Mittelberger, G. (translated by Carl Eben). *Journey to Pennsylvania in the Year 1750 and Return to Germany in the Year 1754.* John Joseph McVey, Philadelphia, 1898.
[799] Falconbridge, A. *Account of the Slave Trade on the Coast of Africa.* J. Phillips, London, 1788.
[800] Inikori, J.E. *The Atlantic Slave Trade: Effects on Economies, Societies, and Peoples in Africa, the Americas, and Europe.* Duke University Press, Durham and London, 1992.
[801] http://www.ncbi.nlm.nih.gov/pubmed/1986989
[802] http://www.ncbi.nlm.nih.gov/pubmed/21977356

[803] http://www.ncbi.nlm.nih.gov/pubmed/12746359

[804] Armelagos, G. (2005) *The Slavery Hypertension Hypothesis-Natural Selection and Scientific Investigation: A Commentary.* Transforming Anthropology, Vol. 13, Issue 2, pp. 119-124.

[805] http://www.ncbi.nlm.nih.gov/pubmed/15652604

[806] http://www.ncbi.nlm.nih.gov/pubmed/17541055

[807] http://www.ncbi.nlm.nih.gov/pubmed/21977356

[808] http://www.ncbi.nlm.nih.gov/pubmed/15548830

[809] http://www.ncbi.nlm.nih.gov/pubmed/21722093

[810] http://www.ncbi.nlm.nih.gov/pubmed/9754697

[811] http://www.ncbi.nlm.nih.gov/pubmed/17433557

[812] http://www.ncbi.nlm.nih.gov/pubmed/21300675

[813] http://www.ncbi.nlm.nih.gov/pubmed/19835674

[814] http://www.ncbi.nlm.nih.gov/pubmed/21406647

[815] http://www.ncbi.nlm.nih.gov/pubmed/12562112

[816] http://www.ncbi.nlm.nih.gov/pubmed/20013957

[817] http://www.ncbi.nlm.nih.gov/pubmed/21400640

[818] http://www.ncbi.nlm.nih.gov/pubmed/17567398

[819] http://www.ncbi.nlm.nih.gov/pubmed/21637733

[820] http://www.ncbi.nlm.nih.gov/pubmed/19365086

[821] http://www.ncbi.nlm.nih.gov/pubmed/15950022

[822] http://www.ncbi.nlm.nih.gov/pubmed/20944770

[823] http://www.ncbi.nlm.nih.gov/pubmed/21637629

[824] http://www.ncbi.nlm.nih.gov/pubmed/17875251

[825] http://www.ncbi.nlm.nih.gov/pubmed/19773716

[826] http://www.ncbi.nlm.nih.gov/pubmed/19193347

[827] http://www.ncbi.nlm.nih.gov/pubmed/19646365

[828] http://www.ncbi.nlm.nih.gov/pubmed/19659917

[829] http://www.ncbi.nlm.nih.gov/pubmed/19725254

[830] http://www.ncbi.nlm.nih.gov/pubmed/20039111

[831] http://www.ncbi.nlm.nih.gov/pubmed/16041294

[832] http://www.ncbi.nlm.nih.gov/pubmed/11876672

[833] http://en.wikipedia.org/wiki/Incarceration_in_the_United_States

[834] http://www.ncbi.nlm.nih.gov/pubmed/21879629

[835] http://www.ncbi.nlm.nih.gov/pubmed/16617231

[836] http://www.ncbi.nlm.nih.gov/pubmed/21742345

[837] http://www.ncbi.nlm.nih.gov/pubmed/20031097

[838] http://www.ncbi.nlm.nih.gov/pubmed/21919925

[839] http://www.ncbi.nlm.nih.gov/pubmed/19131944

[840] http://www.ncbi.nlm.nih.gov/pubmed/17700082

[841] http://www.ncbi.nlm.nih.gov/pubmed/19040267

[842] http://www.ncbi.nlm.nih.gov/pubmed/20876085

[843] http://www.ncbi.nlm.nih.gov/pubmed/17470954

[844] http://www.ncbi.nlm.nih.gov/pubmed/16420713

[845] http://www.ncbi.nlm.nih.gov/pubmed/20080984

[846] http://www.ncbi.nlm.nih.gov/pubmed/20876085

[847] Russell, Thaddeus. *A Renegade History of the United States*, 2010 Free Press, a Division of Simon and Schuster, Inc.

[848] Rasmussen, Nicolas. *On speed : the many lives of amphetamine*. 2008 New York University Press, New York and London.

[849] http://www.ncbi.nlm.nih.gov/pubmed/18445805

[850] Kramer, Peter. *Listening to Prozac: The Landmark Book About Antidepressants and the Remaking of the Self, Revised Edition*. 1997, Penguin Group, New York.

[851] Diller, Lawrence. *Running on Ritalin: A physician reflects on children, society, and performance in a pill*. 1998, Bantam Books, New York.

[852] http://www.ncbi.nlm.nih.gov/pubmed/18473654

[853] http://www.ncbi.nlm.nih.gov/pubmed/18473654

[854] http://www.ncbi.nlm.nih.gov/pubmed/19455150

[855] http://www.ncbi.nlm.nih.gov/pubmed/16770765

[856] http://www.ncbi.nlm.nih.gov/pubmed/18093021

[857] http://www.ncbi.nlm.nih.gov/pubmed/18606032

[858] http://www.ncbi.nlm.nih.gov/pubmed/20644990

[859] http://www.ncbi.nlm.nih.gov/pubmed/20610847

[860] http://www.merriam-webster.com/dictionary/sheep

[861] http://www.ncbi.nlm.nih.gov/pubmed/18788325

[862] http://www.ncbi.nlm.nih.gov/pubmed/21262039

[863] http://www.ncbi.nlm.nih.gov/pubmed/21387986

[864] Pechmann, Cornelia, et al (2005). *Impulsive and Self-Conscious: Adolescents' Vulnerability to Advertising and Promotion*, American Marketing Association, Vol 24(2): 202-221 (http://web.gsm.uci.edu/antismokingads/articles/CP_JPPM_05.pdf)

[865] Trudel, Remi, and Murray, Kyle B. (2011). *Why Didn't I Think of That? Self-Regulation Through Selective Information Processing*, Journal of Marketing Research (in print) (http://www.marketingpower.com/AboutAMA/Documents/JMR_Forthcoming/why_didnt_I_think_of_that.pdf)

[866] http://www.ncbi.nlm.nih.gov/pubmed/20597593

[867] Douglas, K., Sutton, R., & Stathi, S. (2010). *Why I am less persuaded than you: People's intuitive understanding of the psychology of persuasion*. Social Influence, 5 (2), 133-148

[868] Moss, S. *Need for Cognition.* Psych-it.com.au, posted June 11, 2008. http://www.psych-it.com.au/Psychlopedia/article.asp?id=207

[869] http://www.panarchy.org/montagu/territorialism.html

[870] http://en.wikipedia.org/wiki/Spock

[871] http://en.wiktionary.org/wiki/get_a_leg_up

[872] Coen, Joel and Ethan. *A Serious Man.* 2009, Relativity Media, StudioCanal, Working Title Films, Mike Zoss Productions, United States.

[873] http://en.wikipedia.org/wiki/Rashi

[874] http://theamericanscene.com/2009/10/09/ Some+Thoughts+on+A+Serious+Man

[875] http://en.wikipedia.org/wiki/Viktor_Frankl

[876] http://www.sorfoundation.org/

[877] http://www.continuingedcourses.net/active/courses/ course003.php

[878] http://en.wikipedia.org/wiki/Occam's_razor

[879] http://www.ncbi.nlm.nih.gov/pubmed/19257888

[880] http://www.ncbi.nlm.nih.gov/pubmed/16209748

[881] http://www.ncbi.nlm.nih.gov/pubmed/14702221

[882] http://www.dsm5.org/Pages/Default.aspx

[883] http://www.dsm5.org/ProposedRevisions/Pages/ proposedrevision.aspx?rid=383# (Accessed 11/13/11)

[884] http://www.dsm5.org/meetus/pages/adhd.aspx

[885] http://www.dsm5.org/research/pages/externalizingdisorders ofchildhood(attention-deficithyperactivitydisorder, conductdisorder,oppositional-defiantdisorder,juven.aspx

[886] http://en.wikipedia.org/wiki/Attention-deficit_hyperactivity_disorder_controversies

Biography

Dr. Sterling was born on March 26, 1946, in San Francisco, California, and named Ronald Murray Sterling (after no particular person).

He has a brother two years younger, also born in San Francisco. The Sterling family moved to Southern California in 1948 and Dr. Sterling attended schools in Hawthorne, Inglewood, and Torrance, California. He has always gone by the name Ron Sterling which often attracted comments about the "Twilight Zone" television show (that was Rod Serling).

In June 1968, Dr. Sterling graduated with a B.A., major in Biology, minor in Chemistry, from Walla Walla College, College Place, Washington. In June 1972, he graduated from Loma Linda University Medical School, Loma Linda, California. In June 1975, he received Certificate of Completion for General Psychiatry from the University of Hawaii Affiliated Psychiatric Residency Program, Honolulu, Hawaii. In June 1999, he received Certificate of Completion for Geriatric Psychiatry Fellowship from the University of Kansas Medical School, Wichita, Kansas.

Dr. Sterling is fully licensed to practice medicine in Washington State. His office is in Bellevue, Washington. To read more about Dr. Sterling, please visit RonSterling.com.

Made in the USA
San Bernardino, CA
22 September 2013